# PEDAGOGICAL ARTICLES

## (INCLUDING THE SCHOOL OF YASNAYA POLYANA AND THE LINEN-MEASURER)

By
COUNT LEO N. TOLSTÓY

Translated from the Original Russian
and edited by
PROFESSOR LEO WIENER

**Fredonia Books
Amsterdam, The Netherlands**

Pedagogical Articles
(Including the School of Yasnaya Polyana and the Linen-Measurer)

by
Leo Tolstoy

ISBN: 1-58963-652-X

Copyright © 2002 by Fredonia Books

Reprinted from the 1904 edition

Fredonia Books
Amsterdam, The Netherlands
http://www.fredoniabooks.com

All rights reserved, including the right to reproduce this book, or portions thereof, in any form.

In order to make original editions of historical works available to scholars at an economical price, this facsimile of the original edition of 1904 is reproduced from the best available copy and has been digitally enhanced to improve legibility, but the text remains unaltered to retain historical authenticity.

# CONTENTS

**PEDAGOGICAL ARTICLES:**

|  | PAGE |
|---|---|
| On Popular Education | 3 |
| On Methods of Teaching the Rudiments | 32 |
| A Project of a General Plan for the Establishment of Popular Schools | 60 |
| Education and Culture | 105 |
| Progress and the Definition of Education | 152 |
| Are the Peasant Children to Learn to Write from Us? | 191 |
| The School at Yásnaya Polyána | 225 |
| Linen-Measurer | 361 |

# PEDAGOGICAL ARTICLES

From the Periodical, *Yásnaya Polyána*

1862

# ON POPULAR EDUCATION

POPULAR education has always and everywhere afforded me an incomprehensible phenomenon. The people want education, and every separate individual unconsciously tends toward education. The more highly cultured class of people — society, the government — strive to transmit their knowledge and to educate the less educated masses. One would think that such a coincidence of necessities would satisfy both the class which furnishes the education and the one that receives it. But the very opposite takes place. The masses continually counteract the efforts made for their education by society or by the government, as the representatives of a more highly cultured class, and these efforts are frequently frustrated. Not to speak of the schools of antiquity, of India, Egypt, ancient Greece, and even Rome, the arrangement of which is as little known to us as the popular opinion of those institutions, this phenomenon seems startling to us in the European schools from the days of Luther to our own times.

Germany, the founder of the school, has not been able during a struggle of two hundred years to overcome the counteraction of the masses to the school. In spite of the appointments of meritorious invalid soldiers as teachers made by the Fredericks; in spite of the law which has been in force for two hundred years; in spite of the preparation according to the latest fashion, which teachers receive in seminaries; in spite of the Germans' feeling of obedience to the law, — compulsory education even to this moment lies as a heavy burden upon the people, and the German governments cannot bring themselves to abolish the law of compulsory education. Germany can pride itself on the education of its people only by statistical data, but the masses, as before, for the greater part take away from the schools nothing but a contempt for them.

France, in spite of the fact that education had passed out of the hands of the king into those of the Directory, and from the hands of the Directory into those of the clergy, has succeeded as little as Germany, and even less, in the matter of popular education, so say the historians of education, judging from official accounts. Serious statesmen even now propose for France the introduction of compulsory education as the only means for overcoming the opposition of the masses.

In free England, where the promulgation of such a law has been and always will be unthinkable, — which, however, many regret, — society, and not the government, has struggled and still struggles with all possible means and more vigorously than elsewhere against the people's expressed opposition to the schools. Schools are conducted there partly by the government and partly by private societies. The enormous dissemination and activity of these religio-philanthropic educational societies in England better than anything else prove the power of resistance with which the educating part of society there meets.

Even the new country, the United States of North America, has not evaded that difficulty and has made education semi-compulsory.

It is, of course, even worse in our own country, where the masses are even more enraged against the idea of the school; where the most cultivated people dream of the introduction of the German law of compulsory education; and where all the schools, even those intended for the higher classes, exist only as bait for preferments of rank and for the advantages accruing therefrom.

So far the children are everywhere sent to school by force, while parents are compelled to send their children to school by the severity of the law, or by cunning, or by offering them advantages, whereas the masses everywhere study of their own accord and regard education as good.

How is this? The need of education lies in every man; the people love and seek education, as they love and seek the air for breathing; the government and society burn with the desire to educate the masses, and yet, notwithstanding all the force of cunning and the persistency of governments and societies, the masses constantly manifest their dissatisfaction with the education which is offered to them, and step by step submit only to force.

As at every conflict, so also here, it was necessary to solve the question: What is more lawful, the resistance, or the action itself? Must the resistance be broken, or the action be changed?

So far, as may be seen from history, the question has been solved in favour of the state and the educating society. The resistance has been acknowledged to be unlawful, men seeing in it the principle of evil inherent in man, and so, without receding from its mode of action, that is, without receding from that form and from those contents of education, which society already possessed, the state has made use of force and cunning in order to annihilate the people's resistance.

It must be supposed that the educating society had some reasons to know that the education which it possessed in a certain form was beneficial for a certain people at a certain historical epoch.

What were these reasons? What reasons has the

school of our day to teach this, and not that, thus, and not otherwise?

Always and in all ages humanity has endeavoured to give and has given more or less satisfactory answers to these questions, and in our time this answer is even more necessary than ever. A Chinese mandarin who never leaves Pekin may be compelled to learn by rote the sayings of Confucius, and these saws may be beaten into children with sticks; it was possible to do that in the Middle Ages, — but where are we to get in our time that strong faith in the indubitableness of our knowledge, which would give us the right of forcibly educating the masses?

Let us take any mediaeval school, before and after Luther; let us take all the learned literature of the Middle Ages, — what strength of faith and of firm, indubitable knowledge of what is true and what false, is to be seen in those people! It was easy for them to know that the Greek language was the only necessary condition of an education, because Aristotle was written in that language, the truth of whose propositions no one doubted for several centuries afterward. How could the monks help demanding the study of Holy Writ which stood on a firm foundation? It was natural for Luther peremptorily to demand the study of Hebrew, for he knew full well that God Himself had in that language revealed the truth to men. Of course, so long as the critical sense of humanity was still dormant, the school had to be dogmatic, and it was natural for students to learn by heart the truths which had been revealed by God and by Aristotle, and the poetical beauties of Vergil and Cicero. For several centuries afterward no one could even imagine a truer truth or a more beautiful beauty.

But what is the position of the school in our day, which has persevered in the same dogmatic principles, when, side by side with the class where the scholar learns by heart the truth about the immortality of the soul, they try to make it clear to him that the nerves, which are common to man and to a frog, are that which anciently used to be called a soul; when, after the story of Joshua, the son of Nun, which is transmitted to him without explanations, he finds out that the sun had never turned around the earth; when, after the beauties of Vergil have been explained to him, he finds the beauties in Alexandre Dumas, sold to him for five centimes, much greater; when the only faith of the teacher consists in the conviction that there is no truth, that everything existing is sensible, that progress is good and backwardness bad; when nobody knows in what this universal faith in progress consists?

After all this, compare the dogmatic school of the Middle Ages, where truths were indubitable, with our school, where nobody knows what truth is, and to which the children are nevertheless forced to go and the parents to send their children. More than that. It was an easy matter for the mediæval school to know what ought to be taught, what first, and what later, and how it was all to be taught, so long as there was but one method and so long as all science centred in the Bible, in the books of St. Augustine, and in Aristotle.

But how are we, in this endless variety of methods of instruction, proposed to us on all sides, in this immense mass of sciences and their subdivisions, which have been evolved in our time, — how are we to select one of the many proposed methods, one certain branch of the sciences, and, which is most difficult, how are we to select that sequence in the instruction of these sciences which would be sensible and just? More than that. The discovery of these principles is the more difficult in our time, in comparison with the mediæval school, for the reason that then education was confined to one definite class which prepared itself to live in certain well-defined conditions, while in our time, when the whole people has declared its right to be educated, it appears much more difficult and much more necessary for us to know what is needed for all these heterogeneous classes.

What are these principles? Ask any pedagogue you please why he teaches this and not that, and this first and not later. If he will understand you, he will say that he knows the God-revealed truth, and that he considers it his duty to transmit it to the younger generation and to educate it in those principles which are unquestionably true; but he will give you no answer in regard to the subjects which do not refer to religious education. Another pedagogue will explain to you the foundation of his school by the eternal laws of reason, as expounded by Fichte, Kant, and Hegel. A third will base his right of compulsion on the fact that the schools have always been compulsory and that, in spite of this, the result of these schools has been real education. Finally, a fourth, uniting all these principles, will tell you that the school has to be such as it is, because religion, philosophy, and experience have evolved it as such, and that that which is historical is sensible. All these proofs may be, it seems to me, divided into four classes: *religious, philosophical, experimental, and historical.*

Education which has for its basis religion, that is, divine revelation, the truth and legality of which nobody may doubt, must indisputably be inculcated on the people, and in this — only in this — case is violence legal. Even thus missionaries do at the present time in Africa and in China. Thus they have proceeded up till now in the schools of the whole world as regards religious instruction, Catholic, Protestant, Hebrew, Mohammedan, and so forth. But in our time, when religious education forms but a small part of education, the question what ground the school has to compel the young generation to receive religious instruction in a certain fashion remains unanswered from the religious point of view

Maybe the answer will be found in philosophy. Has philosophy as firm a foundation as religion? What are these principles? By whom, how, and when have these principles been enunciated? We do not know them. All the philosophers search for the laws of good and evil; having discovered these laws, they, coming to pedagogy (they could none of them help touching upon that subject), compel the human race to be educated in conformity with these laws. But each of these theories, in a series of other theories, appears incomplete and furnishes only a new link in the perception of good and evil inherent in humanity. Every thinker expresses only that which has been consciously perceived by his epoch, consequently the education of the younger generation in the sense of this consciousness is quite superfluous: this consciousness is already inherent in the living generation.

All the pedagogico-philosophical theories have for their aim and problem the bringing up of virtuous men. However, the conception of virtue either remains the same or develops infinitely, and, notwithstanding all the theories, the decadence and bloom of virtue do not depend on education. A virtuous Chinaman, a virtuous Greek, Roman, or Frenchman of our time, are either equally virtuous, or equally remote from virtue.

The philosophical theories of pedagogics solve the question of how to bring up the best man according to a given theory of ethics, which has been evolved at one time or other, and which is accepted as indisputable. Plato does not doubt the truth of his own ethics, and on its basis he builds up education, and on that education he constructs the state. Schleiermacher says that ethics is not yet an accomplished science, and therefore the bringing up and the education must have for their aim the preparation of men who should be able to enter upon such conditions as they find in life, and who should at the same time be able to work vigorously upon their future improvement. Education in general, says Schleiermacher, has for its aim the presentation of a member all prepared to the state, church, public life, and science. Ethics alone, though it is not a finished science, gives us an answer to the question what kind of a member of these four elements of life an educated man shall be.

Like Plato, so all the philosophical pedagogues look to ethics for the problem and aim of education, some regarding this ethics as well-known, and others regarding it as an eternally evolving consciousness of humanity; but not one theory gives a positive answer to the question of what and how to teach the masses. One says one thing, another another, and the farther we proceed, the more their propositions become at variance. There arise at one and the same time various contradictory theories. The theological tendency struggles with the scholastic, the scholastic with the classical, the classical with the real, and at the present time all these directions exist, without contending with each other, and nobody knows what is true and what false. There arise thousands of various, strangest theories, based on nothing, like those of Rousseau, Pestalozzi, Froebel, and so forth; there appear side by side all the existing schools: the real, the classical, and the theological establishments. Everybody is dissatisfied with what is, and nobody knows that something new is needed and possible.

If you follow out the course of the history of the philosophy of pedagogics, you will find in it, not a criterion of education, but, on the contrary, one common idea, which unconsciously lies at the foundation of all the pedagogues, in spite of their frequent divergence of opinion, — an idea which convinces us of the absence of that criterion. All of them, beginning with Plato and ending with Kant, tend to this one thing, to the liberation of the school from the historical fetters which weigh heavily upon it. They wish to guess what it is that man needs, and on these more or less correctly divined needs they build up their new school.

Luther wants people to study Holy Writ in the original, and not according to the commentaries of the holy fathers. Bacon enjoins the study of Nature from Nature, and not from the books of Aristotle. Rousseau wants to teach life from life itself, as he understands it, and not from previously instituted experiments. Every step forward taken by the philosophy of history consists only in freeing the school from the idea of instructing the younger generations in that which the elder generations considered to be science, in favour of the idea of instructing it in what are the needs of the younger generations. This one common and, at the same time, self-contradictory idea is felt in the whole history of pedagogy: it is common, because all demand a greater measure of freedom for the school; contradictory, because everybody prescribes laws based on his own theory, and by that very act that freedom is curtailed.

The experience of past and of existing schools? But how can this experience prove to us the justice of the existing method of compulsory education? We cannot know whether there is not another, more legal method, since the schools have heretofore not yet been free. It is true, we see at the highest rung of education (universities, public lectures) that education strives to become ever more free. But that is only a supposition. Maybe education at the lower steps must always remain compulsory, and maybe experience has proved to us that such schools are good.

Let us look at these schools, without consulting the statistical tables of education in Germany, but by trying to know the schools, and learn their influence on the masses in reality.

This is what reality has shown to me: A father sends his daughter or son to school against his wish, cursing the institution which deprives him of his son's labour, and counting the days up to the time when his son will become *schulfrei* (this expression alone shows how the people look at the schools). The child goes to school with the conviction that the only power of which he knows, that of his father, does not approve of the power of the state, to which he submits upon entering school.

The information which he receives from his older companions, who were in that institution before, is not calculated to enhance his desire to enter school. Schools present themselves to him as an institution for torturing children, — an institution in which they are deprived of their chief pleasure and youthful needs, of free motion; where *Gehorsam* (obedience) and *Ruhe* (quiet) are the chief conditions; where he needs a special permission to go out "for a minute;" where every misdeed is punished with a ruler (although in the official world corporal punishment with the ruler is declared abolished) or by the continuation of study, — the more cruel condition for the child.

School justly presents itself to the child's mind as an establishment where he is taught that which nobody understands; where he is generally compelled to speak not his native *patois*, *Mundart*, but a foreign language; where the teacher for the greater part sees in his pupils his natural enemies, who, out of their own malice and that of their parents, do not wish to learn that which he has learned; and where the pupils, on their side, look upon their teacher as their enemy, who only out of personal spite compels them to learn such difficult things. In such an institution they are obliged to pass six years and about six hours every day.

What the results must be, we again see from what they really are, not according to the reports, but from actual facts.

In Germany nine-tenths of the school population take

away from school a mechanical knowledge of reading and writing, and such a strong loathing for the paths of science traversed by them that they never again take a book into their hands.

Let those who do not agree with me show me the books that the people read; even the Badenian Hebel, and the almanacs, and the popular newspapers are read as rare exceptions. As an incontrovertible proof that the masses have no education serves the fact that there is no popular literature and, above all, that the tenth generation has to be sent to school with the same compulsion as the first.

Not only does such a school breed loathing for education, but in these six years it inculcates upon these pupils hypocrisy and deceit, arising from the unnatural position in which the pupils are placed, and that condition of incoherence and confusion of ideas, which is called the rudiments of education. During my travels in France, Germany, and Switzerland I tried to discover the information held by pupils, their conception of school, and their moral development, and so I proposed the following questions in the primary schools and outside of schools to former pupils: What is the capital of Prussia or Bavaria? How many children did Jacob have? Tell the story of Joseph!

In the schools they sometimes delivered themselves of tirades learned by rote from books; those who had finished the course never answered the questions. If not learned by heart, I hardly ever could get an answer. In mathematics I discovered no general rule: they sometimes answered well, and sometimes very poorly.

Then I asked them to write a composition on what they had been doing on last Sunday. All the girls and boys, without a single exception, replied the same, that on Sunday they had used every possible chance of praying, but that they had not played. This is a sample of the moral influence of the school.

To my question, which I put to grown men and women, why they did not study after leaving school, or why they did not read this or that book, they invariably replied that they had all been to confirmation, that they had passed the quarantine of the school, and that they had received a diploma for a certain degree of education,— for the rudiments.

In addition to that stupefying influence of school, for which the Germans have invented such a correct appellation, "*verdummen*," which properly consists in a continuous contortion of the mental faculties, there is another, a more injurious influence, which consists in the fact that during the long study hours, when the child is dulled by his school life, he is for a long period of time, so valuable at his age, torn away from all those necessary conditions of development which Nature herself has made.

One frequently hears or reads the statement that the home conditions, the rudeness of the parents, the field labour, the village games, and so forth, are the chief hindrances to school education. It may be that they really interfere with that school education, as pedagogues understand it; but it is time to convince ourselves that these conditions are the chief foundation of all education, and that they are far from being inimical and hindrances to the school, but that they are its prime and chief movers. A child could never learn to distinguish the lines which form the distinctive letters, nor numbers, nor could he acquire the ability to express his thoughts, if it were not for these home conditions. It seems strange that this coarse domestic life should have been able to teach the child such difficult things and should all of a sudden become unfit to instruct him in such easy things as reading, writing, and so forth, and should even become injurious for such an instruction. The best proof of this is found in the comparison of a peasant boy who has never had any instruction with a gentleman's son who has been for five years under the care of a tutor: the superiority of mind and knowledge is always on the side of the first.

More than that. The interest in knowing anything whatever and the questions which it is the problem of the school to answer are created only by these home conditions. Every instruction ought to be only an answer to the question put by life, whereas school not only does not call forth questions, but does not even answer those that are called forth by life. It eternally answers the same questions which had been put by humanity several centuries back, and not by the intellect of the child, and which he is not interested in. Such questions are: How was the world created? Who was the first man? What happened two thousand years ago? What kind of a country is Asia? What is the shape of the earth? How do you multiply hundreds by thousands? What will happen after death? and so forth.

But to the questions which life presents to him he receives no reply, the more so since, according to the police regulation of the school, he has no right to open his mouth even to ask to be allowed to go out, which he must do by signs in order not to break the silence and not to disturb the teacher.

The school is arranged in such a manner because the aim of the state school, established from above, is, for the main part, not to educate the people, but to educate them according to our method, — above all, that there should be schools, and plenty of them! Are there no teachers? Make them! But there are not enough teachers. Very well! let one teacher teach five hundred pupils: *mécaniser l'instruction, Lancasterian method, pupil teachers*. For this reason the schools which are established from above and by force are not a shepherd for the flock, but a flock for the shepherd.

School is established, not in order that it should be convenient for the children to study, but that the teachers should be able to teach in comfort. The children's conversation, motion, and merriment, which are their necessary conditions of study, are not convenient for the teacher, and so in the schools, which are built on the plan of prisons, questions, conversation, and motion are prohibited.

Instead of convincing themselves that, in order to act successfully on a certain object, it is necessary to study it (in education this object is the free child), they want to teach just as they know how, as they think best, and in case of failure they want to change, not the manner of their teaching, but the nature of the child itself. From this conception have sprung and even now spring (Pestalozzi) such systems as would allow to *mécaniser l'instruction*, — that eternal tendency of pedagogy to arrange matters in such a way that, no matter who the teacher and who the pupil may be, the method should remain one and the same.

It is enough to look at one and the same child at home, in the street, or at school: now you see a vivacious, curious child, with a smile in his eyes and on his lips, seeking instruction in everything, as he would seek pleasure, clearly and frequently strongly expressing his thoughts in his own words; now again you see a worn-out, retiring being, with an expression of fatigue, terror, and ennui, repeating with the lips only strange words in a strange language, — a being whose soul has, like a snail, retreated into its house. It is enough to look at these two conditions in order to decide which of the two is more advantageous for the child's development.

That strange psychological condition which I will call the scholastic condition of the soul, and which all of us, unfortunately, know too well, consists in that all the higher faculties, imagination, creativeness, inventiveness, give way to other, semi-animal faculties, which consist in pronouncing sounds independently from any concept, in counting numbers in succession, 1, 2, 3, 4, 5, in perceiving words, without allowing imagination to substitute images for these sounds, in short, in developing a faculty for crushing all higher faculties, so that only those might be evolved which coincide with the scholastic condition of fear, and of straining memory and attention.

Every pupil is so long an anomaly at school as he has not fallen into the rut of this semi-animal condition. The moment the child has reached that state and has lost all his independence and originality, the moment there appear in him various symptoms of disease, — hypocrisy, aimless lying, dulness, and so forth, — he no longer is an anomaly: he has fallen into the rut, and the teacher begins to be satisfied with him. Then there happen those by no means accidental and frequently repeated phenomena, that the dullest boy becomes the best pupil, and the most intelligent the worst. It seems to me that this fact is sufficiently significant to make people think and try to explain it. It seems to me that one such fact serves as a palpable proof of the fallacy of the principle of compulsory education.

More than that. Besides this negative injury, which consists in removing the children from the unconscious education which they receive at home, at work, in the street, the schools are physically injurious, — for the body, which at this early age is inseparable from the soul. This injury is especially important on account of the monotony of the scholastic education, even if it were good. For the agriculturist it is impossible to substitute anything for those conditions of labour, life in the field, conversation of elders, and so forth, which surround him; even so it is with the artisan and, in general, with the inhabitant of the city. Not by accident, but designedly, has Nature surrounded the agriculturist with rustic conditions, and the city dweller with urban conditions. These conditions are most highly instructive, and only in them can each develop. And yet, school lays down as the first condition of education the alienation from these conditions.

More than that. School is not satisfied with tearing the child away from life for six hours a day, during the best years of the child, — it wants to tear three-year-old children away from the influence of their mothers. They have invented institutions (*Kleinkinderbewahranstalt*, infant schools, *salles d'asile*) of which we shall have occasion to speak more in detail. All that is lacking now is the invention of a steam engine to take the place of wet-nurses.

All agree that schools are imperfect (I, on my side, am convinced that they are injurious). All admit that many, very many, improvements must be made. All agree that these improvements must be based on a greater comfort for the pupils. All agree that these comforts may be found out only through studying the needs of the children of school age and, in general, of every class in particular.

Now, what has been done for the study of this difficult and complex subject? For the period of several centuries each school has been based on the pattern of another, itself founded on the pattern of one before it, and in each of these schools the peremptory condition is discipline, which forbids children to speak, ask questions, choose this or that subject of instruction, — in short, all measures are taken to deprive the teacher of all possibility of making deductions in regard to the pupils' needs.

The compulsory structure of the school excludes the possibility of all progress. And yet, when we consider how many centuries have passed in answering the children's questions which it did not occur to them to put, and how far the present generations have departed from that ancient form of culture, with which they are inoculated, it becomes incomprehensible to us how it is these schools still exist. School, so it would appear to us, ought to be an implement of education and, at the same time, an experiment on the young generation, constantly giving new results. Only when experiment will be at the foundation of school, only then when every school will be, so to speak, a pedagogical laboratory, will the school not fall behind the universal progress, and experiment will be able to lay firm foundations for the science of education.

But perhaps history will answer our fruitless question: On what is the right based of compelling parents and pupils to be educated? The existing schools, it will tell us, have been worked out historically, and just so they must continue to evolve historically, and to change in conformity with the demands of society and of time; the farther we go, the better the schools become.

To this I will reply: in the first place, that exclusively philosophic arguments are just as one-sided and false as exclusively historical arguments. The consciousness of humanity forms the chief element of history; consequently, if humanity becomes conscious of the inadequacy of its schools, this fact of consciousness becomes a chief historical fact, upon which ought to be based the structure of the schools. In the second place, the farther we proceed, the schools do not get better, but worse, — worse as regards that level of education to which society has attained.

School is one of those organic parts of the state which cannot be viewed and valued separately, because its worth consists only in a greater or lesser correspondence to the remaining parts of the state. School is good only when it has taken cognizance of the fundamental laws by which the people live. A beautiful school for a Russian village of the steppe, which satisfies all the wants of its pupils, will be a very poor school for a Parisian; and the best

school of the seventeenth century will be an exceedingly
bad school in our time; and, on the other hand, the very
worst school of the Middle Ages was in its time better
than the best in our time, because it better corresponded
to its time, and at least stood on a level with the general
education, if not in advance of it, while our school stands
behind it.

If the problem of the school, admitting the most general
definition, consists in transmitting everything which the
people have worked out and have become cognizant of,
and in answering those questions which life puts to man,
then there is no doubt but that in the mediæval school
the traditions were more limited and the questions which
presented themselves in life were easier of solution, and
this problem of the school was more easily satisfied. It
was much easier to transmit the traditions of Greece and
Rome from insufficient and improperly worked out sources,
the religious dogmas, the grammar, and that part of mathematics which was then known, than to impart all those
traditions which we have lived through since, and which
have removed so far the traditions of antiquity, and all
that knowledge of the natural sciences, which are necessary in our day as answers to the every-day phenomena of
life. At the same time the manner of imparting this has
remained the same, and therefore the school has had to
fall behind and get, not better, but worse. In order
to maintain the school in the form in which it has been,
and not to fall behind the educational movement, it has
been necessary to be more consistent: it not only became
incumbent to make education compulsory, but also to
keep this education from moving forward by any other
path, — to prohibit machines, roads of communication,
and the art of printing.

So far as we know from history, the Chinese alone have
been logical in this respect. The attempts of the other
nations to restrict the art of printing, and, in general, the

restriction of the educational movement, have been only temporary and insufficiently consistent. Therefore, the Chinese of all the nations may, at the present time, pride themselves on a good school, one that completely corresponds to the general level of education.

If we are told that the schools are perfected historically, we shall only reply that the improvement of schools must be understood relatively, but that in respect to school, on the contrary, the compulsion becomes worse and worse in every year and with every hour; that is, they more and more depart from the general level of education, because their progress is disproportionate to the progress of education since the days of the invention of printing.

In the third place, in reply to the historical argument that schools have existed and therefore are good, I shall myself adduce a historical argument. Last year I was in Marseilles, where I visited all the schools for the working people of that city. The proportion of the pupils to the population is very great, and so the children, with few exceptions, attend school three, four, and even six years.

The school programmes consist in learning by heart the catechism, Biblical and universal history, the four operations of arithmetic, French orthography, and bookkeeping. In what way bookkeeping could form the subject of instruction I was unable to comprehend, and not one teacher could explain it to me. The only explanation I was able to make to myself, when I examined the books kept by the students who had finished the course, was that they did not know even three rules of arithmetic, but that they had learned by heart to operate with figures and that, therefore, they had also learned by rote how to keep books. (It seems to me that there is no need of proving that the *tenue des livres*, *Buchhaltung*, as it is taught in Germany and England, is a science which demands about fifteen minutes of explanation in case of a pupil who knows the four operations in arithmetic.)

Not one boy in these schools was able to solve, that is, to put the simplest problem in addition and subtraction. And yet, they operated with abstract numbers, multiplying thousands with ease and rapidity. To questions from the history of France they answered well by rote, but if asked at haphazard, I received such answers as that Henry IV. had been killed by Julius Cæsar. The same was the case with geography and sacred history. The same with orthography and reading. More than one half of the girls cannot read any other books than those they have studied. Six years of school had not given them the faculty of writing a word without a mistake.

I know that the facts which I adduce seem so incredible that many will doubt them; but I could write whole books about the ignorance which I have witnessed in the schools of France, Switzerland, and Germany. Let any one who has this thing at heart study the schools, not from the reports of public examinations, but from extended visits and conversations with teachers and pupils in the schools and outside the schools. In Marseilles I also visited a lay school, and another, a monastic school, for grown persons. Out of 250,000 inhabitants, less than one thousand, of these only two hundred men, attend these schools. The instruction is the same: mechanical reading, which is acquired in a year or in longer time, bookkeeping without the knowledge of arithmetic, religious instruction, and so forth. After the lay school, I saw the daily instruction offered in the churches; I saw the *salles d'asile*, in which four-year-old children, at a given whistle, like soldiers, made evolutions around the benches, at a given command lifted and folded their hands, and with quivering and strange voices sang laudatory hymns to God and to their benefactors, and I convinced myself that the educational institutions of the city of Marseilles were exceedingly bad.

If, by some miracle, a person should see all these estab-

lishments, without having seen the people in the streets, in
their shops, in the cafés, in their home surroundings, what
opinion would he form of a nation which was educated in
such a manner? He certainly would conclude that that
nation was ignorant, rude, hypocritical, full of prejudices,
and almost wild. But it is enough to enter into relations,
and to chat with a common man in order to be convinced
that the French nation is, on the contrary, almost such as
it regards itself to be: intelligent, clever, affable, free from
prejudices, and really civilized. Look at a city workman
of about thirty years of age: he will write a letter, not
with such mistakes as are made at school, often without
mistakes; he has an idea of politics, consequently of
modern history and geography; he knows more or less
history from novels; he has some knowledge of the
natural sciences. He frequently draws and applies mathematical formula to his trade. Where did he acquire all
that?

I involuntarily found an answer to it in Marseilles,
when, after the schools, I began to stroll down the streets,
to frequent the dram-shops, *cafés chantants*, museums,
workshops, quays, and book-stalls. The very boy who
told me that Henry IV. had been killed by Julius Cæsar
knew very well the history of the "Three Musketeers"
and of "Monte Cristo." I found twenty-eight illustrated
editions of these in Marseilles, costing from five to ten
centimes. To a population of 250,000 they sell thirty
thousand of them, — consequently, if we suppose that ten
people read or listen to one copy, we find that all have
read them. In addition there are the museum, the public
libraries, the theatres. Then the cafés, two large *cafés
chantants*, where each may enter for fifty centimes'
worth of food or drink, and where there are daily as
many as twenty-five thousand people, not counting the
smaller cafés, which hold as many more: in each of these
cafés they give little comedies and scenes, and recite

verses. Taking the lowest calculation, we get one-fifth of the population, who get their daily oral instruction just as the Greeks and Romans were instructed in their amphitheatres.

Whether this education is good or bad is another matter; but here it is, this unconscious education which is so much more powerful than the one by compulsion; here is the unconscious school which has undermined the compulsory school and has made its contents to dwindle down almost to nothing. There is left only the despotic form with hardly any contents. I say with hardly any contents, because I exclude the mere mechanical ability of putting letters together and writing down words, — the only knowledge which is carried away after five or six years' study. Here it must be remarked that even the mere mechanical art of reading and writing is frequently acquired outside of school in a much shorter period, and that frequently the pupils do not carry away from school even this ability, or it is lost, finding no application in life, and that there where the law of compulsory school attendance exists there is no need of teaching the second generation to read, write, and figure, because the parents, we should think, would be able to do that at home, and that, too, much easier than at school.

What I saw in Marseilles takes place in all the other countries: everywhere the greater part of one's education is acquired, not at school, but in life. There where life is instructive, as in London, Paris, and, in general, in all large cities, the masses are educated; there where life is not instructive, as in the country, the people are uneducated, in spite of the fact that the schools are the same in both. The knowledge acquired in cities seems to remain; the knowledge acquired in the country is lost. The direction and spirit of the popular education, both in the cities and in the villages, are absolutely independent from and generally contrary to the spirit which it is intended to instil into the schools. The education goes on quite independently of the schools.

The historical argument against the historical argument is found in considering the history of education, where we do not find that the schools have progressed in proportion to the people's development, but that, on the contrary, they have fallen and have become an empty formality in proportion with the people's advancement; that the more a nation has progressed in general education, the more has education passed away from school to life, making the contents of the school meaningless.

Leaving aside all the other means of education, the development of commercial relations, the improved intercommunication, the greater measure of personal liberty, and the participation of the individual in affairs of state, — leaving aside meetings, museums, public lectures, and so forth, it suffices to look at the mere art of printing and its evolution, in order to understand the difference in the condition of the old school and the new. The unconscious education of life and the conscious scholastic education have always gone side by side, complementing each other; but in the absence of the art of printing what insignificant amount of education could life afford in comparison with the school! Science then belonged to a few elect, who were in possession of the means of education. See, now, what share has fallen to the education afforded by life, when there is not a man who has not a book; when books are sold at an insignificant price; when public libraries are open to all; when a boy, as he comes from school, carries with him, not only his note-books, but also some cheap illustrated novel carefully concealed; when in our country two primers are sold for three kopeks, and any peasant of the steppe will buy a primer and will ask a transient soldier to show and teach him all the wisdom, which the latter had in former years learned in the course of many years from a sexton; when a gymnasiast abandons the gymnasium and from books alone prepares himself for the entrance examination at the university; when young people leave the university and, instead of studying the professors' notes, work directly on the sources; when, sincerely speaking, every serious education is acquired only from life, and not in school.

The last and, in my opinion, the most important argument consists in this: granting even that the Germans have a right to defend the school historically, on the ground of its existence for the period of two hundred years, what reason have we to defend the public school which we do not yet possess? What historical right have we to say that our schools must be such as the other European schools are? We have not yet a history of public education. But if we examine closely the universal history of popular education, we shall not only become convinced that we can in no way establish seminaries for teachers according to the German pattern, work over the German sound method, the English infant schools, the French lyceums and special schools, and thus catch up with Europe, but also that we Russians are living under exceptionally fortunate conditions as regards the popular education; that our school must not issue, as it had in mediæval Europe, from the conditions of civil life; must not serve certain governmental or religious ends; must not be evolved in the darkness of uncontrolling public opinion and of an absence of the highest degree of vital education; must not with new pain and labour pass through and get out of that vicious circle, through which the European schools passed so long, and which consists in the assumption that the school was to move the unconscious education, and the unconscious education was to move the school. The European nations have vanquished this difficulty, but of necessity have lost much in the struggle.

Let us be thankful for the labour which we are called

to make use of, and let us not forget that we are called to accomplish a new labour in this field. On the basis of what humanity has already experienced and in consideration of the fact that our activity has not yet begun, we are able to bring to bear a greater consciousness upon our labour, and, therefore, we are obliged to do so.

In order to borrow the methods of the European schools, we are obliged to distinguish that which in them is based on the eternal laws of reason from that which owes its origin to historical conditions. There is no general sensible law, no criterion, which justifies the violence which the school exercises against the people; therefore, every imitation of the European school will be not a step in advance, but a retrogression as regards our people, — it will be a treason to its calling.

It is intelligible why in France there has been evolved a school of discipline with the predominance of the exact sciences, — mathematics, geometry, and drawing; why in Germany there has been evolved a graduated educational school with the predominance of singing and analysis; it is intelligible why in England there have developed such a mass of societies founding philanthropic schools for the proletariat, with their strictly moral and, at the same time, practical tendencies; but what school is to be evolved in Russia is not known to us and never will be known, if we do not permit it to be worked out freely and in proper season, that is, in conformity with that historical epoch in which it is to develop, in conformity with its own history and still more with universal history. If we become convinced that popular education is advancing on the wrong path in Europe, then, by doing nothing for our popular education, we shall be doing more than if we should force upon it all that which seems good to us.

So the little educated people want to be better educated, and the educated class wants to educate the masses, but the masses submit to education only under constraint.

We have looked in philosophy, experience, and history for those principles which would give the educating class such a right, but we have found none; on the contrary, we have convinced ourselves that human thought is constantly striving after freeing the people from constraint in matters of education.

In looking for a criterion of pedagogics, that is, for a knowledge of what ought to be instructed and how to do it, we found nothing but the most contradictory opinions and institutions, and we have come to the conclusion that the farther humanity advanced, the less possible did such a criterion become. Looking for this criterion in the history of education, we have come to the conclusion that for us Russians the historically evolved schools cannot serve as patterns, and that, moreover, these schools, with every step in advance, fall more and more behind the common level of education, and that, therefore, their compulsory character becomes more and more illegal, and that, finally, education itself in Europe has, like oozing water, chosen another path for itself, — it has obviated the schools and has poured forth in the vital tools of education.

What are we Russians to do at the present moment? Shall we all come to some agreement and take as our basis the English, French, German, or North American view of education and any one of their methods? Or, shall we by closely examining philosophy and psychology, discover what in general is necessary for the development of a human soul and for making out of the younger generation the best men possible according to our conception? Or, shall we make use of the experience of history, — not in the sense of imitating those forms which history has evolved, but in the sense of comprehending those laws which humanity has worked out through suffering, — shall we say frankly and honestly to ourselves that we do not know and cannot know what the future generations may need, but that we feel ourselves obliged to study these wants and that we wish to do so? that we do not wish to accuse the people of ignorance for not accepting our education, but that we shall accuse ourselves of ignorance and haughtiness if we persist in educating the people according to our ideas?

Let us cease looking upon the people's resistance to our education as upon a hostile element of pedagogics, but, on the contrary, let us see in it an expression of the people's will which alone ought to guide our activities. Let us finally profess that law which so plainly tells us, both from the history of pedagogics and from the whole history of education, that for the educating class to know what is good and what bad, the classes which receive the education must have the full power to express their dissatisfaction, or, at least, to swerve from the education which instinctively does not satisfy them, — that the criterion of pedagogics is only liberty.

We have chosen this latter path in our pedagogical activity.

At the basis of our activity lies the conviction that we not only do not know, but we cannot know, wherein the education of the people is to consist; that not only does there not exist a science of education, — pedagogics, — but that the first foundation of it has not yet been laid; that the definition of pedagogy and of its aims in a philosophical sense is impossible, useless, and injurious.

We do not know what education is to be like, and we do not acknowledge the whole philosophy of pedagogy because we do not acknowledge the possibility of a man's knowing what it is he ought to know. Education and culture present themselves to us as historical facts of one set of people acting upon another; therefore, the problem of the science of education, in our opinion, is only the discovery of the laws of this action of one set of people upon another. We not only do not acknowledge in our generation the knowledge, nor even the right of a knowledge of what is necessary for the perfecting of man, but are also convinced that if humanity were possessed of that knowledge, it would not be in its power to transmit, or not to transmit such knowledge. We are convinced that the cognition of good and evil, independently of man's will, lies in humanity at large and is developed unconsciously, together with history, and that it is impossible to inculcate upon the younger generation our cognition, just as it is impossible to deprive it of this our cognition and of that degree of a higher cognition to which the next step of history will take it. Our putative knowledge of the laws of good and evil, and our activity in regard to the younger generation on the basis of these laws, are for the greater part a counteraction to the development of a new cognition, which is not yet worked out by our generation, but which is being worked out in the younger generation, — it is an impediment, and not an aid to education.

We are convinced that education is history, and therefore has no final end. Education, in its widest sense, including the bringing up, is, in our opinion, that activity of man, which has for its base the need of equality, and the invariable law of educational progress.

A mother teaches her child to speak only that they may understand each other; the mother instinctively tries to come down to the child's view of things, to his language, but the law of educational progress does not permit her to descend down to him, but compels him to rise to her knowledge. The same relation exists between the author and the reader, the same between the school and the pupils, the same between the state and society, — the people. The activity of him who gives the education has one and the same purpose. The problem of the science of education is only the study of the conditions under which a coincidence of these two tendencies for one common end takes place, and the indication of those conditions which retard this coincidence.

Thus the science of education, on the one hand, becomes easier to us in that it no longer puts the questions: what is the final aim of education, and for what must we prepare the younger generation? and so forth; on the other, it is immeasurably more difficult. We are compelled to study all the conditions which have aided in the coincidence of the tendencies of him who educates, and of him who is being educated; we must define what that freedom is, the absence of which impedes the coincidence of both the tendencies, and which alone serves as our criterion of the whole science of education; we must move step by step, away from an endless number of facts, to the solution of the questions of the science of education.

We know that our arguments will not convince many. We know that our fundamental convictions that the only method of education is experiment, and its only criterion freedom, will sound to some like trite commonplace, to some like an indistinct abstraction, to others again like a visionary dream. We should not have dared to violate the quiet of the theoretical pedagogues and to express these convictions, which are contrary to all experience, if we had to confine ourselves to the reflections of this article; but we feel our ability to prove, step after step, and fact after fact, the applicability and legality of our so wild convictions, and to this end alone do we devote the publication of the periodical *Yásnaya Polyána*.

# ON METHODS OF TEACHING THE RUDIMENTS

VERY many people are at the present time very seriously busy finding, borrowing, or inventing the best method for the instruction of reading; very many have invented and found this best method. We frequently meet in literature and in life with the question: By what method do you teach? I must, however, confess that this question is generally heard from people who are very little educated, and who for a long time have been instructing children as a trade, or from people who sympathize with the popular education from their cabinets, and who, to help it along, are ready to write an article, and to take up a contribution for the printing of a primer according to the best method, or from people who are biassed in favour of their one method, or, finally, from people who have never had anything to do with teaching, — from the public who repeat that which the majority of men say. People who seriously busy themselves with it and who are cultured no longer ask such questions.

It seems to be an accepted truth with everybody that the problem of the public school is to teach reading, that the knowledge of reading is the first step in education, and that, therefore, it is necessary to find the best method for its instruction. One will tell you that the

sound method is very good; a second assures you that
Zólotov's method is the best; a third knows a still better
method, the Lancasterian, and so forth. Only a lazy man
does not make fun of teaching "*buki-az — ba*,"[1] and
all are convinced that for the sake of disseminating
education among the people all that is necessary is to
send for the best method, to contribute three roubles
in silver, rent a house, and hire a teacher, or, from the
superabundance of their own education, to offer a small
particle of it, on Sunday, between mass and visits, to the
unfortunate people that are perishing in ignorance, — and
the deed is done.

Some clever, cultivated, rich people have come together:
a happy thought flashes through the head of one of them,
and that is, to confer a benefit on the terrible Russian
people. "Let us do it!" All agree to it, and a society
is born, the aim of which is to foster popular education,
to print good, cheap books for the masses, to found
schools, to encourage teachers, and so forth. By-laws are
written up; ladies take part in it; they go through all
the formalities of such societies, and the society's activity
begins at once.

To print good books for the masses! How simple and
easy it looks, just like all great ideas. There is just one
difficulty: there are no good books for the people, not only
in our country, but even not in Europe. In order to
print such books they must be written first, but not one
of the benefactors will think of undertaking this task.
The society commissions somebody, for the collected
roubles, to compose, or select and translate the very best
(it is so easy to select it!) from the European popular
literature, — and the people will be happy, and will march
with rapid strides toward education, and the society is
very much satisfied.

[1] The Slavic names of the first two letters are *az*, *buki*, hence
*azbuka* = alphabet.

This society proceeds in just the same way in respect to the other side of the schools' activity. Only the rarest, swayed by self-sacrifice, apportion their precious leisure to the instruction of the masses. (These people do not take into consideration the circumstance that they have never read a single book on pedagogy, and have never seen any other school than the one in which they have studied themselves.) Others encourage the schools. Again it looks so simple, and again there is an unexpected perplexity, which is, that there is no other way of promoting education except by learning and completely devoting oneself to this matter.

But beneficent societies and private individuals somehow do not notice this perplexity, and continue in this manner to struggle on the arena of popular education, and remain very much satisfied. This phenomenon is, on the one hand, amusing and harmless, because the activity of these societies and of these people does not embrace the masses; on the other, this phenomenon is dangerous in that it casts a denser mist over our still unformed view of popular education. The causes of this phenomenon may be partly the irritable condition of our society, and partly the universal human weakness to make out of every honest idea a plaything for vanity and idleness. The fundamental cause, it seems to us, is in the great misapprehension of what the rudiments are, the dissemination of which forms the aim of all the educators of the people, and which has caused such strange discussions in our country.

The rudiments, a conception which exists not only in our country, but in all Europe, are acknowledged to be the programme of the elementary school for the people. *Lesen und schreiben, lire et écrire, reading and writing.* What are these rudiments? and what have they in common with the first step in education? The rudiments are the art of composing words out of certain signs and of representing them. What is there in common between the rudiments and education? The rudiments are a definite skill (*Fertigkeit*); education is a knowledge of facts and their correlations. But maybe this skill of composing words is necessary in order to introduce man into the first step of education, and maybe there is no other road? This we do not see at all; we very frequently perceive the diametrically opposite, if, in speaking of education, we shall understand not alone the scholastic, but also the vital education.

Among people who stand on a low level of education we notice that the knowledge or ignorance of reading and writing in no way changes the degree of their education. We see people who are well acquainted with all the facts necessary for farming, and with a large number of interrelations of these facts, who can neither read nor write; or excellent military commanders, excellent merchants, managers, superintendents of work, master mechanics, artisans, contractors, and people simply educated by life, who possess a great store of information and sound reasoning, based on that information, who can neither read nor write. On the other hand, we see those who can read and write, and who on account of that skill have acquired no new information. Everybody who will seriously examine the education of the people, not only in Russia, but also in Europe, will involuntarily come to the conclusion that education is acquired by the people quite independently of the knowledge of reading and writing, and that these rudiments, with the rare exceptions of extraordinary ability, remain in the majority of cases an unapplied skill, even a dangerous skill, — dangerous because nothing in life may remain indifferent. If the rudiments are inapplicable and useless, they must become injurious.

But perhaps a certain degree of education, standing above those examples of the rudiment-less education which we have adduced, is impossible without the rudiments? Very likely it is so, but we do not know that, and have no reason to suppose that for the education of a future generation. All we know is that the degree of education which we have, and outside of which we are not able and do not want to imagine any other, is impossible. We have an example in the primary school, which, in our opinion, forms the corner-stone of education, and we do not want to know all the degrees of education which exist, not below, but entirely outside, and independently of, our school.

We say: All those who do not know the rudiments are equally uneducated,—they are Scythians for us. The rudiments are necessary for the beginning of education, and we persist in leading the masses by that road up to our education. Considering the education which I possess, it would please me very much to agree with that opinion; I am even convinced that the rudiments are a necessary condition of a certain degree of education, but I cannot be convinced that my education is good, that the road over which science is travelling is the right one, and, above all, I cannot leave out of account three-fourths of the human race, who receive their education without the rudiments.

If we by all means must educate the people, let us ask them how they educate themselves, and what their favourite instruments for attaining this end are. If we want to find the foundation, the first step of education, why should we look for it perforce in the rudiments, and not much deeper? Why should we stop at one of the endless number of the instruments of education and see in it the alpha and omega of education, whereas it is only one of the incidental, unimportant circumstances of education?

They have been teaching the rudiments for quite a time in Europe, but still there is no popular literature; that is, the masses — the class of people exclusively occupied

## ON TEACHING THE RUDIMENTS

with physical labour — nowhere read books. We should think that this phenomenon would deserve attention and elucidation, whereas people imagine that the matter is improved by continuing to teach the rudiments. All the vital questions are extremely easy and simple of solution in theory, and it is only when it comes to applying them that they prove not so easy of solution and break up into thousands of difficult questions.

It looks so simple and so easy to educate the masses: teach them the rudiments, if necessary, by force, and give them good books, and the deed is done. But in reality something quite different takes place. The masses do not want to study the rudiments. Well, we can force them. Another impediment: there are no books. We can order them. But the ordered books are bad, and it is impossible to order people to write good books. The main difficulty is that the masses do not want to read these books, and no one has as yet invented a method of compelling them to read these books; besides, the masses continue getting their education in their own way, and not in the primary schools.

Maybe the historical time for the people's participation in the common education has not yet arrived, and it is necessary that they study the rudiments for another hundred years. Maybe the people are spoilt (as many think); maybe the people must write their own books; maybe the best method has not yet been found; maybe, too, the education by means of the book and of the rudiments is an aristocratic means less adapted to the working classes than other instruments of education which have been evolved in our day. Maybe the chief advantage of instruction by means of the rudiments, which consists in the possibility of transmitting science without its auxiliary means, does not in our time exist for the masses. Maybe it is easier for a workman to study botany from plants, zoology from animals, arithmetic from the abacus, with which he has to deal, than from books. Maybe the workman will find time to listen to a story, to look at a museum or an exhibition, but will not find time to read a book. Maybe, even, the book method of instruction is absolutely contrary to his manner of life and composition of character. Frequently we observe attention, interest, and a clear comprehension in the workingman, if a knowing person tells or explains to him something; but it is difficult to imagine that same labourer with a book in his blistered hands, trying to make out the sense of a science popularly expounded to him on two printing sheets. All these are only suppositions of causes, which may be quite erroneous, but the very fact of the absence of a popular literature, and of the people's resistance to education by means of the rudiments, nevertheless exists in all of Europe. Even thus the educating class in all of Europe looks upon the primary school as the first step to education.

The origin of this apparently unreasonable conception will become very clear when we look closely at the historical progress of education. First were founded, not the lower, but the higher schools: at first the monastic, then the secondary, then the primary schools. From this standpoint, Smarágdov's text-book, which on two printing sheets presents the whole history of humanity, is just as necessary in the county school, as the rudiments are needed in the primary school. The rudiments are in this organized hierarchy of institutions the last step, or the first from the end, and therefore the lower school is to respond only to the exigencies of the higher schools.

But there is also another point of view, from which the popular school appears as an independent institution, which is not obliged to perpetuate the imperfections of the higher institution of learning, but which has its independent aim of the popular education. The lower we descend on this ladder of education, instituted by the state, the more the necessity is felt at each step of making the education independent and complete. From the gymnasium only one-fifth enter the university; from the county school only one-fifth enter the gymnasium; from the popular school only one-thousandth enter the higher institutions of learning. Consequently, the correspondence of the popular school to the higher institution is the last aim to be pursued by the popular school. And yet, only by this correspondence can be explained the view which looks upon the popular schools as upon schools of the rudiments.

The discussion in our literature of the usefulness or injuriousness of the rudiments, which it was so easy to ridicule, is in our opinion a very serious discussion, which will elucidate many questions. However, this discussion has existed elsewhere, too. Some say that it is injurious for the masses to be able to read books and periodicals, which speculation and political parties put into their hands; they say that the ability to read takes the labouring class out of their element, inoculates them with discontent with their condition, and breeds vices and a decline of morality. Others say, or infer, that education cannot be injurious, but must always be useful. The first are more or less conscientious observers, the others are theorists. As is always the case in discussions, both are entirely right. The discussion, we think, is due to the fact that the questions are not clearly put.

The first quite justly attack the rudiments as a separately inoculated ability to read and write without any other information (as is actually done by the vast majority of the schools, for that which is learned by rote is forgotten, and all that is left is the art of reading); the last defend the rudiments, understanding by it the first step in education, and are mistaken only in the wrong conception of the rudiments. If the question were put like this: Is the primary education useful to the people, or not? no one could answer it in the negative. But if we ask: Is it useful, or not, to teach the people to read when they cannot read and have no books for reading? I hope that every unbiassed man will answer: I do not know, just as I do not know whether it would be useful to teach the whole nation to play the violin or to make boots.

Looking more closely at the result of the rudiments in the form in which they are transmitted to the masses, I think the majority will express themselves against the rudiments, taking into consideration the protracted compulsion, the disproportionate development of memory, the false conception of the completeness of science, the loathing for a continued education, the false vanity, and the habit of meaningless reading, which are acquired in these schools. In the school at Yásnaya Polyána all the pupils who come to it from the primary schools constantly fall behind the pupils who enter from the school of life; they not only fall behind, but their backwardness is in proportion to the time they have spent in the primary school.

What the problem and, therefore, the programme of the popular school consists in, we cannot explain here, and do not even regard such an explanation as possible. The popular school must respond to the exigencies of the masses, — that is all which we can positively assert in regard to this question. What these exigencies are, only a careful study of them and free experiment can teach. The rudiments constitute only one small, insignificant part of these exigencies, in consequence of which the primary schools are probably very agreeable to their founders, but almost useless and frequently hurtful to the masses, and in no way even resemble the schools of primary education

For the same reason, the question how to teach the rudiments in the shortest possible time and by what method is a question of little importance in the matter of popular education. For the same reason, people who out

## ON TEACHING THE RUDIMENTS 41

of amusement busy themselves with primary schools will do much better if they will exchange this occupation for a more interesting one, because the business of popular education, which does not consist in the mere rudiments, presents itself not only as very difficult, but of necessity demands immediate, persistent labour and a study of the masses.

The primary schools make their appearance in measure as the rudiments are necessary for the masses, and they exist of their own accord to the extent to which they are wanted. These schools exist with us in large number for the reason that the teachers of these schools can impart nothing else of their knowledge but the rudiments, and that the people have the need of knowing a certain amount of these rudiments for practical purposes, — in order to read a sign, write down a figure, read the psalter over a deceased person for money, and so forth.

These schools exist like workshops for tailors and joiners; even the view held by the masses in respect to them and the methods of those who study are the same. The pupil in time somehow manages to learn by himself, and as the master employs the apprentice for his own needs, sending him to fetch brandy, chop wood, clean the gutter, just so there is here a period of apprenticeship. And just like the trade, the rudiments are never used as a means for further educating themselves, but only for practical purposes. A sexton or a soldier is the teacher, and the peasant sends one of his three sons to be an apprentice at the rudiments, as he would send him to a tailor, and the legal exigencies of both are satisfied. But it would be a crime and a mistake to see in this a certain degree of culture, and on this foundation to construct the state school, putting all the fault only on the method of the primary instruction, and to inveigle and force the people into it.

But in the school of popular education, as you under

stand it, they will tell me the teaching of the rudiments will still form one of the first conditions of education, both because the need of knowing the rudiments lies in the popular conception of education, and because the great majority of the teachers know the rudiments best of all, and thus the question of the method of primary instruction after all remains a difficult question and one demanding a solution.

To this we will reply that, in the majority of schools, on account of our insufficient knowledge of the masses and of pedagogy, education actually begins with primary instruction, but that the process of teaching the printed signs and the art of writing presents itself to us as very insignificant and long known. The sextons teach reading in three months by the "*buki-az — ba*" method; an intelligent father or brother teaches by the same method in much less time; according to the Zólotov and *Lautirmethode*, they say, reading may be learned faster still; but, whether they learn to read by one or the other method, nothing is gained if the children do not learn to comprehend what they read, which is the chief problem of primary instruction; and yet no one hears anything about this necessary, difficult, and undiscovered method. For this reason the question of how to teach the rudiments most conveniently, although demanding a reply, appears exceedingly insignificant to us, and the persistency in finding a method, and the waste of energy, which finds a more important application in the more advanced education, seem to us to be a great misunderstanding arising from an improper comprehension of the rudiments and of education.

So far as we know, all the existing methods may be classified into three methods with their combinations.

1. The method of "*azes*," of letter combinations and spelling, and the learning by rote of one book, — *Buchstabirmethode*.

## ON TEACHING THE RUDIMENTS 43

2. The method of vowels with the attachment of consonants which are expressed only in connection with a vowel.

3. The sound method.

Zólotov's method is a clever combination of the second and third, just as all the other methods are only combinations of these three fundamental methods.

All these methods are equally good; every one has its advantages over the others from some one side, or in regard to a given language, or even in respect to a certain ability of a pupil, and every one has its difficulties. The first, for example, makes the learning of the letters easy, by calling them *az, buki, vyedi,* or *apple, book,* and so forth, and transfers all the difficulty to spelling, which is partly learned by heart and partly acquired instinctively from reading a whole book by heart with a pointer.

The second facilitates the spelling and the consciousness of the vowellessness of the consonants, but complicates the study of the letters, the pronunciation of the semi-vowels, and in the case of the triple and quadruple syllables, especially in our language. This method in Russian makes matters difficult on account of the complexity and greater variety of shades in our vowels. " ' " and all the vowels formed with it, $'a = ya,$ $'e = ye,$ $'u = yu,$ are impossible; *ya* with *b* before it will be *b'ya,* and not *bya.* In order to pronounce *bya* and *byu, b'* and *bye,* the pupil must learn the syllables by rote, else he will say *b'ya b'yu, b,* and *b'ye.*

The sound method, one of the most comical monstrosities of the German mind, presents greater advantages in compound syllables, but is impossible in the study of the letters. And, notwithstanding the regulation of the seminaries which do not acknowledge the *Buchstabirmethode,* the letters are learned by the old method, only, instead of frankly pronouncing as before *ef, i, scha,* teacher and pupil contort their mouths in order to pronounce *f-i-sh*, and, at that, *sh* consists of *sch*, and is not one letter.

Zólotov's method presents great conveniences in combining syllables into words and in gaining the consciousness of the vowellessness of the consonants, but offers difficulty in learning the letters and in complicated syllable combinations. It is more convenient than the rest only because it is a combination of two methods, but it is still far from being perfect, because it is — a method.

Our former method, which consisted in learning the letters, naming them *be, ve, ge, me, le, se, fe*, and so forth, and then spelling aloud, by throwing off the useless vowel *e* and vice versa, also offers its conveniences and disadvantages, and is also a combination of three methods. Experience has convinced us that there is not one bad and not one good method; that the failure of a method consists in the exclusive adherence to one method, and that the best method is the absence of all method, but the knowledge and use of all methods and the invention of new ones according to the difficulties met with.

We have divided the methods into three categories, but this division is not essential. We only did so for clearness' sake; properly speaking, there are no methods, and each includes all the rest. Everybody who has taught another to read has made use for the purpose, though he may not know it, of all the existing methods and of all those that may ever exist. The invention of a new method is only the consciousness of that new side from which the pupil may be approached for his comprehension, and therefore the new method does not exclude the old, and is not only no better than the old, but even becomes worse, because in the majority of cases the essential method is divined in the beginning. In most cases the invention of the new method has been regarded as the annihilation of the old, although in reality the old method has remained the essential one, and the inventors, by consciously refuting the old methods, have only complicated matters and have fallen behind those who consciously had used the old and unconsciously the new and the future methods.

Let us adduce as an example the oldest and the newest methods: the method of Cyril and Methodius[1] and the sound method, the ingenious *Fischbuch*, in use in Germany. A sexton, a peasant, who teaches as of old *az*, *buki*, will always hit upon explaining to the pupil the vowellessness of the consonant by saying that *buki* is pronounced as *b*. I once saw a peasant who was instructing his son and who explained the letters as *b*, *r*, and then again continued to teach by the composition and spelling of the words. Even if the teacher does not hit upon it, the pupil will himself comprehend that the essential sound in be is *b*. That is the sound system. Nearly every old teacher, who makes the pupil spell a word of two or more syllables, will cover one syllable and will say: This is *bo*, and this *go*, and this *ro*, and so forth. This is in part the artifice of Zólotov's method and of the method of vowels. Every one who makes a pupil study the primer points to the representation of the word *God* and at the same time pronounces *God*, and thus he reads the whole book with him, and the process of spelling is freely acquired by the pupil, by uniting the organic with the dismembered elements, by uniting the familiar speech (the prayer, as to the necessity of the knowledge of which there can be no question in the child's mind) with the analysis of that speech into its component parts.

Such are all the new methods and hundreds of other artifices which every intelligent old teacher unconsciously employs in order to explain the process of reading to his pupil, giving him all liberty to explain to himself the process of reading in a manner most convenient to the pupil.

[1] The proto-apostles of the Slavs, the inventors of the Slavic alphabet, of which the Russian is but a variation.

Leaving out the fact that I know hundreds of cases of rapid acquisition of the art of reading by the old method *buki-az — ba*, and hundreds of cases of very slow acquisition by the new methods, I only affirm that the old method has this advantage over the new, that it includes all the new methods, even though it be only unconscious, while the new excludes the old, and also this other advantage that the old method is free, while the new is compulsory. What, free? they will tell me, when with the old methods the spelling was beaten in with rods, and with the new children are addressed as "you" and politely asked to comprehend?

It is right here that the strongest and most injurious violence is practised on the child, when he is asked to comprehend in precisely the same manner that the teacher comprehends it. Anybody who has himself taught must have noticed that *b, r, a* may be combined in as many different ways as 3, 4, and 8 may be added up. With one pupil 3 and 4 = 7, and 3 more = 10, and 5 is left; even so *a*, or *az*, and *r*, or *rtsy*, and *b* in front of *ra* makes *bra*. With another 8 and 3 = 11, and 4 more = 15; even so *buki, rtsy* must be *bra*, because they had been spelling *bra, vra, gra*, and so forth, and if not *bra*, then *bru*, and a thousand other ways, out of which *b, r,* and *a* will make *bra*, and this will be one, and, in my opinion, one of the last. One must never have taught and know nothing of men and children, to imagine that, since *bra* is only the combination of *b, r*, and *a*, every child needs only to learn *b, r*, and *a*, in order to be able to pronounce it. You tell him: *B, r, a* is what sound? He says *ra*, and he is quite right, — he hears it so; another says *a*, a third *br*, just as he will pronounce *shch* as *sch*, and *f* as *khv*,[1] and so forth. You tell him *a, e, i, o, u* are the main letters, but to him *l, r* are the chief letters, and he catches entirely different sounds from what you want him to.

[1] In the popular speech every *f* is in Russian changed into *khv*, etc.

## ON TEACHING THE RUDIMENTS 47

This is not the worst yet. A teacher from a German seminary, who has been instructed by the best method, teaches by the *Fischbuch*. Boldly, self-confidently he sits down in the class-room, — the tools are ready: the blocks with the letters, the board with the squares, and the primer with the representation of a fish. The teacher surveys his pupils, and he already knows everything which they ought to understand; he knows what their souls consist of, and many other things, which he had been taught in the seminary.

He opens the book and points to a fish. "What is this, dear children?" This, you see, is the *Anschauungs-unterricht*. The poor children will rejoice at this fish, if the report from other schools or from their elder brothers has not yet reached them, what the sauce is which·goes with this fish, how they are morally contorted and vexed for the sake of that fish.

However it be, they will say: "This is a fish."

"No," replies the teacher (what I am telling here is not a fiction, a satire, but the recital of facts which I saw in all the best schools of Germany and in those schools of England where they have succeeded in borrowing this most beautiful and best of methods). "No," says the teacher. "What do you see?"

The children are silent. You must not forget that they are obliged to sit orderly, each in his place, without moving — *Ruhe und Gehorsam*.

"What do you see?"

"A book," says the most stupid child. All the intelligent children have in the meantime thought of a thousand things which they see, and they know by instinct that they will never guess that which the teacher wants them to say and that they ought to say that a fish is not a fish, but something else which they cannot name.

"Yes, yes," joyfully says the teacher, "very good, — a book."

The brighter children get bolder, and the stupid boy does not know himself what he is praised for.

"And what is in the book?" says the teacher.

The quickest and brightest boy guesses what it is, and with proud joy says, "Letters."

"No, no, not at all," the teacher replies, almost dolefully, "you must think what you say."

Again all the bright boys keep a sullen silence and do not even try to guess, but begin to think what kind of glasses the teacher has, why he does not take them off, but keeps looking over them, and so forth.

"Well, what is there in the book?"

All are silent.

"What is here?"

"A fish," says a bold little lad.

"Yes, a fish, but not a living fish?"

"No, not a living fish."

"Very well. Is it dead?"

"No."

"Very well. What kind of a fish is it?"

"*Ein Bild,* — a picture."

"Yes, very well."

All repeat that it is a picture and imagine that all is ended. No, they ought to have said that it is a picture representing a fish. And this is precisely the way by which the teacher gets the pupils to say that it is a picture representing a fish. He imagines that the pupils reason, and does not have enough shrewdness to see that if he is ordered to get the pupils to say that it is a picture representing a fish, or that if he himself wants them to say so, it would be much simpler to make them frankly learn that wise saying by heart.

Fortunate are the pupils if the teacher will stop here. I myself heard one make them say that it was not a fish, but a thing — *ein Ding,* and that thing only was a fish. This, if you please, is the new *Anschauungsunterricht* in connection with the rudiments, — it is the art of making the children think. But now this *Anschauungsunterricht* is ended, and there begins the analysis of the word. The word *Fisch*, composed of letters, is shown on charts. The best and most intelligent pupils hope to redeem themselves, and at once to grasp the forms and names of the letters, but that's where they are mistaken.

"What has the fish in front?"

The intimidated ones keep silent, and finally a bolder boy says: "A head."

"Good, very good. Where is the head?"

"In front."

"Very well. And what comes after the head?"

"The fish."

"No, think!"

They must say: "The body — *Leib*." They finally say it, but they lose every hope and confidence in themselves, and all their mental powers are strained to comprehend that which the teacher needs. "The head, the body, and the end of the fish — the tail. Very well! Say all together: A fish has a head, a body, and a tail. Here is a fish composed of letters, and here is a painted fish."

The fish which is composed of letters is suddenly divided into three parts: into *F*, into *i*, and into *sch*. The teacher, with the self-satisfaction of a sleight-of-hand performer who has showered flowers on the audience, instead of sprinkling wine on them, removes the *F*, points to it, and says: "This is the head, *i* is the body, *sch* is the tail," and he repeats: "*Fisch, ffff iiii shshshsh*. This is *ffff*, this is *iiii, shshshsh*."

The poor children writhe, and hiss, and blow, trying to pronounce the consonants without vowels, which is a physical impossibility. Without being conscious of it, the teacher himself uses a semivowel, something between *u* in *urn* and *y* in *pity*. At first the pupils are amused by that hissing, but later they observe that they are supposed to memorize these *ff, ii, shsh,* and they say *shif, shish, fif,* and absolutely fail to recognize their word *Fisch, ffff — iiii — shshshsh.* The teacher, who knows the best method, will not come to their rescue, but will advise them to remember *f* from the words *Feder, Faust,* and *sch* from *Schürze, Schachtel,* and so forth, and will continue to ask them to say *shshshsh;* he will not only not come to their rescue, but will absolutely prohibit their learning the letters from the pictorial A B C, or from phrases, such as *a* stands for *apple, b* stands for *boy;* he will not permit them to learn syllables and to read what is familiar to them, without knowing syllabication; in short, to use a German expression, he ignores, — he is obliged not to know any other method but *Fisch,* and that a fish is a thing, and so forth.

There is a method for the rudiments, and there is a method for the primary development of thinking — *Anschauungsunterricht* (see Denzel's "*Entwurf*"); both are connected, and the children must pass through these eyes of needles. All measures have been taken so that there should be no other development at school, except along this path. Every motion, every word and question are forbidden. *Die Hände seien zusammen. Ruhe und Gehorsam.* And there are people who ridicule *buki-az — ba,* insisting that *buki-az — ba* is a method which kills all the mental faculties, and who recommend the *Lautirmethode in Verbindung mit Anschauungsunterricht;* that is, who recommend to learn by heart a fish is a thing, and *f* is a head, *i* a body, and *sch* the tail of a fish, and not to learn by rote the psalter and the Book of the Hours. English and French pedagogues proudly pronounce the difficult word *Anschauungsunterricht,* and say that they are introducing it with the primary instruction. For us this *Anschauungsunterricht,* of which I shall have to say more in detail, appears like something entirely incomprehensible. What is this object-teaching? What other kind of teaching can there be, if not object-teaching? All five senses take part in the instruction, therefore there has always been and always will be an *Anschauungsunterricht*.

For the European school, which is trying to get away from mediæval formalism, there is some sense in the name and idea of object-teaching as opposed to the former mode of instruction, and some excuse for the mistakes, which consist in retaining the old method and in changing only the external manner; but for us, I repeat it, *Anschauungsunterricht* has no meaning. Up to the present I have, after vain endeavours to find this *Anschauungsunterricht* and Pestalozzi's method in all Europe, discovered nothing but the statements that geography is to be taught from surface maps, if they can be had, colours from colours, geometry from drawings, zoology from animals, and so forth, something which each of us has known ever since our birth, which it was not at all necessary to invent because that has long ago been invented by Nature herself, so that anybody who is not brought up under contrary views knows it well.

And it is these methods and others similar to them, and the methods of preparing teachers according to given methods, which are in all seriousness proposed to us, who are beginning our schools in the second half of the nineteenth century, without any historical ballast and blunders weighing us down, and with an entirely different cognition than that which lay at the foundation of the European schools. Even leaving out of discussion the falseness of these methods and the violence exercised upon the spirit of the pupils, — why should we, with whom the sextons teach to read in six months, borrow the *Lautiranschauungsunterrichtsmethode*, under which they have to study a year and more?

We have said above that, in our opinion, every method is good and, at the same time, one-sided; each of them is convenient for a certain pupil and for a certain language and nation. For this reason the sound method and every other un-Russian method will be worse for us than *buki-az—ba*. If the *Lautiranschauungsunterricht* has produced such inglorious results in Germany, where several generations have been taught to think according to certain laws, defined by a Kant or a Schleiermacher, where the best teachers are trained, where the *Lautirmethode* was begun in the seventeenth century, — what would happen with us if a certain method, a certain *Lesebuch* with moral sayings should be adopted by law? What would be the result of an instruction according to any newly introduced method which is not assimilated by the people and by the teachers?

I will tell a few cases near at hand. This autumn a teacher, who had studied in the Yásnaya Polyána school, had opened a school in a village, where out of forty pupils one-half had been instructed according to the *azes* and syllabications, and one-third could read. After two weeks the peasants expressed their universal dissatisfaction with the school. The chief points of accusation were that the teacher taught in German *a, be,* and not *az, buki,* that he taught fairy-tales and not prayers, and that there was no order at school. Upon meeting the teacher I informed him of the opinion of the peasants. The teacher, a man with a university training, explained to me with a contemptuous smile that he taught *a, be,* instead of, *az, buki,* in order to facilitate spelling; that they read fairy-tales in order to get used to understanding what was read according to the pupils' intellects; and that, in conformity with his new method, he considered it unnecessary to punish the children, and that, therefore, there could not be that strict order to which the peasants were accustomed, who had seen their children with pointers on the syllables.

I visited this school two weeks later. The boys were

divided into three classes, and the teacher carefully went from one division to another. Some, of the lower division, were standing at the table and memorizing certain parts of a paper chart, on which there were the letters. I began to ask them questions: more than one-half of them knew the letters and named them: *az, buki*, and so forth; others knew even syllabication; one could read, but was learning anew, pointing with his finger and repeating *a, be, ve*, imagining that he was getting something entirely new; others again, of the middle division, were spelling *s, k, a — ska*, one asking questions and the others answering them. This they had been doing for more than two weeks, although one day is more than enough to acquire this process of casting off the superfluous letter *e*. Among these I also found some who knew syllabication in the old fashion and who could read. These, just like the others, were ashamed of their knowledge and recanted it, imagining that there was no salvation except in spelling *be, re, a — bra*. The third, in fine, were reading. These unfortunate ones were sitting on the floor and, each of them holding a book right before his eyes and pretending that he was reading, were repeating aloud these two verses:

"There where ends the vaulted sky,
People eat nor wheat nor rye—"

Having finished these verses, they began anew the same with saddened and anxious faces, now and then squinting at me, as much as to ask me whether they were doing well.

It is terrible and incredible to mention: of these boys some could read well, and others could not spell; those who could read kept themselves back from a feeling of friendship; those who could not, had for the last three weeks been repeating these two verses from the most abominable remodelling of Ershóv's poor fairy-tale, so far as the masses are concerned.

I began to examine them in sacred history: nobody knew anything, because the teacher, according to the new method, did not make them memorize, but told them stories from the abbreviated sacred history. I examined them in arithmetic: nobody knew anything, although the teacher had, again according to the new method, been showing all the pupils together numbers up to millions all at once, without making them learn by heart. I examined them in the prayers: not one knew anything; they said the Lord's Prayer with mistakes, as they had learned it at home. And all of them were excellent boys, full of life, and intelligence, and eagerness for instruction! The most terrible thing about it is that it was all done according to my method! Here were all the devices employed at my school: the study of the letters written by all at once with chalk, and the oral spelling, and the first intelligible reading for the child, and the oral account of sacred history, and mathematics without memorizing. At the same time, in everything could be felt the device, most familiar to the teacher, of learning by rote, which he consciously avoided, and which alone he had mastered and against his will applied to entirely different materials: he made them memorize not the prayers, but Ershóv's fairy-tale, and sacred history not from the book, but from his own poor, dead recital; the same was true of mathematics and spelling. It is impossible to knock it into the head of this unfortunate teacher of university training that all the accusations of the rude peasants are a thousand times just; that a sexton teaches incomparably better than he; and that if he wants to teach, he can teach reading according to the *buki-az — ba*, by making them memorize, and that in that way he could be of some practical benefit. But the teacher with the university training had, to use his own words, studied the method of the Yásnaya Polyána school, which he for some reason wanted to take as a pattern.

Another example I saw in the county school of one of our capitals. After having listened with trepidation to the best pupil of the highest class, as he rattled off the waterways of Russia, and to another, in the middle class, who honoured us with the story of Alexander the Great, my companion, with whom I was visiting the schools, and I were on the point of leaving, when the superintendent invited us to his room to look at his new method of primary instruction, invented by him and in preparation for the press. "I have selected eight of the most indigent boys," he said to us, "and am experimenting on them and verifying my method."

We entered: eight boys were standing in a group. "Back to your places!" cried the superintendent, in the voice of the most ancient method. The boys stood in a circle in soldierly fashion. He harangued us for about an hour, telling us that formerly this beautiful sound method had been in use in the whole capital, but that now it was left only in his school, and that he wanted to resuscitate it. The boys were standing all the time. Finally, he took from the table a chart with the representation of *c-a-t*. "What is this?" he said, pointing to cat. "*Cow*," replied a boy. "What is this? — *c*." The boy said *c*. "And this is *a*, and this *t*, together — *cat*. Add *mp* to this, and you will get *camp*." The children had the greatest difficulty in reciting to us these memorized answers. I tried to ask them something new, but nobody knew anything but *cat* and *cow*. I wanted to know how long they had been studying. The superintendent had been experimenting for two years. The boys were between the ages of six and nine, — all of them wide-awake, real boys, and not dummies, but living beings.

When I remarked to the superintendent that in Germany the sound method was used differently, he explained to me that in Germany the sound method was unfortunately falling into disuse. I tried to convince him of the opposite, but he, in proof of his idea, brought me from another room five German A B C's of the thirties and forties, composed by another than the sound method. We were silent and went away, while the eight boys were left to the superintendent to be further experimented upon. This happened in the fall of the year 1861.

How well this same superintendent might have taught these eight boys reading, by putting them orderly at tables with A B C books and pointers, and even pulling their toplocks, just as the old deacon, who had taught him, had pulled his! How very, very many examples of such teaching according to new methods may be found in our day which is so prolific in schools, not to mention the Sunday schools that swarm with such inconsistencies!

And here are two other examples of an opposite character. In a village school, which was opened last month, I in the very beginning of the instruction noticed a sturdy, snub-nosed fourteen-year-old boy who, whenever the boys repeated the letters, kept mumbling something and smiling self-contentedly. He was not inscribed as a pupil. I spoke to him and found that he knew all the letters, now and then falling into *buki*, *rtsy*, and so forth; as with others, so he, too, was ashamed of it, supposing that it was prohibited and something bad. I asked him syllabication and he knew it; I made him read, and he read without spelling out, although he did not believe he could do it.

"Where did you study?"

"In the summer I was with a fellow shepherd; he knew, and he taught me to read."

"Have you an A B C book?"

"Yes."

"Where did you get it?"

"I bought it."

"How long have you been studying?"

"During the summer: I studied whenever he showed me in the field."

Another pupil of the Yásnaya Polyána school, who had studied before from a sexton, a boy ten years of age, once brought his brother to me. This boy, seven years old, read well, and had learned to do so from his brother during the evenings of one winter. I know many such examples, and whoever wants to look for them among the masses will find very many such cases. What use is there, then, in inventing new methods and by all means abandoning the *az-buki — ba*, and to regard all methods as good except *buki-az — ba*?

Besides all that, the Russian language and the Cyrillian alphabet surpass all the other European languages and alphabets by their distinctive features, from which must naturally spring the especial mode of teaching reading. The superiority of the Russian alphabet consists in this fact, that every sound in it is pronounced just as it is, which is not the case in any other language. *Ch* [which we throughout this work transliterate as *tskh*] is pronounced *tskhe*, and not *she*, as in French, and not *khe* as in German; *a* is *a*, and not *i, e, a,* as in English; *s* is *s*, and *c* [*ts*] is *ts*, and not *ch* and *k*, as in Italian, not to mention the Slavic languages that do not possess the Cyrillian alphabet.

What, then, is the best method for teaching the reading of Russian? Neither the newest sound method, nor the oldest of the *azes*, letter combination, and syllabication, nor the method of the vowels, nor Zólotov's method. The best method for a given teacher is the one which is most familiar to the teacher. All other methods, which the teacher will know or invent, must be of help to the instruction which is begun by any one method. In order to discover the one method, we need only know according to what method the people have been studying longest; that method will in its fundamental features be most adapted to the masses. For us it is the method of letters, combinations, syllables, — a very imperfect one, like all methods, and therefore capable of improvement by means of all inventions, which the new methods offer us.

Every individual must, in order to acquire the art of reading in the shortest possible time, be taught quite apart from any other, and therefore there must be a separate method for each. That which forms an insuperable difficulty to one does not in the least keep back another, and vice versa. One pupil has a good memory, and it is easier for him to memorize the syllables than to comprehend the vowellessness of the consonants; another reflects calmly and will comprehend a most rational sound method; another has a fine instinct, and he grasps the law of word combinations by reading whole words at a time.

The best teacher will be he who has at his tongue's end the explanation of what it is that is bothering the pupil. These explanations give the teacher the knowledge of the greatest possible number of methods, the ability of inventing new methods, and, above all, not a blind adherence to one method, but the conviction that all methods are one-sided, and that the best method would be the one which would answer best to all the possible difficulties incurred by a pupil, that is, not a method, but an art and talent.

Every teacher of reading must be well grounded in the one method which has been evolved by the people, and must further verify it by his own experience; he must endeavour to find out the greatest number of methods, employing them as auxiliary means; must, by regarding every imperfection in the pupil's comprehension, not as a defect of the pupil, but as a defect of his own instruction, endeavour to develop in himself the ability of discovering new methods. Every teacher must know that every method invented is only a step, on which he must stand in order to go farther; he must know that if he himself will not do it, another will assimilate that method and

## ON TEACHING THE RUDIMENTS 59

will, on its basis, go farther, and that, as the business of teaching is an art, completeness and perfection are not obtainable, while development and perfectibility are endless.

# A PROJECT OF A GENERAL PLAN FOR THE ESTABLISHMENT OF POPULAR SCHOOLS

---

## I.

THE other day I read the Project of a General Plan for the Establishment of Popular Schools. That reading produced upon me an effect such as a man must experience when he receives the sudden news that the young grove, which he has known and loved so much, and which he has seen growing up under his eyes, is to be changed into a park, by cutting out here, clearing off and lopping there, by pulling out young shoots by the root and laying out pebble walks in their place.

The general idea of the Project is this: Considering it necessary to disseminate popular instruction, and surmising that the education of the masses has not yet begun and that it is hostile toward its future education; surmising that the statute of the year 1828, prohibiting persons not specially entitled to do so from opening schools and teaching, is still in force; surmising that the masses will never consider their own education without compulsion from without, or that, having undertaken it, they will not be able to carry it on,— the government imposes on the people a new, the largest of all the existing taxes, the school tax, and entrusts the officials of the ministry with the management of all the newly opened schools, that is, the appointment of teachers and choice of programmes and manuals. The government, in consideration of the new levy, puts itself under obligation before the people of finding and appointing fifty thousand teachers and of founding at least fifty thousand schools. However, the government has constantly felt its inadequacy in managing the existing parochial and county schools. All know that there are no teachers, and nobody dissents from that view.

This idea, so strange in all the barrenness of its expression to any Russian who knows his country, is in the Project shrouded in all kinds of excuses, expressions of intentions, and grants of privileges, which not one Russian has heretofore ever thought of doubting. However, it is not a new idea. It has been applied in one of the greatest countries of the world, namely, in the North American States. The results of the application of this idea in America have been comparatively very brilliant; nowhere has public education developed so fast and so universally. That is quite true. But, if America, beginning its schools after the European States, has been more successful in its public education than Europe, all that follows from it is that it has fulfilled its historic mission, and that Russia, in her turn, must fulfil hers. By transplanting on her soil the American compulsory system (by means of levies), she would commit the same mistake that America would have committed if, in founding its schools, it should have applied the German or the English system. The success of America is due to the fact that its schools have developed in accordance with the time and the surroundings. Russia, it seems to me, ought to proceed in the same way; I am firmly convinced that for the Russian system of public education not to be worse than the other systems (taking into consideration all the conditions of the times it must be better), it must be independent and not like any other system.

The law of the school tax has been enacted in America by the people itself. If not the whole nation, at least the majority was convinced of the necessity of the proposed system of education, and had its full confidence in the government, to which it has entrusted the establishment of schools. If the levy has appeared in the nature of a compulsion, only an insignificant minority is affected by it.

As is well known, America is the only country in the world which has no peasant class, not only *de jure*, but even *de facto*, in consequence of which there could not in America exist that difference of education and that difference of opinion concerning education, which exists in our country between the peasant and the non-peasant population. Besides, America, in establishing its schools, was, I suppose, convinced that it had the essential element for the establishment of schools, — the teacher.

It we compare Russia and America in all their respects, the impropriety of transferring the American system upon Russian soil will become manifest to us.

I now turn to the Project itself. Chapter I. *General Considerations.*

§1. *In order to strengthen the masses in their religious and moral concepts and offer the whole peasantry and the lower classes of the urban population primary, general, and necessary information, schools in sufficient number, in proportion to the population, are to be established throughout the Empire by rural and urban Communes.*

What does it mean "establish"? By what process? We may be convinced that the people will take no part in the establishment of these schools; the people will only look upon the school tax as an increased burden.

## A PROJECT FOR POPULAR SCHOOLS 63

Who will select the place to build the school on? Who will appoint the teacher? Who will invite the children and will get the parents interested to send them? All those are questions to which I found no answer in the Project. All that will be done by officials of the Ministry of Public Instruction and by the justices of the peace with the coöperation of the local police; but in what manner and on the basis of what data?

*Are to be established throughout the Empire in sufficient number, in proportion to the population.* Leaving out of consideration the impossibility of subjecting the whole population of Russia to the same treatment as regards popular education, it seems to me, in addition, to be exceedingly inconvenient and dangerous in this manner forcibly to bring education to one common level. There are Governments, counties, and districts where there is a great need of schools (where the need is as great as two and three hundred pupils to every thousand of population), and where there is a need of schools with more extended programmes. On the other hand, there are localities where the need has not yet risen as high as fifty or even ten in every thousand of the population, and where the compulsory school will either be injurious, or, at the very least, the means set aside for the popular education will be wasted uselessly.

I know localities within a distance of twenty versts of each other; in one of these there is a free school, and nobody sends his children there; in the other, children are glad to walk a distance of three versts, and their parents are only too glad to pay fifty kopeks a month. The compulsory establishment of the school, in proportion to the population, produces in the first mentioned locality nothing but suspicion of the school and rage against it, while in the second the average proportion of the whole of Russia will be insufficient. Consequently the compulsory establishment of schools in proportion to the population would be partly an injurious and partly a useless waste of the money set aside for the popular education.

§2. *The popular schools have a course of primary instruction as defined by the Ministry of Public Instruction.*

It seems to me impossible to define a course for the popular schools.

Chapter VI. gives us a fine example of such an impossibility. There, for example, writing is not included in the programme, and, according to the sense of a note, writing may be taught only by special permission of the educational authorities.

§3. *The popular schools are open institutions, that is, they are intended only for day scholars.*

This article belongs to that order of many similar articles in the law, where a circumspect and serious explanation is given of that which nobody would doubt in the least. The appearance of such negative articles involuntarily makes us think that they were written solely in order to swell the volume of the Project, or because there happened to be some members on the committee who had insisted that the popular schools be made boarding-schools.

§4. *For the purpose of a constant and immediate control of each school, the Communes and municipalities, at whose expense the schools are supported, are entitled to elect curators of either sex; where such curators shall not be elected, the inspection of the school is incumbent on the justice of the peace.*

Who will chose these curators? Who will want to be a curator? And what do these curators mean? What is meant by inspection of schools? All that does not appear from the law.

The money will not be in the hands of the curator; the appointment and discharging of the teachers does not depend on the curator; the change of the school programme is not in the curator's power; what, then, I ask, is a curator? People who take delight in the name and who for it will sacrifice their money. Out of respect to the human race, I cannot admit that any one will be willing to assume that strange office, or that the municipalities and Communes will want to elect anybody to such a doubtful honour.

§5. *In their scholastic relations all the popular schools of the Empire are in charge of the Ministry of Public Instruction, and are governed by specially appointed directors of schools for each of the Governments.*

§6. *The material part of each school is managed by each Commune, at whose expense the school is maintained.*

§7. *No pay for the instruction of the pupils is levied except in the cases provided for in Arts. 25, 26.*

Art. 7, with its reference to Arts. 25, 26, belongs to the category of those serio-official articles which have been mentioned before. It means that the peasants who have already paid thirty kopeks a head for the school are fully privileged not to pay a second time for their children.

Articles 6 and 7 are far from being definite. What means the *educational part*, the maintenance of which is left to the director of schools, and what is the *material part*, which is left to the Commune? The appointment and dismissal of teachers, the arrangement of the school, the choice of a place for it, the teacher's pay, the choice of books and programmes, — all that depends on the Ministry of Public Instruction. What, then, does the remaining part, which is left in charge of the Commune, consist in? In the purchase of dampers and latches, in the choice of the left or right side to cut a door through, in the hire of a janitor for the school, in washing the floors, and so forth. Even in this case the Commune is granted only the right to pay for everything out of its own money. What is to be built and how, — all that is attended to by the law, and will be carried out by the educational authorities.

According to Art. 5 there is to be a director of schools.

Each director will have from three to five hundred schools under his charge. It will be impossible for him to visit all the schools once a year, consequently the business of the director of schools will be carried on from his office.

Chapter II. *The Establishment of Schools.*

I shall omit Articles 8 and 9, which deal with the town schools, which I have not studied and about which I, consequently, cannot judge.

§10. *In the rural districts every parish is obliged to have at least one popular school.*

The word "*obliged*" leaves no doubt as to whether the peasants, in accordance with the meaning of the Project, will be compelled to open schools, or not. The only questions that arise are : (1) What is a parish (the writers of the Project must have had in mind a township) ? and (2) What will be the procedure in case (which will happen most frequently) the peasants will refuse to take any interest whatever in the establishment of the schools, and will pay their school tax only under the pressure of police measures ? Who will select the place, the building, the teacher, and so forth ?

§11. *The parishes, whose means are not sufficient for the maintenance of schools, may, in lieu of establishing a school, hire a teacher at the Commune's expense for the purpose of giving instruction gratis to the children of said parish in a house set aside for him, or in the assembly house, or by rotation in the houses of the peasants.*

§12. *The rules laid down in the preceding Art. 11 will also guide the separate settlements, remote from parish churches, when, on account of such remoteness and unconvenient communication, it becomes difficult to send the children to the respective parish school.*

Articles 11 and 12 are, on the one hand, quite incomprehensible, and, on the other, belong to the category of elucidatory official articles, mentioned above.

When the parishes hire a teacher and rent a hut, what

keeps this from being a school, and why *may* the parishes only do it? I used to think that when we have pupils, a teacher, and a place in which to teach, we have a school; why, then, are a teacher, a schoolroom, and pupils not a school? But if we are to understand that small, remote Communes have the right to choose their own teachers, without conforming to the law about the maintenance of the teacher, as laid down in the Project, and without writing the word "School" over the hut, — then no one has ever doubted this right, and all have made use of this right, and always make use of it, notwithstanding the prohibition of the law, which is unable to keep a father, uncle, or godfather from teaching one, two, three, or fifteen boys. All it says in this article is that the teacher is to be hired by the Commune, but this is in the majority of cases inconvenient, because all schools which are freely established are generally maintained by contributions from the parents, and not from the whole Commune, which is both more convenient and more just.

§§13, 14, and 15. *Where no possibility presents itself of arranging a separate school for girls, boys and girls shall be taught in one and the same school, by one and the same teacher, but at different hours of the day or on different days of the week. In places where there is no separate school for girls, the Commune may hire a lady teacher to help out the male teacher. Girls up to the age of thirteen years may be admitted to instruction with the boys of the same age.*

The girls, of whom mention is made in Art. 13, being above the age of thirteen years, are called maidens by the people, — and to suppose that the maidens would be permitted by their parents, or would themselves choose, to go to school with small boys, and to prescribe rules for them, in order to secure the popular morality, is the same as to prescribe laws for what is not and never can be. With the present popular view of education even the thought of it is out of the question. Even if such a case should arise in the next generation, Art. 14 has provided for it, giving the Commune the unheard-of right to hire, again at their own expense, a lady teacher. The instruction of women in schools has not yet begun, and I dare think that Articles 13, 14, and 15 have not divined all possible cases that may arise during such instruction. It seems to me in general that it is exceedingly difficult to vest in legal forms that which is not yet, and has not yet begun.

Chapter III. *The Maintenance of the Schools.*

I omit the articles dealing with the town municipalities.

Articles 20, 21, 22, and 23 decree a compulsory levy on the parish for the maintenance of the schools and for a Government fund.

We must repeat once more that, in spite of the seeming definiteness of these articles, we do not comprehend many very essential things; namely: Who apportions the necessary amount of money for the schools? Who receives this money, and under what conditions? Have the Communes the right to declare themselves poor on the basis of Articles 10 and 11? I am sure that all the Communes without exception will be anxious to invoke this right, and therefore its elucidation is exceedingly important. From the above mentioned articles it appears only that the writers of the Project propose to burden the rural population with a tax, which is to be used for the establishment of schools and for the formation of a Governmental fund. By an extremely faulty calculation, attached to the law, twenty-seven and one-half kopeks from each soul will fall to the share of each peasant. This tax is enormous, and in reality it will be more than increased sixfold, for (p. 18) the calculation there adduced is based on the statistical data furnished by Academician Veselóvski, in a memoir of the Imperial Russian Geographical Society, and not only is groundless, but must contain some typographical error. It is hard to believe that the

members of the committee should have known so little
the conditions of the country in which they live, and the
conditions of the popular education, to which they have
devoted their labours.

*The number of children subject to primary instruction,
that is, of those between the ages of eight to ten years, forms
about five per cent. of the whole mass of the population.*

The number of children subject to primary instruction
will be three times the figure mentioned, because, no
doubt, it is known to everybody who takes the trouble
of visiting a popular school that the normal school age is
not from eight to ten years, but rather from seven to thirteen, or, more correctly, from six to fourteen years. At
the present time, with the insufficient dissemination of
schools, there are in the Yásenets township 150 pupils
to one thousand souls, in the Golovénkov township sixty
pupils to four hundred souls, and in the Trásnen township
seventy pupils to five hundred souls. With the present
undeveloped condition of the schools there are everywhere
not five per cent., but twelve per cent. and fifteen per cent.
It must be kept in mind that by far not all the children
study now, and that the girls form but one-twentieth of
all the pupils.

*Consequently, to one thousand of the male population,*
proceeds the Project, *we must assume about fifty boys who,
on account of age, are subject to primary instruction, and
in the same number of the female population there will be
about fifty girls. The teaching of such a number will not
be too burdensome for one teacher.*

We have pointed out above that there will be three
times as many pupils, and it is not only burdensome, but
simply impossible to teach fifty boys and girls together.
But that is not the worst of the typographical blunder.
Every Russian knows that in Russia there are six months
of winter, with frosts and snow-storms, while in summer
the peasant children are doing some field labour, and in

winter few have enough warm clothing to venture out
any distance; they run about the street with their
father's short fur coat thrown over their heads, and back
again to the hut, and upon the oven. In Russia the
great majority of the population is scattered in settlements of from fifty to one hundred souls, at a distance
of from two to three versts from each other. How can
one in Russia get as many as fifty pupils together in one
school? As facts have shown to me, one cannot count
on more than ten to fifteen pupils for one school.

If there was no mistake in the calculation, and the
Project was really meant to be executed, then, on the
basis of the blunder in the calculation concerning the percentage of the school population, the taxes will have
to be increased threefold, because there will be three
schools instead of one, of fifty pupils in each. On account of the blunder in the calculation, which brings
together fifty pupils into one school, the tax will have
to be doubled, that is, by supposing as high as twenty-five
pupils to each school, and six schools to each one thousand souls, we get six times twenty-seven and one-half
kopeks, which, deducting the ten per cent. of the Government fund, makes at least one rouble and a half to each
soul, without counting what is necessary for the establishment and for the repairs of the school, and for the
support of the teacher in kind. It is an impossible levy.
In a note to Art. 23, which is based *on an observation
deduced from practice, that the expenses of teaching frequently keep the uneducated parents from sending their
children to school*, it says that the appliances of education
and the text-books are not bought by the parents themselves, but by the person mentioned in the Project as
having charge of the expenses for the maintenance of
the school.

This observation deduced from practice is not true,
for, on the contrary, it has always and at all times been

observed that the parents prefer to buy their own books, slates, and pencils for their sons, in order that the things may always remain in the house, rather than give the money for the purchase of these things by the school; besides, these things are safer and more useful at home than at school.

In spite of it being mentioned in Art. 24 that *the expenses for the maintenance of the school are allowed by the village elder and audited by the village meeting,* I affirm that it does not appear from the Project who is entrusted with the expense for the maintenance of the school. Who is to put up a school building, where, when, what kind of a house? Who buys the school appliances? What books and pencils, and so forth, and how many are to be bought? All this is either passed by in the Project, or it is entrusted to the director of schools. The Communes have only the right to collect the money and give it away, also to rent or build a house, also to cut off half a desyatína of land for the teacher, also to travel to town for the purpose of buying dampers, and also, which is most flattering of all, to audit the accounts over which they have no control. All that is done, as it says in the Project, *in order to awaken in the Communes a greater readiness to provide the means for the support of the school.*

It is ordered *to give the Communes full liberty both in the apportionment and collection of the sum necessary for the maintenance of the school and in the material care of acquiring everything necessary for the schools.*

It seems to me that in this matter there is a lack of sincerity in the Project; it would have been simpler to say that the Communes are granted no rights whatever in the matter of the school government, but that, on the contrary, a new burden is imposed upon them, which is to acquire certain necessary things and look after the school accounts.

Art. 25 imposes the obligation of finding proper quarters for the school and for the teacher, and for providing heat for them. The obligation is very dimly defined, very burdensome, and, on account of its indefiniteness, liable to give rise to abuses on the side of the school authorities.

Art. 26 refers to towns.

In Art. 27 it is carefully explained that especial payment may be made by persons who have not contributed at large.

§28. *Towns and village parishes, which, on account of their sparse population and poverty of inhabitants, are really unable to support schools and even to hire a teacher, may receive aid, at the discretion of the Minister of Public Instruction, from the general reserve school fund.*

As has been pointed out above, all the Communes without exception will, if they understand the meaning of the Project, be anxious to fall under the provision of Art. 28, and they will quite justly remark that the majority of the inhabitants are poor. (Poverty, especially as regards money, is a well-known common condition of the Russian peasantry.) Who is to define what Commune falls under the provision of Art. 28 ? Which first, and which later ?

On what basis and by whom will similar questions be decided ? The Project tells us nothing concerning it, and yet, it is our opinion, these questions will universally arise.

Art. 29 again repeats that the Commune has the right to cut a door on the right or left side, to make pine or oak seats, and even not to be embarrassed in the manner of their acquisition; that is, they have the full right to buy them, or to build them from their own timber.

Art. 30 is the only one which, being a promise to find means for cheapening the text-books, meets with our full sympathy.

Articles 31, 32, and 33 do not properly refer to the establishment of village schools, but deal with the formation of the Government fund. We cannot agree with the wisdom of a measure which alienates from the Communes a certain part of their moneys and transfers it to the Government, which is again to use it for these Communes. It seems to us that this money could be more justly and more usefully applied to each Commune from which any amount is taken.

Chapter IV. *The Personnel of the Popular Schools.*

In Art. 34 it says that in every school there must be a teacher and a religious teacher, which is quite just. In addition to these, the Commune has the right to elect curators of either sex. The following articles explain that the curators have no meaning whatever and no rights whatever, and that in order to be elected they need have no qualifications.

Art. 37 explains *that the curators enter upon their duties immediately after the election, informing the director of schools of the Government of having entered upon said duties.*

In addition to this, Art. 38 declares that the curators are *not subject to, but only confer with* the educational authorities; they, therefore, do not write reports, but communications which is both exceedingly flattering and definite.

On the other hand, in Art. 36, where it says that the curators supervise the teachers in the correct fulfilment of their duties, and see to it that the teachers receive their pay promptly, that everything necessary is supplied to the school in proper time, and that the external order is preserved in the school, nothing is said as to what a curator can and must do in case of the teacher's improper execution of his duties. He may only communicate the fact to the director; he may do so justly or unjustly, with the knowledge of the matter, or, as may be supposed, more frequently, without the knowledge of the matter. It is not to be supposed that the interference of an entirely superfluous outsider could be of any use.

Articles 39, 40, 41, and 46 define the relations of the teacher of religion to the school.

Art. 42 says directly, without leaving the slightest doubt about the matter, that the management of the schools in each Government, in spite of the imaginary *complete independence* of the Communes and in spite of the incomprehensible invention of curators, is left to one person, — the director of schools, since the discharge and the appointment of a teacher form, according to our opinion, the only essential management of a school. We shall have occasion, later on, to speak at greater length of the inconvenience connected with the centralization of such an enormous power in the person of one man.

Art. 43 promises the training of teachers, although, as a promise, this article does not even enter into the composition of the Project; I cannot withhold the remark that the attempts at training any teachers whatever, both in our Pedagogical Institute, as also in the German seminaries and French and English normal schools, have so far led to no results, and have only convinced us of the impossibility of training teachers, especially for the popular schools, just as it is impossible to train artists and poets. Teachers are educated only in proportion to the general demands of education and with the raising of the general level of education.

Articles 44 and 45 explain that the belonging to a certain class is no impediment to a man's carrying on the duties of a teacher, and that people belonging to the clerical profession and those who are not of the gentry may be teachers; here it also says that if a clergyman undertakes to be a teacher, he must teach by all means! That is all very true. In a note to Art. 45 it says that the curator or justice of the peace recommends teachers for vacancies to the director of schools. I surmise that a brother or uncle of the curator or justice of the peace may recommend a teacher to the director.

Chapter V. *The Rights of Persons Connected with the Popular Schools.*

In Art. 47 it says that curators are not granted the privilege of wearing cockades and short swords. (I do not omit a single article, and the reader who will consult the Project will convince himself that I am quoting it correctly.)

Articles 48, 49, 50, and 51 define the material position of the teacher.

This position is superb, and we must confess that if the Project is to be put in force, we shall, in this respect, at once outdo Europe.

The village teacher is to get 150 roubles in silver a year, lodgings with heating, which, in our locality, means about fifty roubles. In addition to that, he is to receive, *in grain or flour* (by a provision of the Project the Communes are granted a great freedom in this matter), two puds [1] a month, which, according to our prices, will amount to about twelve roubles a year; he is to get, besides, half a desyatína [2] of land fit for a vegetable garden, which means another ten roubles, and thus the whole amounts to 222 roubles. (All this is to come from the Commune which, by the calculation adduced above, is hardly able to get together an average of twenty pupils.) In addition to this, the Commune is to pay the teacher of religion fifty roubles, for school appliances fifty roubles, and twenty-five roubles interest on the Government fund; it has to build and maintain the school, hire a janitor, which, at the least figure, means eighty roubles more, — and thus the Commune has to pay 427 roubles.

In Art. 50 it says that the Commune has the right to hire also a lady teacher.

[1] A pud is equal to almost thirty-six pounds.
[2] A desyatína is equal to about three acres.

A teacher who has served twenty years receives two-thirds of his yearly salary, and is, besides, exempt from taxation and military service, which will again be burdened upon the Commune to the extent of ten roubles a year. The position of the teacher is brilliant indeed, but I shall allow myself to question the willingness of the Communes to remunerate them so liberally, if they were to pay the teachers according to their deserts, or if the writers of the Project were compelled to draw the means from other sources. (The privileges granted the teachers, according to Articles 52, 56, and 57, namely, the right to be counted as being in government service, and the right of earning a medal or an Alexander ribbon, and to be elected as assistant director of schools, are not a burden to the Commune, but these, I venture to say, will not have that allurement for the teachers that the rights have which they are to enjoy at the expense of the Commune.)

The question of the increase of the salary of the popular school-teachers is a question which has for a long time been agitating the European governments, and which finds its solution only step by step; but with us this question is solved at once by a few lines of the Project. This very simplicity and facility of solution seem suspicious to me. The question involuntarily arises why did they fix it at 150 roubles, and not at 178 roubles and sixteen and one-third kopeks, for by paying 178 roubles and sixteen and one-third kopeks we should get better teachers still. Then again, why not put it at 178 roubles, when the source from which we are deriving the money is in our power, absolutely without any control? Why only half a desyatína of good soil for a vegetable garden, and not eight and two-thirds desyatínas for a field? In a note it says: *Clericals who at the same time occupy the positions of teacher of religion and of a regular teacher, are entitled only to a full teacher's salary and receive only one-half of the amount set aside for the teacher of religion.* These figures, no doubt, are all carefully chosen, since twenty-five roubles are so cautiously apportioned to the teacher of religion. These figures must have been arrived at from positive data. These data must be absolutely known, the more so, since it appears from the data which many of us have collected in our personal experience, that the school-tax which, according to that calculation, is imposed upon the Communes, is immeasurably high, exorbitant; that, in our opinion, not one Commune will agree to pay one-fifth of that tax for school, and that in Russia there is not to be found even one hundredth part of teachers deserving such remuneration.

Chapter VI. *The Course of Instruction in the Popular Schools.*

The first paragraph of Art. 58 defines the programme of the course in religion. Both the instruction and the consideration of this subject are left exclusively in the hands of the clerical profession.

(2) *The native tongue; the reading of books in Russian and in Slavic type; explanatory reading of books adapted to primary instruction.* (3) *Arithmetic: the four operations with integral numbers, abstract and concrete, and an idea of fractions. Note. In addition to these subjects, at the request of Communes, there may be introduced the instruction of church singing, and with the consent of the educational authorities also other subjects.*

We have expressed our conviction that the definition of a course of instruction for the popular schools is quite impossible, especially in the sense in which the Project is trying to make it, — in the sense of setting limits to the subjects of instruction. In this sense was conceived the circular published by the Minister of Public Instruction in reference to Sunday schools; in the same sense was composed the note according to which everything not defined by the programme in the preceding three lines may be taught only with the consent of the educational authorities; in the same providential sense are composed Articles 59, 60, and 61, by which the very method of instruction and the manuals to be used in the instruction of that impossible and narrow programme are to be determined upon by the Ministry of Public Instruction.

I do not mention that this is unjust; that it is injurious to the development of education; that it excludes the possibility of all lively interest of the teacher in his work; that it gives rise to endless abuses (the writer of a programme or of a text-book need only make one mistake, and that mistake becomes obligatory for the whole of Russia). I say only that every programme for the popular school is absolutely impossible, and every such a programme is only words, words, words. I can comprehend a programme which defines the obligation which teachers, or the power establishing the school, take upon themselves; I can understand how one may say to the Commune and to the parents: I am the teacher; I open the school, and I undertake to teach your children this or that, and you have no right to ask of me that which I have not promised you; but to open a school and to promise that one *will not teach* this or that is both imprudent and absolutely impossible. And it is precisely such a negative programme that the Project proposes for all of Russia and for the popular primary schools. In a higher institution, I presume, it is possible for the instructor, without deviation, to stick to one given course. In lecturing on the Roman civil law, a professor can bind himself not to speak of zoology or chemistry, but in a popular school the historical, natural, and mathematical sciences mingle, and at any minute questions arise in all the branches of these sciences.

The most essential difference between the higher and the lower school lies in the degree of subdivisibility of the subjects of instruction. In the lowest school it does not exist at all. Here all the subjects are united in one, and after this they gradually branch out.

Let us look at Articles 2 and 3 of the programme.

What is meant by native tongue? Does it include syntax and etymology? There are some teachers who regard both as the best means for teaching language. What is meant by the reading of books, and by explanatory reading? He who has learned his A B C book can read, and he who reads and understands the *Moscow Gazette* also only reads. How are the books to be explained, say the chrestomathy published by the society for the publication of cheap books? To take through with explanations all the articles of this book, would be tantamount to going through nearly the whole course of human knowledge, — theology, and philosophy, and history, and the natural sciences; and to read through the book by syllables and for the purpose of explanation to repeat each phrase by other incomprehensible words is also explanatory reading. Writing is entirely omitted in the Project; but even if it were allowed, and most precisely defined in the programme, one might understand by writing the mere copying of letters, or the knowledge of the art of the language; which may be acquired only by a whole course of subjects and exercises. The programme defines everything and nothing, nor can it define anything.

*In mathematics.* What is meant by the four operations on abstract and concrete numbers? I, for example, in my teaching, do not use concrete numbers, leaving the so-called concrete numbers for multiplication and division. Arithmetic in general I begin with progression, which every teacher does, for numeration is nothing but decimal progression. It says: *an idea of fractions.* But why only an idea? In my instruction I begin the decimal fractions at once with numeration. Equations, that is, algebra, I begin with the first operations. Consequently, I transcend the programme. Plane geometry is not indicated in the programme, and yet problems from plane geometry are the most natural and the most intelligible applications of the first rules. With one teacher geometry and algebra will enter into the teaching of the four operations; with another teacher the four operations will form only a mechanical exercise in writing with chalk on a blackboard, and for either the programme will be only words, words, words. So much the less is it possible to give the teacher instruction and guidance. For the successful progress of the teaching, the teacher must have the means for his own instruction and full liberty in the choice of his methods. It is convenient for one to teach by the *buki-az — ba* method, and for another by the *be-a*, and for a third by the *b-a* method, each being master of his. For the teacher to assimilate another method, it is not enough to know it and to prescribe it to him, — he must believe that this method is the best, and he must love it.

This refers both to the methods of the instruction itself, as also to the treatment of the pupils.

Circular instructions and prescriptions to the teachers will only embarrass them. More than once have I seen teachers instructing according to the sound method, just as according to the *buki-az — ba* method, memorizing letters, combinations, and syllables, and calling *buki* "*by*," and *dobro* "*dy*," but this was only done in the presence of the authorities, because such was the order.

As to the aim, which the committee may have had in view in writing out the programme, — the aim of warding off the possibility of any baneful influence of evil-minded teachers, — it must be said that no programme will keep a teacher from exerting a baneful influence upon his pupils. With such a programme the presence of a captain of gendarmes would become necessary in every school, for nobody could rely on the statements of the pupils, neither for nor against the teacher. The fact is that such fears are not in the least allayed by the programme, and

# A PROJECT FOR POPULAR SCHOOLS 81

that such fears are quite groundless. No matter how much a Commune is removed from the control over its schools, a father cannot be kept from being interested in that which is being taught to his son; and however compulsory a school may be, a mass of pupils cannot be kept from judging their teacher and giving him just the weight he deserves. I am fairly convinced, both by ratiocination and by experience, that a school is always secure against baneful influences by the control of the parents and by the sentiment of justice in the pupils.

In Art. 62 it says that the Communes may establish libraries; that is, nobody is forbidden to buy books, neither singly, nor in partnership, if they are so minded.

Chapter VII. *Of the Students in the Popular Schools, and of the Distribution of the Time of Study.*

§63. *Children may enter the popular schools with their eighth year. No preliminary knowledge is required of those who enter school.*

Why eight years and not six years and three and one-half months? This question demands just such positive proofs as that other question why teachers are to receive 150 roubles, and not 178 roubles and sixteen and one-third kopeks; and this the more, since I know by personal experience that at least one-fourth of the children going to school are below eight years of age, and that during this age, of from six to eight years, the children learn to read more rapidly, more easily, and better. All the children I know of, who are instructed at home, also begin much earlier than at eight years. That is the freest time for a peasant child, — a period during which he is not yet employed at domestic labour, and unreservedly devotes himself to the school until his eighth year. Why, then, did the writers of the Project take such a dislike to that age? It is absolutely necessary to know the ground on which children before the age of eight are excluded from the schools.

In the second part of the article there is a statement that no preliminary knowledge is required in those who enter. We cannot comprehend what that is for. Are those who enter obliged to wear canvas blouses in the summer, and the well-known uniform in winter?

If everything which is not needed is to be defined, this, too, ought to be stated.

In Art. 64 it says: *No definite period of instruction in the popular school is established; every pupil is declared to have finished his course of instruction whenever he has sufficiently acquired that which is taught in the school.*

We vividly imagine the joy and happiness of some Akhramyéy when he is declared to have finished a course.

§65. *In the village popular schools instruction shall begin from the time the field labours are ended, and shall last until the beginning of work in the following year, conforming to the local conditions of peasant life.*

Here the authors of the Project, apparently trying wisely to submit to the exigencies of actuality, again are in error, despite the shade of practicalness which this article has. What are the beginning and the end of rural labours? So long as there is a law upon it, this ought to be defined. The teacher, who in everything will comply with the law, will execute it promptly. And in this case, if the 1st of April is to be the last day, he will not teach a day too much. Let alone that it is difficult to define the period, in many localities a number of pupils will stay through the summer, and there will nearly everywhere be about a third of them. The peasants are everywhere firmly convinced, on account of the method of memorizing in vogue with them, that what has been learned will soon be forgotten; and so only those who are in need of their children unwillingly take them out for the summer, but even then they beg to have their children recite at least once a week. If it comes at all to writing a

Project, to conforming to the needs of the people, this ought to be written down too.

Art. 66 directs the attention to the fact that instruction is given during week-days, and not on holidays, with which one cannot help agreeing, as in the case of all such decrees, written down no one knows why, and expressive of absolutely nothing.

But Art. 67 again makes us stagger. There it says that *the pupils shall have but one session, and shall study not more than four hours, with a recess.*

It would be interesting to see the progress made by at least fifty pupils (and maybe even one hundred, as is intended by the calculation) studying only during the winter, and not more than four hours a day, with a recess! I have the boldness to consider myself a good teacher, but if I were given seventy pupils under such conditions I should say in advance that half of them would be unable to read in two years. As soon as the Project shall be confirmed, not one teacher, in spite of the half desyatína of garden land, will add one hour of work contrary to the regulation, lest, by not complying with the philanthropic foresight of the Project, he should exhaust the youthful minds of the peasant children. In a sufficiently large number of schools, which I know, the children study from eight to nine hours a day, and remain overnight at school so as to be able in the evening once more to recite to the teacher, and neither the parents nor the teachers observe any evil consequences from it.

According to Art. 69 there is to be an annual public examination. This is not the place to prove that examinations are injurious, and more than injurious, — that they are impossible. I have mentioned this in the article "The School at Yásnaya Polyána." In reference to Art. 69 I will limit myself to the question: "For what and for whom are these examinations?"

The bad and baneful side of the examinations in a

popular school must be evident to anybody: they lead to official deceit, forgery, useless mustering of children, and the consequent interruption of the customary occupations. The usefulness of these examinations is totally incomprehensible to me. It is injurious by means of examinations to awaken a spirit of rivalry in children eight years old, and it is impossible by means of an examination of two hours' duration to determine the knowledge of eight-year-old pupils and to judge of the merits of a teacher.

According to Art. 70 the pupils received stamped documents, called diplomas. As to what these documents are to be used for, nothing is said in the Project. No rights and no privileges are connected with them, and so I suppose that the deceptive idea that it is very flattering to have a stamped document will long be current among the people or will serve as an incitement for attending school. Even though at first the masses may be deceived as to the meaning of these papers, they will soon come to see their error.

Art. 71 grants the same right of stamped documents to people who have been instructed outside the school, and who, in my opinion, will still less be flattered by such a privilege.

Art. 72, with a note to it, on the contrary, deserves our full confidence, and, more than all the others, corresponds to the aim and spirit of the Project. It runs as follows: *At the end of each scholastic year, the teacher reports to the director of the Government, on the enclosed blank, as to the number of pupils in the popular school, and as to the number of those who have been subjected to examination for the purpose of receiving a diploma.*

*Note. This information contains statistical data, necessary for the final report to the Ministry of Public Instruction, and therefore its form must always agree with the questions, as defined by that report. The director of schools shall furnish the schools with printed blanks of such information, the expenses for printing to be credited to the sum allowed him for office appliances.*

How well everything is thought out! How everything has been provided for, — even the printing of the blanks, even the sum from which the expense is to be met! One simply feels the stern regularity and immutability of form and even of contents of the future reports, such as the government wants to get: not reports of what is to be in reality, not even of what is, — for the chief part of the education in private schools will slip away from these reports, — but of what ought to be according to the impracticable decrees of the government. With this article ends the whole Project of the state schools. Then follows:

Chapter VIII. *Private Popular Schools.*

Three articles of this chapter grant all persons the right to open private schools, define the conditions under which they may be opened, limit the programmes of such schools to the mere rudiments in the narrower sense, and establish the control of the clergy over them. One may be sure that in the *Nord* and in other foreign papers the granting of such a privilege will be received and esteemed as a new step toward progress which we are taking. The critic of the Project, who is unacquainted with Russian life, will take down the law of 1828, according to which the opening of schools and private instruction is prohibited, and, comparing the older restrictive measures with the new Project, in which one is only asked to give information of the opening of a school, will say that in matters of public education the Project gives incomparably greater freedom than was the case before. But for us, who are living a Russian life, the matter appears different.

The law of the year 1828 was only a law, and it never occurred to any one to comply with it; all, both society and the executors of the law, acknowledged its impracticability and the impossibility of carrying it out. There have existed and still exist thousands of schools without permission, and not one superintendent or director of a gymnasium has ever raised his hand to close these schools, because they do not comply with the articles of the law of 1828. By tacit consensus of opinion, society and the executors of the law accepted the law of 1828 as non-existing, and, in reality, in the teaching and opening of schools men were guided by a complete time-honoured liberty of action. The law passed by entirely unnoticed. I opened a school in 1849, and only in March of 1862 did I learn, upon the occasion of the promulgation of the Project, that I had no right to open such a school. Out of a thousand teachers and founders of schools scarcely one knows of the existence of the law of 1828. It is known only to the officials of the Ministry of Public Instruction.

For this reason it seems to me that Articles 73, 74 and 75 of the Project offer new rights only as regards supposedly existing restrictions, but when compared with the existing order of things, they only impose new restrictive and impracticable conditions. Nobody will be willing to establish schools, if he is not to have the right of appointing and dismissing teachers, himself choosing text-books, and of getting up his own programme. The majority of teachers and founders of schools — soldiers, sextons, cantonists [1] — will be afraid to report the establishment of their schools; many will not know of this requirement, and, if they want to do so, will know how to elude it in legal form. As I have said in the preceding article, it is impossible to define the limits between a home education and the school. The innkeeper has hired a teacher for his two children, and three others come to his house; the landed proprietor teaches four of the children of his manorial servants and two peasant children with his own; labourers come to me on Sundays, and to some of these

[1] Soldiers raised from boyhood in soldier-colonies.

I read, while others study the rudiments, or look at drawings and models. Are these schools, or not? And yet, what a field for abuses! I am a justice of the peace and am convinced that education is harmful for the masses, and so I fine an old man for having taught his godchild reading, and take away from him the A B C book and the psalter, on the ground that he ought to have informed me of the establishment of the school. There are relations of man to man, which cannot be defined by laws, such as the domestic relations, the relations of him who educates to him who is being educated, and so forth.

Chapter IX. *On the Government of Schools.*

Here it says that the government of the schools is entrusted to the director of schools, one to each province. In the Project there is frequent mention of the subdivision of the schools as regards their government into an educational part and some other kind of a part. I positively cannot comprehend this division, and I can see no other part in a school than the educational, from which springs the material part, naturally subject to it and in no way to be separated from it. According to the Project, everything is left in charge of the one director. The director, to judge from the indistinct expression of Art. 87 (*who has gained experience in matters of education during the period of his service as a teacher*), is to be selected from among the teachers of a gymnasium or from the professors. The director must personally supervise the instruction, and must even show how to act and teach,— there being but one director to three hundred or five hundred schools in the Government. In order to have the right to offer any kind of advice to a teacher, one must for at least a week study up the condition of each school, but, as everybody knows, there are only 365 days in the year. These officials will cost the government about two hundred thousand roubles for the whole of Russia.

In Art. 79 it says that the director is to avoid correspondence, but shall superintend in person.

In the following articles the director is given instructions as to what he is to demand of the teachers.

In Art. 86 the director is furnished with travelling expenses. It is the evident desire of the authors of the Project that the supervision of the director should not be formal, but real. But the very position of this official precludes the possibility of actual observation. An alumnus of the university, a former teacher at a gymnasium, or a professor at a university, that is, a man who has never had anything to do with the masses and with the popular schools, is obliged, living in the city and attending to his office duties, to the appointment of teachers, to rewards, reports, and so forth, to guide the schools which he can visit only once a year, if at all as often as that. I know directors of gymnasia, who are almost in the same situation, who with the greatest possible zeal and love busy themselves with the parochial schools, and who at every step, at revisions, at examinations, at appointments and exchanges of teachers, make blunder after blunder only because their circle of activity is a hundred times wider than it should or could be. One man may manage an army corps and, making one inspection, may know whether the corps is in good or bad order, but to manage a dozen schools is more than one man can do.

Everybody who knows the popular schools must know how difficult and how impossible it is by inspection or by an examination to ascertain the degree of success and the direction of a certain school. How often a conscientious teacher, with a feeling of his dignity and not allowing himself to show off his pupils, will appear in a worse light than a soldier-teacher who has been ruining his pupils for a year and who is working only in view of the final parade! And how cunning these unprincipled men

are, and how frequently they succeed in deceiving good
and honest superiors! There is hardly use in speaking
of the terrible injury which such a higher authority does
to the pupils. But even if my readers should not agree
with me on that score, the creation of the office of the
director will be useless and harmful for this reason alone,
if for no other, that one director to a Government will
appoint and discharge teachers and will offer rewards only
by hearsay, by supposition, or arbitrarily, because it is
impossible for one man to know what is going on in five
hundred schools.

Then follows a sample of a report on the number of
pupils, a calculation of the sum necessary for the maintenance of the popular schools, and the personnel of the
Governmental Office of Popular Schools. Then there
comes an explanatory note.

From the explanatory note it appears that the activity
of the committee was divided into two parts: (1) the
finding of measures for the development of the popular
instruction at the present time until the final adjustment
of the rural population; (2) the plan of the Project itself,
which we have been discussing. The preliminary measures have been realized, so far as I know, by a circular of
the Ministry of Internal Affairs as regards the order of the
opening of schools and the obligation of making announcement about them. In reference to the appointment and
dismissal of teachers by the director of the Government, to
the supervision entrusted to the local clergy, and to the
order that the text-books in use should be approved by
the Ministry of Public Instruction and by the Holy
Synod, I do not know, although I am specially interested
in schools, whether that is a request, or a law. It is very
likely that I am committing a crime when I use unapproved books in my school, and that the Communes are
also criminal in changing and appointing teachers without
the director. If such a law has been in force, or is to

be in force, it is not enough to fall back on the first article of the Code of Laws, which declares that the ignorance of the laws does not excuse any one; such new and unexpected laws ought to be read in all the churches and in all the parishes. We are equally ignorant whether the Ministry of Public Instruction has adopted the proposition of the committee of training teachers in the quickest time possible, and where and how many of them are undergoing such training. I have mentioned before that the measure prescribed in the circular of the Ministry of Internal Affairs is not practicable. Let us now turn to some of the thoughts expressed in the explanatory note, which have startled us most.

It would seem that there is no good cause for not being sincere in such a serious matter of state. I have in mind the part, meaning, and influence, which, in matters of education, is given, according to the Project, to our Russian clergy. I vividly present to myself the authors of the Project, who, when writing the note: *and entrusting the parochial clergy with the supervision of the education so that it be carried on in the spirit of Orthodox Christian morality*, etc., — I vividly present to myself the smile of submission and of the consciousness of their certain superiority and, at the same time, of the falseness of this measure, which must have played on the lips of the authors of the Project as they listened to the reading of this article and ordered it written down in the minutes. Just such a smile is produced by it on all experienced men who claim to know life.

"What is to be done? This is natural," say some. Other, inexperienced, intelligent people interested in the matter are provoked and become enraged at the reading of this article. From whom do they wish to conceal the sad truth? No doubt from the masses. But the masses know it better than we. Is it possible that, having lived so many centuries in the closest relations with the clergy, they have not learned to know and value them properly? The people appreciate the clergy and give them such a part and influence upon their education as the clergy deserve. In the Project there are many such insincere, diplomatic articles. As a matter of fact they will all be eluded, and it would make no difference if they had never been written; but these articles, as, for example, the one we have just mentioned, on account of their falseness and obscurity, open an enormous field for abuses which cannot be foreseen. I know some clergymen who say that to teach reading by the *be* method and not by *buki* is a sin; that to translate the Slavic prayers into Russian and to explain them is a sin; that sacred history should be taught only as set down in the A B C book, and so forth.

## II.

I MYSELF feel that my manner of discussing the Project is not sufficiently serious and that it looks as though I were making fun of the Project and as though I had set out to deny everything contained in it. Such a relation to the Project has arisen involuntarily as the result of the oppositeness of my practical view on matters, growing out of my close relations with the people, and from the absolute estrangement from reality, which is evident in the conception and draft of the Project. We occupy such opposite, distantly remote points of view that, in spite of the respect and even terror roused in me by the Project, I somehow cannot bring myself to believe in its reality, and, in spite of the efforts which I am making over myself, I am unable to remain quite serious in respect to it. I can find no retorts in the sphere of ideas in which the committee acted. The essence of my objections is directed, not against the mistakes and omissions of the Project, but against that very sphere of action from which it has emanated, and consists only in the denial of the applicability and possibility of such a Project.

I shall endeavour to transfer myself to that sphere of ideas and actions, from which the Project has emanated. It is clear to me why in the present period of universal reforms in Russia the question of establishing a system of popular education should naturally rise in governmental circles. The government, which has always taken the initiative in all reforms and innovations, must have naturally arrived at the conviction that precisely at this time it was incumbent upon it to establish a system of popular education. Having arrived at such a conviction, it naturally had to entrust the establishment of this system to certain officials of various ministries. Nothing more fundamental and more liberal could have been invented, or might have been expected, than the idea that representatives of all the ministries should take part in the authorship of this Project. (It may, however, be remarked that it is strange that to this committee, whose labours are a thousand times more important than those of the serf committee, no experts were invited, as had been done in the case of the deliberations of the question of the emancipation of the serfs. But this remark has no force because, in our opinion, the Project would have been little changed from what it is, even if so-called experts had been invited.) It was, of course, out of the question to let the people who are concerned in the Project, themselves, by means of their representatives, create that system.

People, very respectable though they be, who have served as officials, who have never studied the masses, nor the questions of popular education, who are no specialists in the business with which they were occupied, continuing their former occupations, having no time to devote dozens of years to the study of the question in hand, began to assemble on certain days of the week and to discuss the greatest question of creation, — popular education *in Russia*. It must also be remarked that the most essential question of the subordination of the schools to the Ministry of Public Instruction had been settled in the committee of the ministers, and that, therefore, the members of the committee were confined to the narrowest possible limits.

I take in advance all the members of the committee to have been highly cultured and moral men, pervaded by love for the masses and by a desire to benefit their country, and yet, in spite of it, I cannot assume that anything else could have resulted under the conditions under which they were working. Nothing but the Project which we are discussing could have resulted. In the whole Project we observe not so much a study of the national needs and a study of education itself and the determination of new laws based on such a study, as a struggle with something unknown, baneful, and deadening. The whole Project, as the readers have seen, is filled with articles stating that *popular schools are open establishments; that priests may teach only if they have the time for teaching; that no privileges are granted a curator; that teachers are not subject to preferments of rank; that there is no conventional form of school buildings; that private individuals may teach; that libraries may be established; that directors of schools shall visit the schools; that men belonging to any class may become teachers; that salaries are paid but once; that teachers are not to be prohibited from passing over to other occupations* (Art. 22 of the explanatory note); *that teachers need not wear any uniform*, etc., etc. The reading of this Project makes one living in the country marvel why such articles are written, and the Project is full of such articles, as may be seen from our analysis.

Working under such conditions of ignorance of the matter and of ignorance of the people and their needs, and, above all, under the restrictions which one feels throughout the whole Project, one can only marvel that it has not turned out much worse.

The question was put like this: There are no means and will be none; the popular education is to be subject to the Ministry of Public Instruction; the clergy must have the power of guiding and directing the spirit of the education; the management of the schools and the schools themselves are to be uniform throughout Russia, — now, make the system the best possible. To invent a Russian system of education, such as would spring from the needs of the people, is a matter of impossibility for a committee or for anybody else in the world, — one has to wait for it to grow out of the people. To divine the measures which may facilitate, and not hamper such a development, takes much time, labour, study, and freedom of view; none of these did the committee possess. To solve the question it was necessary to turn to the European systems. I suppose that officials had been sent to the various countries for the purpose of studying up their systems. (I even saw such investigators aimlessly wandering from place to place and concerned only about the thought of writing up a memoir to be presented to the ministry.)

On the basis of such memoirs, I suppose, all the foreign systems had been discussed in the committee. We cannot be grateful enough to the committee for having selected the least bad of all the inapplicable systems, the American. Having solved the main financial question on the basis of this system, the committee passed over to the administrative questions, being guided only by the predetermination of the committee of the ministers as to subordinating the schools to the Ministry of Public Instruction, and making use, for the information of the facts of the case, of such material as was at hand in St. Petersburg : of the memoir of the Geographical Society for the dissemination of the schools, and of the official reports of the religious department and of the directors for the determination of the number of schools, — and the Project was written up.

From the standpoint of the government, schools will be opened in Russia in proportion to the population, the moment the Project is made effective. In the majority of cases the well-to-do peasants will gladly pay twenty-seven and one-half kopeks for each soul, and in the poor settlements the schools will be opened gratis (from the government fund). The peasants, having such excellent schools, will not let their children be instructed by soldiers, but will gladly bring them to the school. For every thousand inhabitants (all this from the government point of view) there will be a beautiful house, which, although not constructed in a prescribed way, will bear the inscription "School" and will be provided with benches and tables and a reliable teacher appointed by the government.

The children of the whole parish will be gathered here. The parents will be proud of the diplomas which their children will receive; such a diploma will be regarded as the best recommendation for a lad, — and they will be more willing to give him a maiden in marriage and to give him work, if he has a diploma. Three or four years later not only boys, but girls also will attend school. One teacher, by dividing up the hours of the day, will teach one hundred pupils.

The instruction will be successful, in the first place, because by granting a reward the best method will be found, selected, and approved by the Ministry of Public Instruction, and this method will be obligatory for all schools (and after awhile the teachers will all be trained in this one, best method); in the second place, because the text-books will also be the best, being approved by the Ministry, like those of Bertet and Obodóvski. The teacher will be well provided for, and he will be attached to and united with the people, in the midst of whom he will live. The teacher, as in Germany, will with the priest form the aristocracy of the village, and will be the first friend and adviser of the peasants. For every vacancy among the teachers there will be dozens of candidates, from among whom the expert and cultured director will choose the worthiest.

The teacher of religion, for an appropriate remuneration, will confirm the children in the truths of the Orthodox faith. Since nearly all the young generation will be drawn to the school, all possibility of a further spread of the schism will stop.

## A PROJECT FOR POPULAR SCHOOLS

The means of the school will always be sufficient, not only for the teachers' pay, which is secured by means of a twenty-seven-kopek levy, but also for school appliances and for the buildings, the construction of which is left to the discernment of the Commune, so that the Communes will not stint the means, but, on the contrary, will contend in rivalry with each other. Not only will the Communes not spare the means, but each school will have its curators, and these persons, in sympathy with the popular education, — presumably rich people, — will come to the aid of the school, both by furnishing material means and by governing it. The slightest irregularity of the teacher or misunderstanding on the side of the parents will be removed by the curators or justices of the peace, who will gladly devote part of their leisure to the holy work of popular education, which rouses the sympathy of all the enlightened men of Russia.

The time of instruction will not be a burden to the moral powers of the pupils; the whole summer will be devoted to field labour. The course of instruction will contain the most essential knowledge and will coöperate in strengthening in the masses their religious and moral concepts. Evil-minded, coarse, uncultured people, being obliged to report the opening of their schools, will by that very act fall under the control of the educational authorities, and thus will be deprived of the possibility of doing any harm. The government schools will naturally be so good that the competition of the private schools will prove as impossible as it has proved in America, the more so since the government schools will be free.

The provincial authority over the schools will be concentrated in one cultivated, expert, independent person, — the director of schools. This person, materially secure and not bound by any bureaucratic exigencies, will all the time be making the round of the schools, examining, and personally watching over the progress of instruction.

It looks all so nice! One seems to see in his mind's eye large school buildings erected all over Russia, with iron roofs, presented by curators or by Communes; one sees, at the hour appointed by the ministry, the pupils gathering from the various villages, carrying knapsacks over their shoulders; one sees a cultured teacher, who has studied the best method, and a lady curator, filled with love for the work and present during classes and watching the instruction; one sees the director arriving in a carriage drawn by fine horses, for a third or fourth time that year, greeting the teacher and the pupils, nearly all of whom he knows, and giving the teacher practical advice; one sees the happiness and contentment of the parents, who are present at the examinations and who in trepidation are waiting for the rewards and the diplomas of their children; and one sees all over Russia the darkness of ignorance quickly dispelled, and the rude, ignorant people becoming all changed, growing in culture and happiness.

But there will be nothing of the kind. Reality has its laws and its demands. In reality, so far as I know the people, the application of the Project will lead to the following results:

It will be announced through the rural police or through the township offices that the peasants are to levy a tax of twenty-seven and one-half kopeks per head against such and such a date. They will be informed that this money is for the purpose of a school. Then there will be announced another levy for the building of the school; if it will be said that the amount of the levy depends upon them, the peasants will set it at three kopeks, so they will be compelled to make a stated levy. The peasants will, naturally, not comprehend this, and will not believe it. The majority will decide that there is an ukase from the Tsar to increase the tax, and that is all. The money will be collected with difficulty, through threats and use of force. The captain of the rural police will determine the place where the school is to be built and will demand that the Communes choose their own supervisors of the building. The peasants will, naturally, see in this a new tax, and will carry out the command only under compulsion. They will not know what to build or how to build it, and will only carry out the command of the authorities.

They will be told that they may elect a curator for their school; they will not comprehend this under any circumstances, not because they are so stupid and ignorant, but because they will fail to understand how it is they are not to have the right of watching in person over the instruction of their children, while they are to elect for that purpose a person that, in reality, does not possess that right either. The tax of twenty-seven and one-half kopeks, the levy for the building, the obligation to have it erected, — all that will breed in the people such a hostility to the idea and to the word "school," with which they naturally will connect the idea of taxation, that they will not wish to elect anybody, fearing lest they should be mulcted for the curator's salary. The captain and the justice will come down upon them, and they will in terror and trepidation choose the first man who happens to call himself a curator. The curator will be the same justice of the peace, or, nearly always, it will be the first landed proprietor of the village, who will be elected, and thus the curatorship will become his amusement and pastime, that is, the most serious business in the world will become his plaything or will serve him as a means for satisfying his vanity. The justice of the peace, as matters now stand, is not physically able to attend even to his direct duties; and it is an exceedingly difficult matter, demanding great knowledge and conscientious labour, to be the representative of a Commune, in relation to the control exercised by this Commune over the school. The majority of the curators will visit the school two or three times a month, will probably make a present of a home-made blackboard, on Sunday will invite the teacher to the house (and that is the best thing of all), and in case of a vacancy will recommend their godchild, the priest's son expelled from the theological school, or their former office lad.

Having built the school and paid the money, the Communes will conclude that they are through with the taxes, — but that is where they will be mistaken. The captain will announce to them that they are to cut off half a desyatína of the hemp-field for the teacher's use. Again there will be meetings, again the words "school" and "forcible alienation" will mingle in one inseparable idea. The peasants will go through their fields, trying to cut off the desired strip, and they will call each other names, and quarrel, and sin, as they call it, and will come together a second and a third time, and somehow, fulfilling the command of the authorities, will manage to deprive themselves of a piece of valuable garden land. But that is not all: there has to be another meeting in order to apportion the teacher's allowance of grain throughout the parish. (The contributions in kind are the most disliked of all by the peasants.) Finally the school is built, and the maintenance of the teacher is assured.

If the landed proprietor or the justice of the peace has not recommended his office lad, or godchild, the director of schools has to appoint his own teacher. The choice will be either very easy or very hard for the director of schools, for thousands of teachers, expelled from the seminaries, or discharged scribes, will every day be standing in his antechamber, treating his secretary to wine, and in every possible way trying to gain his favour. The director, a former teacher of a gymnasium, will, if he is an absolutely conscientious and cautious man, be guided in his choice of teachers only by the degree of their education, that is, he will prefer one who has finished a course to one who has not, and will thus constantly be making blunders. But the majority of directors, who do not look so severely upon their duties, will be guided by philanthropic recommendations and their good hearts: why not give a piece of bread to a poor man? — and thus they will commit the same blunders as the first. I see no juster means for the director's choice than the casting of lots.

One way or other, the teacher will be appointed. The Communes are informed that they may send their children without any farther expenses to the very school which has come so hard to them. The majority of peasants will everywhere give the same reply to such a proposition: "The devil take that school, — we are sick of it. We have lived so many years without a school, and we shall manage to get along without it; if I want my boy to learn something, I shall send him to the sexton. I know something about that instruction, and God knows what this will be: it may be they will teach my boy something, and then they will take him entirely away from me." Let us suppose that such an opinion will not be universal, that it will disappear in time, and that, seeing the progress of the children who have entered before, others will wish to send theirs; in that case, which I do not at all admit, only those who live in the village where the school building is will send their children there. No gratis instruction will entice the pupils in the winter from villages one verst distant from the school. That would be physically impossible. There will be an average of about fifteen pupils to a school. The remaining children of the parish will study with private people in the villages, or they will not study at all, while they will be counted in as attending school and will be so reported.

The success of the schools will be just the same as, if not worse than, the success obtained with private teachers, sextons, and soldiers. The teachers will be men of the same calibre, seminarists, for there are as yet no others, but with this difference: in the first case they are bound by no repressive conditions and are under the control of the parents who demand results corresponding to the money paid out by them, while in the government school, where they have to submit to methods, manuals, limitations of hours each day, and the interference of curators and directors, the results will certainly be worse.

The director will receive an enormous salary, will be travelling, and now and then bothering good, conscientious teachers, appointing poor teachers, and dismissing good ones, for it is impossible to know the conditions of the schools for a whole Government; as he must supervise them, he will at stated times make reports, which will be as unwittingly false as those are which are made now.

Private schools will exist just as they exist now, without giving information of their existence, and nobody will know anything of them, although in them will take place the chief movement of the popular education.

All that is not the worst, nor the most baneful thing. In all the branches of the Russian administration we are accustomed to the incompatibility of official legislation with actual conditions. It would seem, then, that there might be here the same incompatibility in matters of the popular education. What is faulty and inapplicable in the Project will be eluded, and much will be carried into effect and will be useful. With the Project a beginning of a system of popular education has at least been made, and whether good or bad, small or large, there will be at least one school to every thousand of the Russian population.

This would be quite true if the establishment of the schools, in the administrative and financial respect, were fully and frankly taken up by the government, and if that institution were just as fully and frankly transferred to the Commune, whereas in the Project before us the Commune is made to pay, and the government takes upon itself the organization of the schools. It is from this that naturally will spring that enormous moral evil, though it may not be apparent to all, which for a long time will undermine the development of education in the Russian people. The need of education is just beginning freely to take germ in the masses. After the manifesto of February 19th, the people everywhere expressed their conviction that they now need a greater degree of education and that, in order to acquire this education, they are ready to make certain sacrifices. This conviction has found its expression in the fact that everywhere free schools have been arising in enormous numbers. The masses have been advancing on the path on which the government would like to see them go.

Suddenly, by exerting an oppression on the free schools and by imposing an obligatory school tax upon all, the government not only does not acknowledge the previous educational movement, but, as it were, denies it: the government seems to be imposing the obligation of another, unfamiliar education on the masses, removing them from participation in their own affair, and demanding from them not guidance and deliberation, but only submission. Not only has my own experience shown to me in particular cases, but history and common sense indicate to us, the possible results of such interference: the masses will regard themselves as the martyrs of violence. The old sexton's schools will appear to them as sanctuaries, while the new government schools will seem to them to be sinful innovations, and they will in rage turn away from the very business which they had begun themselves in love, simply because the government has been in a hurry and has not given them a chance to think out the matter to its conclusion, has not given them a chance to select their own road, but has forcibly led them along a path which they do not yet regard as the best.

The realization of the Project will, in addition to its essential imperfections, breed one immeasurable evil: a schism of education, a taciturn negative resistance to the school, and a fanaticism of ignorance or of the old education.

# EDUCATION AND CULTURE

THERE are many words which have no clear definition and are easily taken one for the other, but yet are necessary for the transmission of thought. Such words are "education," "culture," and even "instruction."

Pedagogues sometimes do not acknowledge any distinction between culture and education, and yet are not able to express their thoughts otherwise than by using the words culture, education, instruction, or teaching. There must certainly be separate conceptions corresponding to these words. There may be some reasons why we do not wish to use these conceptions in their precise and real sense; but these conceptions exist and have a right to exist separately.

In Germany there exists a clear subdivision of the concepts as *Erziehung* (education) and *Unterricht* (instruction). It is assumed that education includes instruction, that instruction is one of the chief means of education, and that every instruction has in it an educational element, *erziehliges Element*. But the concept of culture, *Bildung*, is mistaken either for education, or for instruction. The most general German definition will be like this: education is the formation of the best men in conformity with the ideal of human perfection, worked out by a certain period. Instruction which introduces a moral development is a means, though not an exclusive means, toward its attainment; among the other means, outside of instruction, is the placing of the subject under education into certain conditions favourable to the ends of education, — discipline and compulsion, *Zucht*.

The spirit of man, say the Germans, must be broken in as the body is broken in by gymnastics. *Der Geist muss gezüchtigt werden.*

Culture, *Bildung*, in Germany, in society, and sometimes even in pedagogical literature, as already mentioned, is either mistaken for instruction and education, or is represented as a social phenomenon with which pedagogy has nothing to do. In the French language I do not even know a word corresponding to the concept of culture: *éducation, instruction, civilization* are entirely different concepts. Even thus there is no word in English which corresponds to the concept of *obrazovanie* (culture).[1]

The German practical pedagogues sometimes do not acknowledge the subdivisions into education and culture: both are welded into one inseparable whole. In talking once with the famous Diesterweg, I led him up to the question of culture, education, and instruction. Diesterweg spoke with malicious irony of people who made such subdivisions, for according to him all these ran together. And yet we spoke of *education, culture,* and *instruction,* and we clearly understood each other. He himself said that *culture* had an *educational* element which was included in every *instruction.*

What do these words mean? How are they understood, and how should they be understood?

---

[1] The Russian word for "culture," *obrazovanie*, means also "formation," being derived from a word meaning "image" or "form." Tolstóy is mistaken in not finding an equivalent word for it in English, for "culture" very nearly covers it. However, in this essay what is translated by "education" more nearly corresponds to "bringing up," while what is translated by "culture" frequently corresponds to the English connotations of "education," as which it is translated elsewhere in these essays.

I will not repeat the discussions and conversations I have had with pedagogues in respect to this subject, nor will I copy from books those contradictory opinions which are current in literature regarding this matter, — that would be a waste of time, and everybody who has read my first pedagogical article may verify the truth of my words, — but will only try to explain here the origin of these conceptions and the causes of their obscurity.

According to the conceptions of the pedagogues, education includes instruction.

The so-called science of pedagogy is interested only in education, and looks upon a man receiving his culture as upon a being entirely subject to the educator. Only through him does the man in the formative period of culture receive cultural or educational impressions, whether these impressions be books, stories, memorizing, artistic or bodily exercises. The whole external world is allowed to act upon the pupil only to the extent to which the educator finds it convenient. The educator tries to surround his pupil with an impenetrable wall against the influences of the world, and allows only so much to pass through his scientific scholastico-educational funnel as he deems to be useful. I am not speaking of what has been done by so-called unprogressive men, — I am not fighting windmills, — I am speaking of the comprehension and application of education by so-called excellent, progressive educators. Everywhere the influence of life is removed from the cares of the pedagogues; everywhere the school is surrounded with a Chinese wall of book knowledge, through which only so much of the vital cultural influence is admitted as may please the educators. The influence of life is not recognized. Thus the science called pedagogy looks upon the matter, for it assumes the right to know what is necessary for the formation of the best man, and it considers it possible to remove every extra-educational influence from its charge; even thus they proceed in the practice of education.

On the basis of such a view, education and culture are naturally confused, for it is assumed that if there were not education, there would not be culture. Of late, when people have begun dimly to conceive the necessity of a freedom of culture, the best pedagogues have come to the conclusion that instruction is the best means of education, but that the instruction is to be compulsory, obligatory, and thus have begun to confuse all three conceptions of education, culture, and instruction.

According to the conceptions of the theoretical pedagogue, education is the action of one man upon another, and includes three acts: (1) the moral or forcible influence of the educator, — mode of life, punishment; (2) teaching and instruction, and (3) the direction of vital influences upon the person under education. The mistake and confusion of ideas, in our opinion, arises from the fact that pedagogy takes for its subject education, and not culture, and does not perceive the impossibility for the educator of foreseeing, weighing, and defining all the influences of life. Every pedagogue admits that life introduces its influence before school and after school, and, in spite of all efforts to remove it, even into school. This influence is so strong that the whole influence of the school education is for the greater part annihilated; but the pedagogue sees in this only an insufficient development of the science and art of pedagogy, and insists upon regarding as his problem the education of men according to a certain pattern, and not their culture, that is, the study of the paths on which men become cultured, and the cooperation to this liberal culture. I admit that *Unterricht*, teaching, instruction, is part of *Erziehung*, education, but culture includes both.

Education is not the subject of pedagogy, but one of the

phenomena to which pedagogy cannot help paying attention; the subject of pedagogy ought to be and can be only culture. Culture, in its widest meaning, in our opinion, forms the sum total of all those influences which develop a man, give him a wider world conception, and furnish him with new information. Children's games, suffering, punishments of parents, books, work, compulsory and free instruction, the arts, the sciences, life, — everything gives culture.

Culture in general is to be understood as the consequence of all those influences which life exerts on man (in the sense of the culture of a man we say "a cultured man"), or, as the influence itself of all vital conditions upon man (in the sense of the culture of a German, a Russian peasant, a gentleman, we say, "This man has received a good or a bad culture [training]," and so forth). It is only with the last that we have to deal. Education is the action of one man upon another for the purpose of making the person under education acquire certain moral habits (we say, "They have educated him [brought him up] a hypocrite, a robber, or a good man." The Spartans educated brave men, the French educate one-sided and self-satisfied men). Instruction is the transmission of one man's information to another (one may instruct in the game of chess, in history, in the shoemaker's art). Teaching, a shade of instruction, is the action of one man upon another for the purpose of making the pupil acquire certain physical habits (one teaches how to sing, do carpentry, dance, row, declaim). Instruction and teaching are the means of culture, when they are free, and means of education, when the teaching is forced upon the pupil, and when the instruction is exclusive, that is, when only those subjects are taught which the educator regards as necessary. The truth presents itself clearly and instinctively to everybody. However much we may try to weld what is disconnected, and to subdivide what is inseparable, and to subordinate thought to the existing order of things, — truth is apparent.

Education is a compulsory, forcible action of one person upon another for the purpose of forming a man such as will appear to us to be good; but culture is the free relation of people, having for its basis the need of one man to acquire knowledge, and of the other to impart that which he has acquired. Instruction, *Unterricht*, is a means of both culture and education. The difference between education and culture lies only in the compulsion, which education deems itself in the right to exert. Education is culture under restraint. Culture is free.

Education, French *éducation*, German *Erziehung*, are conceptions which are current in Europe; but culture is a concept which exists only in Russia and partly in Germany, where there is an almost exact correspondence in the word *Bildung*. But in France and in England this idea and the word do not exist at all. *Civilization* is enlightenment, *instruction* is a European conception, untranslatable into Russian, which denotes a wealth of scholastic scientific information, or the transmission of such information, but is not culture, which includes the scientific knowledge, and the arts, and the physical development.

I spoke in my first article on the right of compulsion in matters of education, and have endeavoured to prove that, firstly, compulsion is impossible; secondly, that it brings no results or only sad results; thirdly, that compulsion can have no other basis but arbitrary will. (A Circassian teaches to steal, a Mohammedan to kill the infidels.) Education as a subject of science does not exist. Education is the tendency toward moral despotism raised to a principle. Education is, I shall not say an expression of the bad side of human nature, but a phenomenon which proves the undeveloped condition of human thought, and, therefore, it cannot be put at the base of intelligent human activity, — of science.

Education is the tendency of one man to make another just like himself. (The tendency of a poor man to take the wealth away from the rich man, the feeling of envy in an old man at the sight of fresh and vigorous youth, — the feeling of envy, raised to a principle and theory.) I am convinced that the educator undertakes with such zeal the education of the child, because at the base of this tendency lies his envy of the child's purity, and his desire to make him like himself, that is, to spoil him.

I know a usurious innkeeper, who has been making money by all kinds of rascalities, and who, in response to my persuasion and flattery to have him send his fine twelve-year-old boy to my school at Yásnaya Polyána, makes his red mug bloom out into a self-satisfied smile and constantly makes one and the same reply: "That is so, your Serenity, but it is more important for me first to saturate him with my own spirit." And so he takes him about with him and boasts of the fact that his son has learned to cheat the peasants who sell his father wheat. Who does not know the fathers, educated as yunkers and in military schools, who regard as good only that culture which is saturated with the spirit in which the fathers were educated? Do not professors in the universities and monks in the seminaries saturate their students with their own spirit in just such a way?

I do not want to prove that which I have already proved and which is very easy to prove, — that education as a premeditated formation of men according to certain patterns is *sterile, unlawful,* and *impossible.* Here I will confine myself to just one question. There are no rights of education. I do not acknowledge such, nor have they been acknowledged nor will they ever be by the young generation under education, which always and everywhere is set against compulsion in education. *How are you going to prove this right?* I know nothing and assume nothing, but you acknowledge and assume a new and for us non-existing right for one man to make of others just such men as he pleases. Prove this right by any other argument than by the fact that the abuse of power has always existed. Not you are the plaintiffs, but we,— while you are the defendants.

I have several times been answered orally and in print in reply to the ideas expressed in *Yásnaya Polyána*, just as one soothes an unruly child. I was told: "Of course, to educate in the same manner as they educated in the mediæval monasteries is bad, but the gymnasia, the universities, are something quite different." Others told me: "No doubt it is so, but taking into consideration, and so forth, such and such conditions, we must come to the conclusion that it could not be otherwise."

Such a mode of retorting seems to me to betray not seriousness, but weakness of mind. The question is put as follows: Has one man the right to educate another? It will not do to answer, "No, but—" One must say directly, "Yes," or "No." If "yes," then a Jewish synagogue, a sexton's school, have just as much legal right to exist as all our universities. If "no," then your university, as an educational institution, is just as illegal if it is imperfect, and all acknowledge it to be so. I see no middle way, not merely theoretically, but even in practice. I am equally provoked at the gymnasium with its Latin and at a professor of the university with his radicalism and materialism. Neither the gymnasiast nor the student have any freedom of choice. From my own observations even, the results of all these kinds of education are equally freaky to me. Is it not obvious that the courses of instruction in our higher institutions of learning will in the twenty-first century appear as strange and useless to our descendants, as the mediæval schools appear to us now?

It is so easy to come to this simple conclusion that if in the history of human knowledge there have been no absolute truths, but mistakes have constantly given way to other mistakes, there is no reason for compelling the younger generation to acquire information which is sure to prove faulty.

I have been told: "If it has always been that way, then what are you worrying about? It cannot be otherwise." I do not see that. If people have always killed each other, it does not follow that it ought always to be that way, and that it is necessary to raise murder to a principle, especially when the causes of these murders have been discovered, and the possibility of avoiding them has been pointed out.

The main thing is, why do you, who acknowledge the universal human right to educate, condemn bad education? A father condemns it, when he sends his son to the gymnasium; religion condemns it, looking at the universities; the government, society condemn it. Either you grant *everybody* the right, or you grant it to nobody. I see no middle. Science must decide the question whether we have the right to educate, or not. Why not tell the truth? The university does not like the clerical education, saying that there is nothing worse than the seminaries; the clericals do not like the university culture, saying that there is nothing worse than the universities, and that they are only schools of pride and atheism; parents condemn the universities, and the universities condemn the military schools; the government condemns the universities, and vice versa.

Who is right and who wrong? Healthy thought in the living, not the dead, people cannot, in view of these questions, busy itself with making pictures for object study; it must perforce get an answer to these questions. It makes no difference whether this thought will be called pedagogy or not. There are two answers: either we must acknowledge the right to be vested in those to whom we stand nearer, or whom we love most, or fear, even as the majority do (I am a priest, and so I consider the seminary better than anything else; I am a soldier, so I prefer the military school; if I am a student, I recognize only the universities: thus we all do, only that we strengthen our bias by more or less ingenious arguments, not noticing that all our opponents do the same); or the right to educate is not to be vested in anybody. I chose this latter way, and I have tried to prove why.

I say that the universities, not only the Russian universities, but those in the whole of Europe, since they are not entirely free, have no other basis than that of arbitrariness, and are as monstrous as the monastic schools. I beg my future critics not to shade down my deductions: either I am talking nonsense, or else the whole pedagogy is at fault,—there is no middle way. Thus, so long as no proof will be given of the right to educate, I shall not recognize it. Still, though I do not recognize the right to educate, I cannot help recognizing the phenomenon itself, the fact of the education, and I must explain it.

Whence comes education and that strange view of our society, that inexplicable contradiction in consequence of which we say that this mother is bad, she has no right to educate her daughter, let us take her away from her mother, this institution is bad, let us destroy it, this institution is good, let us support it? By dint of what does education exist?

If such an abnormal condition as the use of force in culture — education — has existed for ages, the causes of this phenomenon must be rooted in human nature. I see these causes: (1) in the family, (2) in religion, (3) in the state, and (4) in society (in the narrower sense, which in our country includes the official circles and the gentry).

The first cause is due to the fact that the parents, whoever they be, wish to make their children such as they are themselves, or, at least, such as they should like to be. This tendency is so natural that one cannot be provoked at it. So long as the right of each individual to free development has not yet entered into the consciousness of all the parents, nothing else can be expected. Besides, the parents will, more than anybody else, be dependent on what will become of their sons; consequently their tendency to educate them in their fashion may be called natural, if not just.

The second cause which produces the phenomenon of education is religion. As long as a man — Mohammedan, Jew, or Christian — believes firmly that a man who does not recognize his teaching cannot be saved, and for ever loses his soul, he cannot help wishing, even though by force, to convert and educate every child in his tenets.

I repeat: religion is the only lawful and sensible basis of education.

The third and most essential cause of education is contained in the need which the government has of educating such people as it can employ for certain purposes. On the basis of this need are founded the military schools, the schools of law, engineering, and others. If there were no servants of the government, there would be no government; if there were no government, there would be no state. Consequently, this cause, too, finds its unquestionable justification.

The fourth cause, finally, lies in the need of society, of that society which with us is represented by the gentry, the officialdom, and partly by the merchant class. This society needs helpers, abettors, and accomplices.

It is remarkable, — I beg the reader for clearness' sake to pay special attention to the following circumstance, — it is remarkable that in science and literature we continually meet with attacks made upon the compulsion of domestic education (they say the parents corrupt their children, — whereas it seems so natural for the parents to wish to make their children like themselves), and upon religious education (it seems it was but a year ago that all Europe groaned for a Jew boy who had been brought up by a Christian, whereas there is nothing more lawful than the desire to give the boy, who has fallen into my hands, the means of eternal salvation in the one religion in which I believe), and attacks upon the education of officials and officers; but how is a government, which is necessary for all of us, not to educate its servants for its own sake and for ours? Yet one does not hear any attacks directed against the education of society. Privileged society, with its university, is always right, and yet it educates the students in conceptions contrary to those of the masses, and has no other justification than pride. Why is that so? I think it is so, because we do not hear the voice of him who attacks us; we do not hear it, because it does not speak in print and down from the professor's chair. But it is the mighty voice of the people, which one must listen to carefully in order to hear it.

Take any public institution of our time and of our society, — from the popular school and the home for poor children to the female boarding-school, to the gymnasia and the universities, — in all of these institutions you will find one incomprehensible phenomenon which does not startle anybody. The parents, beginning with the peasants and burghers, and ending with the merchants and the gentry, complain that their children are educated in ideas foreign to their circle. The merchants and gentlefolk of the old style say: "We do not want universities and gymnasia which will make atheists and freethinkers of our children." The peasants and merchants do not want any schools, homes, or boarding-schools, because they do not want their children to become "white-hands" and scribes, instead of ploughmen.

All this time all the educators, without exception, from the popular schools to the higher institutions of learning, are concerned only about bringing up the children under their charge in such a way as not to resemble their parents. Some educators naïvely declare themselves to be, some, without declaring it, consider themselves to be, samples of what their pupils ought to be, and their pupils' parents they regard as samples of that rudeness, ignorance, and vice which they are not to be.

The lady teacher, a freaky creature, contorted by life, who places the whole perfection of human nature in the art of bowing, putting on a collar, and in speaking French, will inform you confidentially that she is a martyr to her duties; that all her educational efforts are lost in vain on account of the impossibility of completely removing the children from the influence of their parents; that her charges, who had already begun to forget Russian and to speak poor French, who had begun to forget their friendships with the cooks and their associations with the kitchen, and their running about barefoot, and who, thank God, had learned all about Alexander the Great and about Guadeloupe, upon meeting their home folk,— alas! — forget all that and acquire anew their trivial habits. This teacher will, without being embarrassed by the presence of her pupils, speak in derision of their mothers or in general of all women who belong to their circle, considering it her special merit, by means of ironical remarks upon the former circle of the pupils, to change their view and ideas.

I do not mention those artificial material surroundings which must entirely change the whole view of the pupils. At home all the comforts of life, the water, the cakes, good food, the well-prepared dinner, the cleanliness and comfort of the house, — all that depended on the labours and cares of the mother and of the whole family. The more labour and care, the more comforts; the less labour and care, the less comfort. It is a simple thing, but, I dare think, it is more instructive than French and

Alexander the Great. In the public education this constant vital reward for labour is removed to such an extent that, no matter whether the pupil will think of it or not, her dinner will be neither better nor worse, her pillow-slips will be neither cleaner nor more soiled, the floors will be waxed neither better nor worse; she has not even her own little cell, her corner, which she may fix up as she pleases, or not; nor has she a chance to make something for herself out of ribbons and odd pieces.

"Well, who would strike a prostrate person," nine-tenths of my readers will say, "so what sense is there in talking about the boarding-schools?" and so forth. No, they are not prostrate, they are up and about, leaning safely on the right of education. The boarding-schools are no way more monstrous than the gymnasia and the universities. At the base of all of them lies one and the same principle, which is, the right, delegated to one man, or to a small group of men, to make of other people anything they please. The boarding-schools are not prostrate, — thousands of them exist, and will exist, because they have the same right to furnish culture as the educational gymnasia and universities. The only difference is, if any, that we do not for some reason recognize the family's right to educate as they please, — we tear the child away from her corrupt mother and place her in a home, where a corrupt lady teacher will straighten her out.

We do not recognize the right of a religion to educate; we exclaim against the seminaries and monastic schools; we do not recognize the state's right to educate; we are dissatisfied with the military schools, with the schools of law, and so forth; but we lack the courage to deny the legality of the institutions in which society, that is, not the masses, but the higher society, claim the right to educate as they please, — the boarding-schools for girls and the universities. The universities? Yes, the universities. I will take the liberty of analyzing also this temple of wisdom. From my point of view it has not advanced one step beyond the boarding-school; more than that, in it lies the root of evil,— the despotism of society, against which no hand has yet been raised.

Just as the boarding-school has decided that there is no salvation without the instrument called a piano, and without the French language, even so one wiseacre, or a company of such wiseacres (I do not care if by this company will be understood the representatives of European science, from which we supposedly have borrowed the organization of our universities, — in any case this company of wiseacres will be very insignificant in comparison with that mass of students for whom the university is organized in the future), have established a university for the study of positively *all* sciences in their highest, their very highest development, and, you must not forget it, have established such institutions in Moscow, St. Petersburg, Kazán, Kíev, Dorpat, Khárkov, and to-morrow will establish some more in Sarátov and in Nikoláev; wherever they please, they will establish an institution for the study of all the sciences in their highest development. I doubt if these wiseacres have thought out the organization of such an institution.

The boarding-school teacher has an easier task: she has a model — herself. But here the models are too varied and too complex. But let us suppose that such an organization is thought out; let us suppose, which is less probable, that we possess people for these institutions. Let us look at the activity of such an institution and at its results. I have already spoken of the impossibility of proving the programme of any institution of learning, much less of a university, as of one which prepares not for any other institution, but directly for life. I will only repeat --- in which all unbiassed people must necessarily agree with me — that there is no possibility of proving the necessity of subdividing the department of study.

Both the boarding-school teacher and the university regard it as the first condition of admitting people to the participation in the culture that they be detached from the circle to which they originally belonged. The university, as a general rule, admits only students who have passed a seven years' apprenticeship at a gymnasium, and who have lived in large cities. A small proportion of special students pass the same gymnasium course with the aid of private teachers, instead of the gymnasium.

Before entering the gymnasium, a pupil has to pass through a course of instruction at a county and popular school.

I will try, by leaving aside all learned references to history and all ingenious comparisons with the state of affairs in European countries, to speak simply of what is taking place under our eyes in Russia.

I hope that all will agree with me that the purpose of our educational institutions consists chiefly in the dissemination of culture among all classes, and not in the conservation of culture in some one class which has taken exclusive possession of it, that is, that we are not so much concerned about the culture of the son of some nabob or dignitary (these will find their culture in a European, if not in a Russian, institution), as that we should give culture to the son of an innkeeper, of a merchant of the third guild, of a burgher, of a priest, of a former manorial servant, and so forth. I leave out the peasant, for that would be an entirely unrealizable dream. In short, the aim of the university is the dissemination of culture among the greatest possible number of men.

Let us take, for example, the son of a small town merchant or a small yeoman. At first the boy is sent to school to learn the rudiments. This instruction, as is well known, consists in the memorizing of incomprehensible Slavic words, which lasts, as is well known, three or four years. The information taken away from such instruction proves inapplicable to life; the moral habits, taken away from there, consist in disrespect for his elders and teachers, sometimes in the theft of books, and so forth, and, above all, in idleness and indolence.

It seems to me that it is superfluous to prove that a school in which it takes three years to learn that which could be acquired in three months is a school of idleness and indolence. A child who is compelled to sit motionless at his book for the period of six hours, studying the whole day that which he ought to learn in half an hour, is artificially trained in the most complete and most baneful idleness.

Upon the children's returning from such a school, nine-tenths of the parents, especially the mothers, find them partially spoilt, physically enfeebled, and alienated; but the necessity of making successful men of the world of them urges the parents to send them on, to the county school. In this institution the acquisition of habits of idleness, deceit, hypocrisy, and the physical deterioration continue with greater vigour. In the county school one sometimes sees healthy faces, in the gymnasium rarely, in the university hardly ever. In the county school the subjects of instruction are even less applicable to life than in the first. Here begin Alexander the Great and Guadeloupe, and what purports to be an explanation of the phenomena of Nature, which give the pupil nothing but false pride and contempt for his parents, in which he is supported by the example of his teachers. Who does not know those pupils who have an utter contempt for the whole mass of uneducated people on the ground that they have heard from the teacher that the earth is round, and that the air consists of hydrogen and oxygen!

After the county school, that foolish mother, whom the writers of novels have so pleasantly ridiculed, worries still more about her physically and morally changed child. There follows the course in the gymnasium, with the same artifices of examinations and compulsion, which evolve hypocrisy, deceit, and idleness, and the son of a merchant or of a petty yeoman, who does not know where to find a workman or clerk, studies by rote French or Latin grammar, the history of Luther, and, in a language not familiarly his own, makes vain endeavours to write a composition on the advantages of a representative mode of government. In addition to all this totally inapplicable wisdom, he learns to make debts, to cheat, to extort money from his parents, to commit debauches, and so forth, acquiring sciences which will receive their final development in the university. Here, in the gymnasium, we see the final alienation from home.

Enlightened teachers endeavour to raise him above his natural surroundings, and for this purpose have him read Byelínski, Macaulay, Lewes, and so forth, not because he may have an exclusive bent for something in particular, but in order to develop him, as they call it. And the gymnasiast, on the basis of dim conceptions and of words corresponding to them, — progress, liberalism, materialism, historical evolution, etc., — looks with contempt and hostility at his past. The aim of the instructors is attained, but the parents, especially the mother, with still greater misgivings and sadness look at their emaciated, self-confident and self-satisfied Ványa, speaking a strange language, thinking with a strange mind, smoking cigarettes, and drinking wine. "The deed is done, and there are others like him," think his parents; "no doubt that is the way it ought to be," and Ványa is sent to the university. The parents dare not tell themselves that they were mistaken.

In the university, as was said before, you will rarely see a healthy, fresh face, and you will not see one who looks with respect, or even without respect, if only calmly, at the circle from which he has emanated, and in which he will have to live; he looks at it with contempt, loathing, and supercilious compassion. Thus he looks at the people of his circle and at his relatives, and even thus he looks at the activity which ought to be his according to his social standing. Only three careers exclusively present themselves to him surrounded by a golden aureole: the learned, the literary, and the official.

Among the subjects of instruction there is not one which is applicable to life, and they are taught in precisely the same manner in which the psalter and Obodóvski's geography are studied. I exclude only the experimental subjects, such as chemistry, physiology, anatomy, and even astronomy, where the students are compelled to work; all the other subjects, such as philosophy, history, law, philology, are learned by rote, with the only purpose in view that of being able to answer questions at the examinations, whatever the examinations be, for promotion or final,—it makes no difference which.

I see the haughty contempt of the professors as they read these lines. They will not even honour me with an expression of their anger, and will not descend from the height of their grandeur in order to prove to a writer of stories that he does not understand anything in this important and mysterious business. I know that, but that does not by any means stop me from pointing out the deductions of reason and of observation.

I cannot with the professors recognize the mystery of culture, invisibly performed on the students, independently from the form and the contents of the lectures of the professors. I recognize nothing of the kind, just as I do not recognize the mysterious, unexplained cultural influence of the classical education, which they no longer deem it necessary to discuss. No matter how many universally recognized wiseacres and respectable people may affirm that for the development of a man nothing is more useful than the study of Latin grammar, and Greek and Latin verses in the original, when it is possible to read them in translation, I will not believe it, just as I cannot believe that it is good for a man's development to stand three hours on one foot. That has to be proved by something more than experience.

By experience everything imaginable may be proved. The reader of the psalter proves by experience that the best method for teaching reading is to make one study the psalter; the shoemaker says that the best way to learn his art is to make the boys for two years fetch water, chop wood, and so forth. In this manner you may prove anything you please. I say all this so that the defenders of the university may not tell me of the historical meaning, of the mysterious cultural influence, of the common bond of the governmental educational institutions, that they may not adduce to me as an example the universities of Oxford and Heidelberg, but that they may allow me to discuss the matter according to good common sense, and that they themselves may do so.

All I know is that when I enter the university at the age of from sixteen to eighteen years, the circle of my knowledge is already defined for me, as it was in the department which I entered, and it is defined quite arbitrarily. I come to any one of the lectures prescribed for me by the department, and I am supposed not only to hear all the professor is lecturing about, but even to commit it to memory, if not word for word, at least sentence for sentence. If I do not learn it all, the professor will not give me the necessary diploma at the final or at the biennial examinations. I do not speak of the abuses which are repeated a hundred times. In order to receive this diploma, I must have certain habits which the professor approves of: I must either always be sitting on the first bench and take down notes, or I must have a frightened or a merry look at the examination, or I must share the professor's opinions, or I must regularly attend his evenings at home (these are not my suppositions, but the opinions of the students, which one may hear at any university). While listening to the professor's lecture, I may differ from his view, I may, on the basis of my readings in regard to this subject, find that the professor's lectures are bad, — I still must listen to them or, at least, memorize them.

In the universities there exists a dogma which is not promulgated by the professors: it is the dogma of the professor's papal infallibility. Moreover, the culture is imparted to the student by the professor precisely as is done with all priests, secretly, in the cell, and with a demand for reverential respect from the uninitiated and from the students. As soon as a professor is appointed, he begins to lecture, and though he be naturally dull, and duller during the performance of his duties, though he may have fallen entirely behind science, though he have an unworthy character, — he continues to read as long as he lives, and the students have no means of expressing their satisfaction or discontent. Moreover, that which the professor lectures upon remains a secret to all but the students. It may be this is due to my ignorance, but I do not know of any manuals composed from the lectures of a professor. If there have existed such courses, the proportion of them will be about one in the hundred.

What is that? A professor lectures on a science in a higher cultural institution, — let us say the history of Russian law, or civil law, — consequently he knows this science in its highest development, consequently he has been able to combine all the different views held in respect to this science, or to select one of them, the most modern, and to prove why it is so; why, then, does he deprive us, and all of Europe, of the fruits of his wisdom, and why does he impart them only to the students who attend his lectures? Does he not know that there are good publishers who pay good sums for good books, that there exists a literary criticism, which appreciates literary productions, and that it would be far more convenient for the students to read his book at home, lying on the bed, than to write out his lectures? If the science is changed and made fuller each year, then there may appear each year new supplementary articles. Literature and society would be grateful to him. Why do not the professors print their courses?

I should like to ascribe this to an indifference to literary success, but, to my misfortune, I see that these same high priests of science do not refuse to write a light political article, one that often does not touch upon their subject. I am afraid that the mystery of our university instruction is due to the fact that ninety out of every one hundred courses would not, if they were printed, stand our undeveloped literary criticism. Why is it absolutely necessary to lecture? Why can't the students be given a good book, their own or somebody else's, one or two, or ten good books?

The condition of university instruction, that the professor must lecture and that his lectures must be absolutely something of his own, belongs to the dogmas of university practice, in which I do not believe, and which it is impossible to prove. "The oral transmission impresses the minds better, and so forth," I shall be told; all that is not true. I know myself and many others, who are not an exception but form the common rule, and who understand nothing when told orally, but who comprehend well only when they quietly read a book at home. The oral transmission would only then have a meaning if the students had a right to oppose, and the lecture were a conversation, and not a lesson. Only then we, the public, would have no right to demand of the professors that they should publish those manuals from which they for thirty years in succession have been teaching our children and brothers. But as matters now are, the reading of lectures is only an amusing ceremony which has no meaning, particularly amusing on account of the solemnity with which it is performed.

I am not on the lookout for means to mend the universities; I do not say that, by giving the students the privilege of retorting at the lectures, it would be possible to invest the university instruction with some meaning. So far as I know the professors and students, I think that in such a case the students would act like schoolboys and would be given to liberal commonplaces, while the professors would not be able coolly to carry on the discussion, without having recourse to force, and matters would only be worse. But from that, I think, it does not at all follow that the students must by all means be silent and that the professors have the right to say what they please; from this only follows that the whole structure of the university is placed on a false foundation.

I can understand a university, corresponding to its name and its fundamental idea, — as a collection of men for the purpose of their mutual culture. Such universities, unknown to us, spring up and exist in various corners of Russia; in the universities themselves, in the student circles, people come together, read, discuss, until at last the rule establishes itself when to meet and how to discuss. That is a real university. But our universities, in spite of all the empty prattle about the seeming liberalism of their structure, are institutions which by their organization in no way differ from female boarding-schools and military academies. As the military schools train officers, as the schools of law train officials, so the universities train officials and men of university culture. (This is, as all know, a special rank, a calling, almost a caste.)

The late university occurrences find an explanation in the simplest manner possible: the students were permitted to let the collars of their shirts protrude, and to wear their uniforms unbuttoned, and they were no longer to be punished for non-attendance at lectures, whereupon the whole structure came very near to its fall. To mend matters, there is this means: incarcerate them again for non-attendance at lectures, and enforce again the wearing of uniforms. It would be better still, following the example set by the English institutions, to punish them for unsatisfactory progress and for misbehaviour, and, above all, to limit the number of students to the number of men required. This would be consistent, and, under such an arrangement, the universities will give us just the men it gave us before.

The universities, as establishments for the education of members of society, in the sense of the higher official circles, are reasonable; but the moment men wanted to make of them institutions for the culture of the whole Russian society, they proved worthless. I positively cannot understand on what ground uniforms and discipline are recognized as necessary in the military schools, while in the universities, where the instruction is just the same, with examinations, compulsion, and programmes, and without the student's right to retort and keep away from lectures, — why in the universities they speak of freedom and imagine that they can get along without the means employed at the military schools. Let not the example of the German universities confuse us! We cannot take an example from the German universities: with them every custom, every law is sacred, and with us, happily or unhappily, it is the other way.

The whole trouble, both in the matters of university instruction and of culture in general, is caused mainly by people who do not reflect, but who submit to the ideas of the age, and who thus imagine that it is possible to serve two masters at once. Those are the same men who reply to my thoughts expressed before as follows: It is true, the time has passed when children are beaten for their studies and when things are learned by rote,— that is all very true; but you must admit that it is sometimes impossible to get along without the rod, and that the children must be compelled to memorize. You are right, but why go to extremes?" and so forth, and so forth.

You would think that these people reflect charmingly, but it is even they who have become the enemies of truth and freedom. They seem to be agreeing with you in order, having taken possession of your thought, to change and cut and lop it according to their fashion. They do not admit at all that freedom is necessary; they only say so because they are afraid not to bow before the idol of our age. They only, like officials, praise the governor to his face, as long as he has the power in his hands. How many thousand times I prefer my friend the priest, who says directly that there is no reason for reflection as long as people are liable to die unfortunate, without knowing the divine law, and that, therefore, all means must be employed in order to teach the child the divine law, — to save him. He says that compulsion is necessary, that teaching is teaching, and not playing. With him I can debate, but with the gentlemen who serve both despotism and liberty, never.

It is these very gentlemen who breed that peculiar condition of the universities under which we now live, and in which one needs that special art of diplomacy, when, according to Figaro, it is not known who is cheating and who is cheated. The students deceive their parents and instructors; the instructors deceive the parents, the students, and the government, and so forth, in all possible combinations and permutations. We are told that it must be so; we are told: "You, the uninitiated, don't stick your nose into our business, for here a special art and special information are needed, — this is a historical evolution." And yet the affair seems so simple.

Some want to teach and others want to learn. Let them teach as much as they can, and let them learn as much as they will.

I remember, during the very heat of Kostomárov's university project, I defended the project in the presence of a professor. With what inimitable, profound seriousness, almost in a whisper, impressively and confidentially, the professor said to me : " Do you know what that project is ? It is not the project of a new university, it is the project of doing away with universities," and he looked with an expression of terror at me. "What of it ? That would be a good thing," I said, "because the universities are bad." The professor would not discuss any further with me, although he had not been able to prove to me that universities were good, just as nobody else is able to prove it.

All men are human, even professors. Not one labourer will say that we must destroy the factory where he earns a piece of bread, and he will say so not from conviction, but unconsciously. Those gentlemen who are concerned about a greater freedom of the universities resemble a man who, having brought up some young nightingales and concluding that they need freedom, lets them out of the cage and gives them freedom at the end of cords attached to their feet, and then wonders why the nightingales are not doing any better on the cord, but only break their legs and die.

No one has ever thought of establishing universities based on the needs of the people. That was impossible because the needs of the people have remained unknown. The universities were founded to answer certain needs, partly of the government and partly of higher society, and for the universities was established all that preparatory ladder of educational institutions which has nothing in common with the needs of the people. The government needed officials, doctors, jurists, teachers, and the universities were founded in order to train these. Now higher society needs liberals of a certain pattern, and the universities train these. The only blunder is that the masses do not need these liberals at all.

It is generally said that the defects of the universities are due to the defects in the lower institutions. I affirm the opposite: the defects of the popular, especially the county, schools, are mainly due to the false exigencies of the universities.

Let us now take a glance at the practice in the universities. Out of fifty students who compose the audience, ten men in the first two rows of seats have note-books and are taking down notes; of these ten, six keep notes in order to find favour with the professor, from a feeling of subserviency worked out by the lower school and by the gymnasium; the other four take notes from a sincere desire to write down the whole course, which they abandon at the fourth lecture, until only one-fifteenth or one-twentieth of the whole number continue to write down the lectures.

It is very difficult not to miss a lecture. The student consults the manual, and it naturally occurs to him that it is useless to write out the lectures when the same result may be obtained from a manual or from the notes of somebody else. In mathematics, and for all that in any other subject, as every teacher must know, not one student is able all the time to follow the deductions and conclusions of the teacher, however precise, clear, and interesting the teacher may try to be. Very frequently there happens a moment of dulness or absent-mindedness with the student: he ought to ask a question, why, for what purpose, what preceded it; the connection is lost, but the professor goes on. The chief care of the students (I am now speaking only of the very best) is to get notes or a manual, from which it would be possible to prepare for the examinations.

The majority go to lectures either because they have nothing else to do, or because they have not yet grown tired of them, or to please the professor, or, in rare cases, because it is the right thing to do, when one professor in a hundred becomes popular and it is a kind of mental dandyism with the students to attend his lectures. From the point of view of the students, the lectures nearly always are an empty formality, necessary only for the sake of the examinations. The majority of students do not study their subjects during the whole time they are given, but instead busy themselves with other subjects, the programme of which is determined by the circle with which the students fall in. The lectures are looked upon in the same way in which soldiers look upon military exercises, while an examination is to them a parade, a dull necessity.

The programme which circles have laid down of late is not varied; it generally consists of the following: of the reading and re-reading of old articles by Byelínski and of new ones by Chernyshévski, Antonóvich, Písarev, and so forth; then, of the reading of new books which are enjoying great popularity in Europe, without any connection or any relation to the subjects which they study, such as Lewes, Buckle, and so on. But their chief occupation is the reading of prohibited books and the copying of these, such as Feuerbach, Moleschott, Büchner, and especially Gértsen and Ogarév. Books are copied, not according to their worth, but in proportion to their degree of prohibition. I have seen in students' rooms heaps of copied books, incomparably more voluminous than would be the whole four years' course of instruction, and among these copy-books fat books of the most abominable of Púshkin's poems and of the most insipid and most colourless of Rylyéev's poems. Other occupations are meetings at which are discussed the most varied and most important subjects, such as the independence of Little Russia, the dissemination of the rudiments among the masses, the playing of some prank in common on a professor or on the inspector, which is called demanding explanations, the union of the two circles, the aristocratic and the plebeian, and so forth. All that is sometimes ridiculous, but often dear, touching, and poetical, such as idle youth frequently is.

The thing is, that in these occupations lose themselves young men, sons of petty landowners or of merchants of the third guild, whom the parents have sent away to make helpers of them, one, to make his small estate productive, the other, to help him carry on his business more regularly and more profitably. In these circles the following opinions prevail about the professors: one is very stupid, though a worker; another has fallen behind in his science, though an able man; a third is not quite honest and allows only those to pass who fulfil certain demands of his; a fourth is the laughing-stock of the human race, who, for thirty years in succession, has been reading his notes which are written in an abominable language, — and happy is the university which, to fifty professors, has at least one who is respected and beloved by the students.

Formerly, when there were annual examinations, there took place each year, not exactly a study of the subject, but at least a cramming from notes before the examinations. Now such cramming takes place twice: in passing from the second to the third year, and at the final examination. The lot which was then cast four times during university life is now cast twice.

As long as there exist examinations under the present procedure, whether pass examinations or finals, there must necessarily exist the senseless cramming, and the lottery, and the personal likes and dislikes, and the arbitrariness of the professor, and the cheating of the students. I do not know what the founders of the universities felt about the examinations, but as common sense tells me, and as I have experienced it more than once, and as many, many people have agreed with me, — examinations cannot serve as a measure of knowledge, but only as a field for rank arbitrariness on the side of the professors, and of rank deception on the side of the students.

I had to pass examinations three times in my life: the first year I was not promoted from the first course to the second by the professor of Russian history, who had shortly before that had a quarrel with my family, although I had not missed one lecture and knew Russian history; also for number one [1] in German, given me by the same professor, although I knew German incomparably better than all the students of our course. In the following year I received five in Russian history, because, having had a dispute with a fellow student as to who had a better memory, we had learned one question each by heart, and I received at the examination the very question I had memorized, which, as I well remember, was the biography of Mazeppa. That was in the year 1845. In 1848 I went to my candidate's examination in the St. Petersburg University, knowing literally nothing, and having prepared myself but one week before the examinations. I did not sleep for nights, and received candidate's marks in civil and criminal law, having prepared each subject not longer than a week. In this year 1862, I know students who have graduated by preparing their subjects just one week before the examinations. I know also of cases, for this year, where seniors have falsified tickets; I know of one professor who gave a student three instead of five because the student allowed himself to smile. The professor remarked to him: "We may smile, but you must not," and put down three.

I hope that nobody will regard the adduced cases as exceptions. Any one who knows the universities knows

[1] One is the lowest, and five the highest mark.

that the cases adduced form the rule, and not the exception, and that it cannot be otherwise. If there is anybody who doubts it, we will mention millions of cases. There will be found protesters against the Ministry of Public Instruction who will sign their names, as there have been protesters against the Ministry of Internal Affairs and of Justice. What happened in 1848, and in 1862, will also happen in 1872, as long as the organization remains the same. The abolishment of the uniforms and of annual examinations does not further this freedom one hair's breadth; these are only new patches on an old garment, which only tear the old cloth. No man putteth new wine into old bottles.

I flatter myself with the hope that even the defenders of the university will say: "That is so, or partly true. But you forget that there are students who follow the lectures with love and who do not need examinations at all, and, what is most important, you forget the cultural influence of the universities."

No, I forget neither the one nor the other: about the first, the independently working students, I will say that for them there is no need of universities with their organization, — they need only appliances, a library, — not lectures to listen to, but conversations with men who can guide them. But even for that minority the universities will not furnish information corresponding to their circle, if they do not wish to become *littérateurs* or professors; the main thing is that even this minority is subject to the influence which is called cultural, but which I call the corrupting influence of the universities.

The second retort about the cultural influence of the universities belongs to the number of those which are based on faith and first must be proved. Who has proved, and how has it been proved, that the universities have that cultural influence, and whence springs that mysterious cultural influence? There is no communion with the professors, — there is not that confidence and love which spring from it; there is, in the majority of cases, nothing but fear and suspicion. The students will learn nothing new from the professors which they could not as well find out from books. The cultural influence, then, lies in the communion of the young men occupied with the same subjects, I suppose. Doubtless so; but they are for the most part occupied, not with science, as you presume, but with cramming for examinations, cheating the professors, acting the liberals, and all such things as will take possession of young men who are torn away from their surroundings, their family, and who are artificially connected by the spirit of fellowship, raised to a principle and carried to a point of self-contentment, of self-sufficiency.

I am not speaking of the exceptions, of the students living with their families, for they are less subject to the cultural, that is, the corrupting influence of students' life; nor do I speak of those rare exceptions, where men have since childhood been devoted to science, who, being constantly at work, are also only partially subjected to that influence. Indeed, people are being trained for life, for work; every work demands not only familiarity with it, but also order, regularity, and, above all, the ability to live and get along with men. See how the son of a peasant learns to become a farmer, how the sexton's son, reading in the choir, learns to be a sexton, how the son of a Kirgiz cattle-keeper becomes a herder: he enters very early into direct relations with life, with Nature, and with men; he learns early, while working, to be productive, and he learns, being secure on the material side of life, that is, secure as regards a piece of bread, his wearing apparel, his lodging. Now look at a student, who is torn away from home, from the family, cast into a strange city, full of temptations for his youth, without means of support (because the parents provide only the necessary means, while all go out to pass their time well), in a circle of companions who by their society only intensify his defects, without guides, without an aim, having pushed off from the old and having not yet landed at the new. Such, with rare exceptions, is the position of a student. From this results that which alone can result: officials, fit only for the government; or professional officials, or literary officials, fit for society; or people aimlessly torn away from their former surroundings, with a spoiled youth, and finding no place for themselves in life, so-called people with *university culture*, — advanced, that is, irritable, sickly liberals.

The university is our first and our chief educational institution. It is the first to arrogate to itself the right of education, and it is the first, so far as the results, which it obtains, indicate, to prove the illegality and impossibility of education. Only from the social point of view is it possible to justify the truits of the university. The university trains not such men as humanity needs, but such as corrupt society needs.

The course is ended. I presuppose my imaginary alumnus as one of the best in every respect. He comes back to his home: all are strangers to him, — his father, his mother, his relatives. He shares neither their faith, nor their desires, and he prays not to their God, but to other idols. His parents are deceived, and the son frequently wishes to unite with them into one family, but he no longer can do that. What I say is not an empty phrase, not a fancy. I know very many students who, after returning to their families, were at odds with their families in nearly all their convictions, about marriage, about honour, about commerce. But the deed is done, and the parents console themselves with the thought that such is *now* the age; that the *present* education is such that their son will make a career for himself somewhere else, if not in his former surroundings; that he will find his livelihood and means to help them; and that he will be happy in his own way.

Unfortunately, in nine cases out of ten, the parents are again mistaken. Having graduated, their son does not know where to lay down his head. A strange thing it is! The information which he has acquired is of no use to anybody, — no one gives anything for it. Their only application is in literature and in pedagogy, that is, in the science dealing with the education of just such useless men as he is.

Now, this is strange: culture is so rare in Russia, so it ought to be expensive and highly esteemed. In reality, the very opposite takes place. We need machinists, for we have few of them, and we send to all of Europe for machinists and pay them good wages; why, then, do people with a university education say (and there are but few cultured people among us) that they are needed, whereas we not only do not appreciate them, but they even can find no place for themselves? Why does a man who has finished his apprenticeship with a carpenter, stone-mason, or stucco-worker, get at once from fifteen to seventeen roubles, if he is a workman, and twenty-five roubles a month, if he is a master mechanic, a boss, while a student is glad if he gets ten (I except literature and officialdom, but speak only of what a student can get in a practical activity)? Why do landed proprietors, who have land left that must be made productive, pay from three hundred to five hundred roubles to peasant farmers, when they will not pay even two hundred roubles to agricultural students and natural science graduates? And why do peasant, and not student bosses control thousands of workmen at the railroads? Why is it that if a student gets a place with a good salary, he gets it not for what knowledge he has acquired in the university, but for what he has learned later? Why do law students become officers and mathematicians and natural science students officials? Why does a ploughman, after living a year in sufficiency, bring home from fifty to sixty roubles, while a student leaves after a year's existence, a debt of one hundred roubles? Why do the masses pay a popular school-teacher eight, nine, ten roubles a month, whether he be a sexton, or a student? Why does a merchant employ as a clerk, take as a son-in-law into his house, not a student, but a peasant lad?

Because, I shall be told, society does not yet know how to appreciate education; because a student teacher will not cheat workmen and enslave them by advance payments; because a student merchant will not give wrong measures and weights; because the fruits of culture are not so palpable as the fruits of routine and ignorance.

This may be so, I shall reply, only experience has taught me the opposite. A student does not know how to manage an affair, neither honestly, nor dishonestly, or if he does know how, he manages it in conformity with his nature, with that general structure of his moral habits, which life, independently of school, has evolved in him. I know an equal number of honest students and of other people, and vice versa. But let us even suppose that the university training develops the feeling of justice in man, and that, in consequence of this, uneducated people prefer uneducated men to students and value them higher than students. Let us suppose that that is so. Why, then, can we, so-called cultured people and men of means, the gentry, the *littérateurs*, the professors, make no other use of the students than in government service? I leave out the government service on the ground that the remuneration in that service cannot be taken as a measure of deserts or of knowledge.

Everybody knows that a student, an ex-officer, a landed proprietor who has squandered his estate, a foreigner, and so forth, travels to the capital, the moment he for some reason must earn a livelihood, and, according to his connections and the influence brought to bear, receives a place in the administration, or, if he does not receive it, he regards himself as insulted. It is for that reason that I do not speak of the remuneration in the service; but I ask why does that same professor, who has imparted that culture to the students, give fifteen roubles a month to his janitor, or twenty roubles to a carpenter, while to the student who comes to him he says that he is very sorry, that he cannot give him a place, that all he can do is to try for him among the officials, or he offers him a ten-rouble place as copyist or proof-reader of the work which he happens to be publishing; that is, he offers him a place in which there is to be applied the knowledge which he has taken away from the county school, — the ability to write? There are no places where the knowledge of Roman law, Greek literature, and integral calculus may be applied, and there can be none.

Thus, in the majority of cases, the son returning from the university to his father does not justify the hopes of the parents, and, in order that he may not become a burden to the family, he is obliged to accept a place in which all the knowledge he needs is the ability to write, and in which he enters into competition with all the Russians who know the rudiments. The only advantage he has is his rank, which does him good only in service, where connections and other conditions are more effective; another advantage is his liberalism, which is not applicable to anything. It seems to me that the percentage of men who occupy places with good remuneration outside the government service is exceedingly small. Trustworthy statistical data about the activity of graduates would be an important material for the science of culture, and, I am convinced, would mathematically prove the truth which I am trying to elucidate from *a priori* reasoning and from data at hand, — the truth that people with a university education are of little use, and that they direct their chief activity to literature and pedagogy; that is, to repeating that eternal circle of culture and to creating just such useless people for actual life.

But I have not foreseen one retort, or rather one source of retorts, which naturally will arise with the majority of my readers: Why does this same highest culture, which turns out to be so fruitful in Europe, become so inapplicable with us? The European societies are more cultured than ours, why, then, cannot Russian society travel along the same path which the European societies have traversed?

This retort would be insuperable, if it were proved, first, that the path over which the European nations have travelled, is the best; secondly, that all humanity travel over the same path; and thirdly, that culture is being grafted upon our people. The whole East has been educated by entirely different paths than the European humanity. If it were proved that a young animal, a wolf or dog, had been brought up on meat and had in this manner received its full development, should I have the right to conclude that, in order to bring up a young horse or a rabbit, I must feed it on meat, in which way alone I can procure its full development? Could I finally conclude from these opposite experiments that, in order to bring up a bear cub, I must feed it on meat or oats? Experience would show me that a bear needs both. Even though I may think that it is more natural for meat to form flesh, and though my previous experiments confirm my supposition, I cannot continue giving the colt meat to eat, if he throws it up every time, and if his organism will not assimilate the food.

The same takes place with the European culture, both in form and contents, when it is transferred to our soil. The organism of the Russian people does not assimilate it; and yet, there must be some other food which will support its organism, for it lives. This food does not seem food for us, just as grass is no food for a carnivorous animal; in the meantime the historico-physiological process is taking place, and that food, unacknowledged though it be by us, is assimilated by the people, and the immense animal is getting stronger and growing up.

Making a résumé of all said above, we arrive at the following conclusions:

(1) Culture and education are two distinct conceptions.

(2) Culture is free, and, therefore, legal and just; education is compulsory, and, therefore, illegal and unjust; it cannot be justified by reason, and, consequently, cannot form the subject of pedagogy.

(3) Education, as a phenomenon, has its origin: (*a*) in the family, (*b*) in faith, (*c*) in the government, (*d*) in society.

(4) The domestic, religious, and governmental bases of education are natural and find their justification in necessity; but the social education has no other foundation than the pride of human reason, and thus bears the most baneful fruits, such as the universities and university culture.

Now, having in part explained our view on education and culture, and having defined the limits of both, we may reply to the questions put by Mr. Glyébov in the periodical *Education* (No. 5, of 1862), — the first questions that naturally must arise during a serious reflection on the matter of culture.

(1) *What shall a school be if it is not to take part in the business of education?*

(2) *What is meant by non-interference of the school in matters of education?*

*And* (3) *Is it possible to separate education from instruction, especially from primary instruction, when the educational element is brought to bear on the youthful minds even in the higher schools?*

(We have already pointed out that the form of the higher institutions of learning, where the educational element is present, by no means serves us as a model. We deny the plan of the higher institutions of learning as much as that of the lower, and we see in it the beginning of all evil.)

In order to answer the questions put to us, we will only transpose them: (1) What is meant by non-interference of the school in education? (2) Is such a non-interference possible? (3) What must the school be, if it is not to interfere in education?

To avoid misunderstandings, I must first explain what I mean by the word "school," which I used in the same sense in my first article. By the word "school" I understand not the house in which the instruction is given, not the teachers, not the pupils, not a certain tendency of instruction, but, in the general sense, *the conscious activity of him who gives culture upon those who receive it*, that is, one part of culture, in whatever way this activity may find its expression: the teaching of the regulations to a recruit is a school; public lectures are a school; a course in a Mohammedan institution of learning is a school; the collections of a museum and free access to them for those who wish to see them are a school.

I reply to the first question. The non-interference of the school in matters of culture means the non-interference of the school in the culture [formation] of beliefs, the convictions, and the character of him who receives that culture. This non-interference is obtained by granting the person under culture the full freedom to avail himself of the teaching which answers his need, which he wants, and to avail himself of it to the extent to which he needs and wants it, and to avoid the teaching which he does not need and which he does not want.

Public lectures, museums are the best examples of schools without interference in education. Universities are examples of schools with interference in matters of education. In these institutions the students are confined to certain limits by a definite course, a programme, a code of selected studies, by the exigencies of the examinations, and by the grant of rights, based chiefly on these examinations, or, more correctly, by the deprivation of rights in case of non-compliance with certain prescribed conditions. (A senior taking his examinations threatened with one of the most terrible punishments, — with the loss of his ten or twelve years of labour in the gymnasium and in the university, and with the loss of all the advantages in view of which he bore privations for the period of twelve years.)

In these institutions everything is so arranged that the student, being threatened with punishments, is obliged in receiving his culture to adopt that educational element and to assimilate those beliefs, those convictions, and that character, which the founders of the institution want. The compulsory educational element, which consists in the exclusive choice of one circle of sciences and in the threat of punishment, is as strong and as patent to the serious observer, as in that other institution with corporal punishment, which superficial observers oppose to the universities.

Public lectures, whose number is on the continuous increase in Europe and in America, on the contrary, not only do not confine one to a certain circle of knowledge, not only do not demand attention under threat of punishment, but expect from the students certain sacrifices, by which they prove, in contradistinction to the first, the complete freedom of choice and of the basis on which they are reared. That is what is meant by interference and non-interference of school in education.

If I am told that such non-interference, which is possible for the higher institutions and for grown-up people, is not possible for the lower schools and for minors, because we have no example for it in the shape of public lectures for children, and so forth, I will answer that if we are not going to understand the word "school" in the narrowest sense, but will accept it with the above-mentioned definition, we shall find for the lower stages of knowledge and for the lower ages many influences of liberal culture without interference in education, corresponding to the higher institutions and to the public lectures. Such is the acquisition of the art of reading from a friend or a brother; such are popular games of children, of the cultural value of which we intend writing a special article; such are public spectacles, panoramas, and so forth; such are pictures and books; such are fairy-tales and songs; such are work and, last, the experiments of the school at Yásnaya Polyána.

The answer to the first question gives a partial answer to the second: is such a non-interference possible? We cannot prove this possibility theoretically. The one thing which confirms such a possibility is the observation which proves that people entirely uneducated, that is, who are subject only to the free cultural influences, the men of the people are fresher, more vigorous, more powerful, more independent, juster, humaner, and, above all, more useful than men no matter how educated. But it may be that even this statement need be proved to many.

I shall have to say a great deal about these proofs at a later time. Here I will adduce one fact. Why does the race of educated people not perfect itself zoologically? A race of thoroughbred animals keeps improving; the race of educated people grows worse and weaker. Take at haphazard one hundred children of several educated generations and one hundred uneducated children of the people, and compare them in anything you please: in strength, in agility, in mind, in the ability to acquire knowledge, even in morality,— and in all respects you are startled by the vast superiority on the side of the children of uneducated generations, and this superiority will be the greater, the lower the age, and vice versa. It is terrible to say this, on account of the conclusions to which it leads us, but it is true. A final proof of the possibility of non-interference in the lower schools, for people, to whom personal experience and an inner feeling tell nothing in favour of such an opinion, can be obtained only by means of a conscientious study of all those free influences by means of which the masses get their culture, by an all-round discussion of the question, and by a long series of experiments and reports upon it.

What, then, must the school be if it is not to interfere in matters of education? A school is, as said above, the conscious activity of him who gives culture upon those who receive it. How is he to act in order not to transgress the limits of culture, that is, of freedom?

I reply: the school must have one aim, — the transmission of information, of knowledge, without attempting to pass over into the moral territory of convictions, beliefs, and character; its aim is to be nothing but science, and not the results of its influence upon human personality. The school must not try to foresee the consequences produced by science, but, in transmitting it, must leave full freedom for its application. The school must not regard any one science, nor a whole code of sciences, as necessary, but must transmit that information which it possesses, leaving the students the right to acquire it or not.

The structure and the programme of the school must be based not on theoretical speculations, not on the conviction held in regard to the necessity of such and such sciences, but on the mere possibilities, that is, the knowledge of the teachers.

I will explain it by an example.

I want to establish an institution of learning. I form no programme which is based on my theoretical conceptions, and on the basis of this programme look about for teachers, but I propose to all people who feel that they are called to furnish information to lecture or teach such subjects as they know best. Of course, my former experience will guide me in the selection of these lessons, that is, we shall not try to offer subjects such as nobody wants to listen to, — in a Russian village we will not teach Spanish, or astrology, or geography, just as a merchant will not open shops of surgical instruments or of crinolines in this village.

We may foresee a demand for what we offer; but our final judge will be only experience, and we do not think we have the right to open a single shop, in which we are to sell tar with this condition, that to every ten pounds of tar every purchaser must buy a pound of ginger or of pomatum. We do not trouble ourselves about the use to which our wares will be put by the purchasers, believing that they know what they want, and that we have enough to do to discover their needs and to provide for them.

It is quite possible that there will turn up one teacher of zoology, one teacher of mediæval history, one of religion, and one of the art of printing. If these teachers will know how to make their lessons interesting, these lessons will be useful, in spite of their seeming incompatibility and accidentalness. I do not believe in the possibility of a theoretically established, harmonious code of sciences, but that every science, being the subject of free instruction, harmonizes with all the others into one code of knowledge for each man.

I shall be told that in such an accidentalness of programme there may enter useless, even injurious, sciences into the course, and that many sciences could not be given because the students would not be sufficiently prepared for them.

To this I will reply that, in the first place, there are no injurious and no useless sciences for anybody, and that we have, as an assurance of that, the common sense and the needs of the students, who, the instruction being free, will not admit useless and injurious sciences, if there were such; that, in the second place, prepared pupils are wanted only for a poor teacher, but that for a good teacher it is easier to begin algebra or analytical geometry with a pupil who does not know arithmetic than with a pupil who knows it poorly, and that it is easier to lecture on mediæval history to students who have not studied ancient history. I do not believe that a professor, who in a university lectures on differential and integral calculus, or on the history of the Russian civil law, and who cannot teach arithmetic, or Russian history in a primary school,— I do not believe that he can be a good professor. I see no use and no merit in good instruction in one part of a subject, and even no possibility of giving it. Above all, I am convinced that the supply will always correspond to the demand, and that at each stage of science there will be found a sufficient number of both students and teachers.

But how, I shall be told, can a person who teaches culture help wishing to produce a certain educational influence by means of his instruction? This tendency is most natural; it is a natural exigency in the transmission of knowledge from him who offers culture to him who receives it. This tendency only imparts strength to the instructor to occupy himself with his subject,— it gives him that degree of enthusiasm which is necessary for him. It is impossible to deny this tendency, and it has never occurred to me to deny it; its existence so much more cogently proves to me the necessity of freedom in the matter of instruction.

A man who loves and teaches history cannot be prohibited from endeavouring to impart to his students that historical conception which he himself possesses, which he regards as useful and absolutely necessary for a man's development; a teacher cannot be prohibited from imparting that method in the study of mathematics or natural science which he considers the best; on the contrary, this prevision of the educational purpose encourages the teacher. The thing is that the educational element of science shall not be imparted by compulsion. I cannot carefully enough direct the reader's attention to this circumstance.

The educational element, let us say in mathematics or in history, is only then imparted to the students when the teacher is passionately fond of his subject and when he knows it well; only then his love is communicated to the students and has an educational influence upon them. In the contrary case, that is, when it has been decided somewhere that such and such a subject has an educational value, and one is instructed to teach, and the others to listen to it, the teaching accomplishes the very opposite results, that is, it not only does not educate scientifically, but also makes the science loathsome.

It is said that science has in itself an educational element (*erziehliges Element*); that is true and not true, and in this very statement lies the fundamental error of the existing paradoxical view on education. Science is science and has nothing in itself. The educational element lies in the teaching of the sciences, in the teacher's love for his science, and in the love with which it is imparted, — in the teacher's relation to his students. *If you wish to educate the student by science, love your science and know it, and the students will love both you and the science, and you will educate them; but if you yourself do not love it, the science will have no educational influence, no matter how much you may compel them to learn it.* Here again there is the one measure, the one salvation, the same freedom for the students to listen or not to listen to the teacher, to imbibe or not to imbibe his educational influence, that is, for them to decide whether he knows and loves his science.

Well, what, then, will the school be with the non-interference in education?

An all-sided and most varied conscious activity directed by one man on another, for the purpose of transmitting knowledge, without compelling the student by direct force or diplomatically to avail himself of that which we want him to avail himself of. The school will, perhaps, not be a school as we understand it, — with benches, blackboards, a teacher's or professor's platform, — it may be a panorama, a theatre, a library, a museum, a conversation; the code of the sciences, the programme, will probably everywhere be different. (I know only my experiment: the school at Yásnaya Polyána, with its subdivision of subjects, which I have described, in the course of half a year completely changed, partly at the request of the pupils and their parents, partly on account of the insufficient information held by the teachers, and assumed other forms.)

"What are we to do then? Shall there, really, be no county schools, no gymnasia, no chairs of the history of Roman law? What will become of humanity?" I hear.

There certainly shall be none, if the pupils do not need them, and you are not able to make them good.

"But children do not always know what they need; children are mistaken," and so forth, I hear.

I will not enter into this discussion. This discussion would lead us to the question: Is man's nature right before the tribunal of man? and so forth. I do not know that it is, and do not take that stand; all I say is that if we can know what to teach, you must not keep me from teaching Russian children by force French, mediæval genealogy, and the art of stealing. I can prove everything as you do.

"So there will be no gymnasia and no Latin? Then, what am I going to do?" I again hear.

Don't be afraid! There will be Latin and rhetoric, and they will exist another hundred years, simply because the medicine is bought, so we must drink it (as a patient said).

# EDUCATION AND CULTURE

I doubt whether the thought, which I have expressed, perhaps, indistinctly, awkwardly, inconclusively, will become the common possession in another hundred years; it is not likely that within a hundred years will die those ready-made institutions, schools, gymnasia, universities, and that within that time will grow up freely formed institutions, having for their basis the freedom of the learning generation.

# PROGRESS AND THE DEFINITION OF EDUCATION

A Reply to Mr. Márkov, *Russian Messenger*, 1862, No. 5

———◆———

THE chief points of Mr. Márkov's disagreement with my view of education are formulated in the following manner:

"(1) We recognize the *right* of one generation to interfere in the education of another. (2) We recognize the *right* of the higher classes to interfere in the popular education. (3) We do not agree with the *Yásnaya Polyána* definition of education. (4) We think that the schools cannot be exempted from the historical conditions, and that they ought not to be. (5) We think that the modern schools more nearly correspond to the modern needs than those of the Middle Ages. (6) We consider our education not injurious, but useful. (7) We think that the full liberty of education, as Count Tolstóy understands it, is injurious and impossible. (8) Finally, we think that the methods of the school at Yásnaya Polyána contradict the convictions of the editor of *Yásnaya Polyána*." (*Russian Messenger*, 1862, No. 5, p. 186.)

Before answering each of these points, we shall endeavour to find the fundamental cause of disagreement in our view and that held by Mr. Márkov, which latter has called forth an expression of universal sympathy from the pedagogical and from the lay public.

This cause lies in the incompleteness of our view as expressed (and so we shall try and make it more complete now), and, on the side of Mr. Márkov and the public in general, in the incorrect and limited comprehension of our propositions, which we shall try to make clearer. It is evident that our disagreement is due to a different comprehension and, consequently, definition of education itself. Mr. Márkov says: "We do not agree with the *Yásnaya Polyána* definition of education." But Mr. Márkov does not overthrow our definition, he merely makes a definition of his own.

The main question is whose definition of education is correct, ours, or Mr. Márkov's. We said: "*Education in its widest sense, including the bringing up, is, in our opinion, that activity of man which has for its base the need of equality and the invariable law of educational progress,*" and we confess that the words to which Mr. Márkov asks the reader to pay special attention need an explanation for the majority of people and for Mr. Márkov. But, before giving this explanation, we deem it necessary to digress a little in order to show why it is that Mr. Márkov and the public in general did not wish to understand this definition and paid no attention whatever to it.

Since the day of Hegel and the famous aphorism, "What is historical is reasonable," there has reigned in the literary and oral debates, especially in our country, a very singular mental hocus-pocus called the historical view. You say, for example, that man has a right to be free and to be judged only on the basis of the laws which he himself regards as just, but the historical view replies that history evolves a certain historical moment, which conditions a certain historical legislation and the people's historical relation to it. You say that you believe in God, and the historical view replies that history has evolved certain religious conceptions and the relations of humanity to it. You say that the Iliad is the greatest epical production, and the historical view replies that the Iliad is only the expression of a nation's historical consciousness at a certain historical moment.

On this foundation the historical view does not contend with you whether liberty is necessary for man, whether there is a God or not, whether the Iliad is good or bad; it does nothing to obtain that liberty for you, after which you have been striving, to persuade or dissuade you of the existence of God, or of the beauties of the Iliad, — it only points out to you that place which your inner need, the love of truth or beauty, occupies in history; it only recognizes, not through direct consciousness, but through historical ratiocinations.

Say that you love something and believe in something, and the historical view tells you, "Love and believe, and your love and faith will find a place for themselves in our historical view." Ages will pass, and we shall find the place which we shall occupy in history; but you must know in advance that that which you love is not unconditionally beautiful, and that that which you believe in is not unconditionally true; but amuse yourselves, children, — for your love and faith will find a place and a proper application for themselves.

Add the word historical to any conception you please, and that conception at once loses its vital, actual meaning and receives an artificial and barren meaning in some kind of an artificially formed historical world conception.

Mr. Márkov says: "The general aim is the result of the whole of life, — the final deduction from the activity of varied forces. It can be seen only at the end, and for the present there is no need of it. Consequently pedagogy is right in that it has no final end; it is right in that it strives after its temporal and local ends, which are most significant in life." (R. M., No. 5, p. 153.)

In his opinion it is useless to look for a criterion of pedagogy. It is enough to know that we are living under historical conditions, and all is well.

Mr. Márkov has perfectly assimilated the historical view to himself; he, like the majority of thinking Russians at the present time, possesses the art of applying the concept of the historical to every phenomenon of life; he knows how to say many learned and ingenious things in the historical sense, and for all occasions is full master of the historical pun.

In our first article we said that education has for its base the need of equality and the invariable law of educational progress. Although expressed without any further proofs, this proposition explained the cause of the phenomenon. It was possible for one not to agree with it and ask for proofs; but it is only the historical view which feels no need of discovering the causes of such a phenomenon as is education.

Mr. Márkov says: "It is desirable that the reader dwell with especial attention upon these words. To me they seem nothing but a fruitless piece of casuistry which only bedims the meaning of things well known to all. What do we want with the need of equality, instinct? What do we want more especially with that *fatum*, that unknown law of motion, which prohibits you from one thing, and orders you to do something else? Who has recognized it or proved it? If we were to deny, as Count Tolstóy does, the educational influence of the grown-up generation on the younger generation, in what would we look for that wonderful law? A mother loves her child, wants to satisfy his wants, and consciously, without the least mystical necessity, feels the need of adapting herself to his incipient reason, to speak the simplest language to him. She does not at all strive after equality with her child, which would be in the highest degree unnatural, but, on the contrary, intentionally tries to transmit to him the whole supply of her knowledge. In this natural transmission of the mental acquisitions of one generation to the next lies the progress of education, which needs no other special laws. Every age casts its handful upon the common heap, and the longer we live, the higher rises this heap, and the higher we rise with it. This is known to the point of triteness, and I see no justification in the attempts to shake such a logically and historically manifest truth."

Here we have the best sample of the historical view. You are looking for an explanation of the most significant phenomenon of life; you surmise that you have found a general law which serves as the foundation of the phenomenon; you imagine you have found the ideal toward which humanity is tending, and the criterion of his activity, — and you are told that there is a heap which grows with every age, and that that is known to the point of triteness. Is it right that it should grow? Why does it grow? To these questions we receive no answer; on the contrary, they wonder why you bother about the solution of such questions.

In another passage Mr. Márkov, paraphrasing our words, says: "Each generation hinders the new in its development: the further we go, the greater the resistance, the worse it gets. What a strange progress! If, without relying on history, we were obliged to believe the *Yásnaya Polyána* theory, we should, probably, have to come to believe that the world has been dreadfully ailing from millennial resistances, and that its death is now not beyond the mountains, but behind its shoulders." (*Ibid.* p. 152.)

"A fine progress!" No, a very bad one, — that is exactly what I have been talking about. I do not hold to the religion of progress: outside of faith, nothing proves the necessity of progress. "Is it possible the world has been ailing all the time?" It is precisely this

that I tried to prove, with this difference, that not all
humanity is ailing, but that part of it which is subjected
to the activity of the education which Mr. Márkov
defends.

But here Mr. Márkov's historical view appears in all
its splendour.

"*Yásnaya Polyána* is disturbed by the circumstance
that at different times people teach different things and
in a different manner. Scholasticism taught one thing,
Luther another, Rousseau in his own way, Pestalozzi
again in his way. It sees in this the impossibility of
establishing a criterion of pedagogy, and on that basis
denies pedagogy. It seems to me that *Yásnaya Polyána*
has pointed out the necessary criterion, by adducing the
above-mentioned examples. The criterion is that one
must teach in conformity with the demands of the time.
It is simple and in absolute harmony with history and
with logic. Luther could be the teacher of a whole century because he himself was the creature of his age, and
thought its thoughts, and acted to its liking. Otherwise
his enormous influence would have been impossible or
supernatural; if he did not resemble his contemporaries,
he would have disappeared fruitlessly, like an incomprehensible, useless phenomenon,— a stranger among his
people, whose language even he did not understand.

"The same is true of Rousseau and of anybody else.
Rousseau formulated in his theories the overboiling hatred
of his age against formalism and artificiality, its thirst for
simple, heartfelt relations. It was an inevitable reaction
against the Versailles mode of life; if Rousseau alone had
felt it, there would not have appeared the age of Romanticism, there would not have appeared the masses to
regenerate humanity, the declaration of rights, the Karl
Moors, and all such things. To rebuke Luther and Rousseau for having unloaded their theories on men, while
arming themselves against the historical fetters, would

be the same as rebuking a whole age for the illegality of its mood. You cannot unload theories on a whole age.

"But one will hardly get rid of his theories. I cannot understand what Count Tolstóy would have of pedagogy. He is all the time troubled about the final end, about the imperturbable criterion. There are none, says he, and so none are needed. Why not consider the life of each individual, say, his own life? He, of course, does not know the final end of his existence, nor the common philosophical criterion for the activity of all the periods of his life. And yet he lives and acts; and he lives and acts only because in his childhood he had one purpose and one criterion, and others in youth, and now others again, and so on. He, no doubt, was a lively boy, — we know what criterion boys have, — and a religious youth, and a poet with liberal tendencies, and a practical man of the world; every such a natural mood made him look differently at the world, expect something different, and be guided by something else. In this constant change of view lies the wealth of human evolution, his philosophic and his every-day experience. Where Count Tolstóy sees a reproach to humanity and pedagogy and a self-contradiction, I see necessity, naturalness, and even advantage." (*Ibid.*, pp. 159–160.)

How much said, you would think! How clever, how instructive, what a calm historical view of everything! You yourself stand on some imaginary height, and below you act Rousseau, and Schiller, and Luther, and the French Revolution. From your historical height you approve or disapprove their historical acts and classify them according to historical patterns. More than that. Each human personality is crawling about somewhere there, subject to the immutable historical laws, which we know; but there is no final end, and there can be none, — there is only the historical view !

But we are asking for something different. We are andeavouring to find that common mental law which has guided man's activity in education, and which, therefore, could be a criterion for the correct human activity in education, whereas the historical view to all our questions answers only by saying that Rousseau and Luther were the products of their time. We are searching for the eternal principle which found its expression in them; and we are told about the form in which it found its expression, and they classify them and determine their orders.

We are told that *the criterion is that one must teach in conformity with the demands of the time,* and we are told that that is very simple. I understand teaching according to the dogmas of the Christian or of the Mohammedan religion, but teaching according to the demands of the time is something of which I fail to comprehend a single word. What are these demands? Who will determine them? Where will they be expressed? It may be very amusing to discuss up and down the historical conditions which compelled Rousseau to express himself in the particular form in which he did express himself, but it is impossible to discover those historical conditions in which a future Rousseau will express himself. I can understand why Rousseau should have written with malice against the artificiality of life; but I positively fail to see why Rousseau appeared, and why he discovered the great truths. I have no business with Rousseau and his surroundings; I am interested only in the thoughts which he expressed, and I can verify and comprehend his thoughts only by thinking, and not by reflecting on his place in history.

It was my problem to express and determine the criterion in pedagogy, whereas the historical view, not following me on that path, replies to me that Rousseau and Luther were in their place (as though they could be in somebody else's place), and that there are different schools (as though we did not know that), and that each carries a kernel to that mysterious historical heap. The historical view can breed many pleasant conversations, when there is nothing else to do, and can explain that which everybody knows; but it is not able to say a word on which to build reality. If it does utter something, it says a commonplace such as that one must teach according to the demands of the time.

Tell us, what are these demands in Syzrán, in Geneva, along the Syr-Darya? Where can we find the expression of these demands and of the demand of the time, — of what time? When it comes to talking about what is historical, I will say that the historical moment is only in the present. One assumes the demands of the year 1825 for the demands of the present; another knows what the demands will be in August, 1892; a third regards the demands of the Middle Ages as our present demands. I repeat that if the phrase *to teach according to the demands of the time*, not one word of which has any meaning for us, is written with due reflection, we ask you, point those demands out to us; we say frankly, with all our heart, that we should like to know those demands, for we do not know them.

We could adduce many more samples of Mr. Márkov's historical view with references to the *Trivium* and the *Quadrivium* of Cassiodorus, of Thomas Aquinas, of Shakespeare, of Hamlet, and with other similar interesting and pleasant discussions. But all these passages give no better answer to our questions, and so we shall confine ourselves to the elucidation of the causes which make the historical view invalid for the solution of philosophical questions.

The cause lies in this: people with the historical view have come to the conclusion that abstract thought, which they abusively call metaphysics, is fruitless the moment it is contrary to historical conditions, that is, to speak more simply, to existing convictions; that this thought is even useless because they have discovered a general law by which humanity advances without the participation of the thought which is contrary to reigning convictions. This supposed law of humanity is called *progress*. The whole reason of our disagreement with Mr. Márkov, and of his complete contempt for our proofs, which he does not take the trouble to answer, lies in the fact that Mr. Márkov believes in progress, and I have no such faith.

What is this conception of progress and the faith based upon it?

The fundamental idea of progress and its expression will be like this: "Humanity is continually changing in form; it lives through the past, retaining the labours begun by that past and its recollections." In the metaphorical sense we call this change of human relations "motion," and the past change we call "back," and the future change we call "forward." In general, in a metaphorical sense we say that humanity moves forward. Though not clearly expressed, this statement is, in a metaphorical sense, quite correct. But back of this undoubted statement, those who believe in progress and the historical evolution make another unproved assertion that humanity in former days enjoyed less well-being, and the farther we go back the less, and the farther forward the more. From this the conclusion is drawn that for a fruitful activity it is necessary to act only in conformity with historical conditions; and that by the law of progress, every historical action will lead to an increase of the general well-being, that is, that all will be well, while all attempts to arrest or even oppose the movement of history are fruitless.

The process of progress has taken place in all humanity from time immemorial, says the historian who believes in progress, and he proves this assertion by comparing, let us say, the England of the year 1685 with the England of our time. Even if it were possible to prove, by comparing Russia, France, and Italy of our time with ancient Rome, Greece, Carthage, and so forth, that the prosperity of the modern nations is greater than that of antiquity, I am still struck by one incomprehensible phenomenon: they deduce a general law for all humanity from the comparison of one small part of European humanity in the present and the past. Progress is a common law of humanity, they say, except for Asia, Africa, America, and Australia, except for one thousand millions of people.

We have noticed the law of progress in the dukedom of Hohenzollern-Sigmaringen, with its three thousand inhabitants. We know China, with its two hundred millions of inhabitants, which overthrows our whole theory of progress, and we do not for a moment doubt that progress is the common law of all humanity, and that we, the believers in that progress, are right, and those who do not believe in it are wrong, and so we go with cannon and guns to impress the idea of progress upon the Chinese. Common sense, however, tells me that if the greater part of humanity, the whole so-called East, does not confirm the law of progress, but, on the contrary, overthrows it, that law does not exist for all humanity, but only as an article of faith for a certain part of it.

I, like all people who are free from the superstition of progress, observe only that humanity lives, that the memories of the past as much increase as they disappear; the labours of the past frequently serve as a basis for the labours of the present, and just as frequently as an impediment; that the well-being of people now increases in one place, in one stratum, and in one sense, and now diminishes; that, no matter how desirable it would be, I cannot find any common law in the life of humanity; and that it is as easy to subordinate history to the idea of progress as to any other idea or to any imaginable historical fancy.

I will say even more: I see no necessity of finding common laws for history, independently of the impossibility of finding them. The common eternal law is written in the soul of each man. The law of progress, or perfectibility, is written in the soul of each man, and is transferred to history only through error. As long as it remains personal, this law is fruitful and accessible to all; when it is transferred to history, it becomes an idle, empty prattle, leading to the justification of every insipidity and to fatalism. Progress in general in all humanity is an unproved fact, and does not exist for all the Eastern nations; therefore, it is as unfounded to say that progress is the law of humanity as it is to say that all people are blond except the dark-complexioned ones.

But we may not yet have defined progress as most understand it. We try to give it a most general and reasonable definition. Maybe progress is a law discovered only by the European nations, but one that is so good that the whole of humanity ought to be subjected to it. In this sense progress is a path over which a certain part of humanity is travelling, and which this part of humanity recognizes as leading it to well-being. In this sense Buckle understands the progress of the civilization of the European nations, including in this general conception of progress the social and the economic progress, the progress of the sciences, the industrial and the fine arts, and especially the invention of powder, printing, and roads of communication.

Such a definition of progress is lucid and intelligible; but there involuntarily arises the question, first, who has decided that this progress leads to well-being? In order to believe that it does, I need that not exceptional people, who belong to an exceptional class, — historians, thinkers, and journalists, — should recognize it as so, but that the whole mass of the people, subject to the action of progress, should recognize that progress leads it to well-being. We, on the contrary, constantly see a phenomenon which contradicts it.

The second question consists in this: What shall be recognized as well-being? Is it the improvement of means of communication, the dissemination of the art of printing, the illumination of the streets by means of gas, the increase of homes for the poor, and so forth? or the virgin wealth of Nature, the woods, the game, the fish, strong physical development, purity of morals, and so forth? Humanity lives at the same time by so many varied sides of its existence that it is impossible for any given man to define the degree of well-being for any given period.

One man sees only the progress of art; another, the progress of virtue; a third, the progress of material comfort; a fourth, the progress of physical force; the fifth, the progress of the social order; the sixth, the progress of science; a seventh, the progress of love, equality, and liberty; the eighth, the progress of illumination by gas, and of sewing-machines. A man who will look at all sides of humanity's life without bias will always find that the progress on the one side is purchased at the expense of a retrogression on the other side of human life.

Have not the most conscientious political actors, who believed in the progress of equality and liberty, convinced themselves each day that in ancient Greece and Rome there was more liberty than in the England of to-day with its Chinese and Indian wars; than in modern France with its two Bonapartes; than in the very newest America with its sanguinary war for the rights of slavery? Have not the most conscientious men, believing in the progress of art, convinced themselves that there are no Phidiases, no Raphaels, no Homers in our day? Have not the most rabid economic progressists convinced themselves that it is necessary to prohibit the working people from procreating children in order to be able to feed the existing population?

Thus, in reply to the two questions which I have put, I say that, first, it is possible only then to recognize a progress which leads to well-being when the whole nation, subjected to the action of progress, will recognize this action as good and useful, whereas now we constantly see the opposite in nine-tenths of the population, in the so-called common, labouring people; and, secondly, when it shall be proved that progress leads to the improvement of all the sides of human life, or that all the consequences of its influence taken together by their good and useful qualities overbalance its bad and injurious results.

The people, that is, the mass of the nation, nine-tenths of all people, are always inimical toward progress and constantly not only do not recognize its usefulness, but positively and consciously recognize its harmfulness for them.

We cannot believe the deductions of the historians, such as Macaulay (the one whom Mr. Márkov adduces to prove the power of the English education), who presume that they have weighed all sides of human life, and who, on the basis of this weighing, have decided that progress has done more good than evil, because these deductions are not based on anything. These deductions manifestly prove to every conscientious and unbiassed judge, in spite of the opposite aim of the writer, that progress has done more evil than good to the people, that is, to the majority, not to mention the State.

I ask the serious reader to read the whole third chapter of the first part of Macaulay's history. The deductions are made boldly and with decision, but it is positively unintelligible to a sound-minded man who is not dulled by the faith in progress, which they are based upon. The important facts are only these:

(1) The population has increased, and that to such an extent that Malthus's theory becomes a necessity. (2) There was no army, and now it has become immense; the same is true of the fleet. (3) The number of petty agriculturists has diminished. (4) The cities have drawn to them the greater part of the population. (5) The land has been stripped of forests. (6) Wages have become half as large again, but the prices have increased on everything and the comforts of life have become fewer. (7) The taxes for the poor have been increased tenfold; there are more newspapers; the illumination of the streets is better; wives and children are beaten less, and English ladies have begun to write without orthographical mistakes.

I ask the reader to read this third chapter with the most conscientious attention, and to remember the simple facts that the army once increased can never be diminished; that the century-old forests, once destroyed, can never be restored; that a population, corrupted by comforts, can never return to its primitive simplicity and moderation. I ask the reader who has no faith in progress, or who for the time being has given up this faith, to read everything which has been written in proof of the good of progress, and to ask himself, with entire disregard of his faith, whether there are any proofs that progress has done people more good than evil. It is impossible to prove this to an unbiassed man; but for the biassed man any paradox is possible, even the paradox of progress, clothed in historical facts.

What a strange and incomprehensible phenomenon! There is no common law of humanity's progress, as the immovable Eastern nations prove to us. It is impossible to prove that the European nations are constantly moving in the direction of the improvement of their well-being, and nobody has ever proved it; and, finally, the most remarkable thing is that nine-tenths of that very European humanity, who are subject to the process of the progress, consciously hate progress and use all the means at their command to resist it, while we recognize the progress of civilization as an unquestioned good. However incomprehensible this phenomenon may appear, it will become quite clear to us if we look at it without prejudice.

Only one small part of society believes in progress, preaches it, and tries to prove its benefit. The other, the greater part of society, resists progress and does not believe in its benefit. From this I conclude that for a small part of society progress is a benefit; but for the majority it is an evil. I conclude this from the reflection that all men consciously or unconsciously strive after the good, and evade the evil. Having made this deduction, I shall verify it by reference to facts.

Who are that small part who believe in progress? They are the so-called cultured society, the leisure classes, to use Buckle's expression. Who are the majority who do not believe in progress? They are the so-called people, the busy classes. The interests of society and of the masses are always opposed to each other. The more advantageous to one set, the more disadvantageous to the other.

My supposition is confirmed in the matter of progress, and I conclude that progress is the more advantageous for society the more disadvantageous it is for the masses. This ratiocination, in addition, gives me a complete explanation of that strange phenomenon why, despite the fact that progress is not a common law of humanity, despite the fact that progress does not lead to an increased well-being of the whole European humanity, despite the fact that nine-tenths of the masses are opposed to it, progress is lauded all the time and is ever more disseminated.

Those who believe in progress are sincere in their

belief, because that faith is advantageous to them, and so they preach their faith with passion and fury. I involuntarily recall the Chinese war, in which three great Powers quite sincerely introduced the belief in progress into China by means of powder and cannon-balls.

But am I not mistaken? Let us see in what may be the advantage of progress for society, and its disadvantage for the masses. Speaking here of facts, I feel the necessity of leaving Europe in peace and speaking of Russia, with which I am familiar. Who with us is a believer, who an unbeliever? The believers in progress are: the educated gentry, the educated merchant and official classes, — the leisure classes, according to Buckle's expression. The unbelievers of progress and its enemies are: the master mechanics, the factory workmen, the peasants, the agriculturists, and the trades-people, men directly occupied with physical labour, — the busy classes. Reflecting upon this distinction, we find that the more a man works the more conservative he is, and the less he works the more he is a progressist. There are no greater progressists than contractors, writers, the gentry, students, officials without places, and manufacturers. There is no greater opponent to progress than the agricultural peasant.

"Man takes possession of the forces of Nature; thought, with the speed of thought, flies from one end of the universe to another. Time is vanquished." All that is beautiful and touching, but let us see for whom that is advantageous. We have in mind the progress of the electric telegraphs. It is apparent that the advantage and application of the telegraph is only for the higher, so-called cultured class. The masses, nine-tenths of the people, hear only the buzzing of the wires and are importuned by the severe laws not to injure the telegraphs.

Over the wires flies the thought that the demand on such and such an article of commerce has increased and that, therefore, the price must be advanced upon it, or the thought that "I, a Russian landed proprietress, living in Florence, have now, thank God, stronger nerves, and embrace my beloved husband and ask him to send me forty thousand francs in the quickest possible time." Without making any exact statistics of telegrams, one may be firmly convinced that all the telegrams belong only to the kind, samples of which I have given here.

A peasant of Yásnaya Polyána, of the Government of Túla, or any other Russian peasant (it must not be forgotten that these peasants form the great mass of the people about whose well-being progress is concerned), has never sent or received, and for a long time to come will never send or receive, a single telegram. All the telegrams which fly over his head cannot add one note to his well-being, because everything he needs he gets from his own field and from his forest, and he is equally indifferent to the cheapness or dearness of sugar or cotton, and to the dethronement of King Otho, and to the speeches made by Palmerston and by Napoleon III., and to the sentiment of the lady writing from Florence. All these thoughts, which with the rapidity of lightning cross the universe, do not increase the productiveness of his field, do not weaken the vigilance in the forests of the landed proprietor and of the Crown, do not add any strength in his work either to him or to his family, do not give him one additional labourer. All these great thoughts can only impair his well-being, instead of fortifying or improving it, and can be interesting to him only in a negative sense.

For the orthodox in progress the telegraphic wires have brought enormous advantages. I am not disputing the advantages; I only try to prove that I must not think and persuade others that that which is advantageous to me is the greatest good for the whole world. This must be proved, or, at least, we must wait for all people to recognize as good that which is advantageous to us. We do not see that at all in the so-called enslavement of space and time. We see, on the contrary, that the advocates of progress in this respect judge precisely as did the old landed proprietors, who assured everybody that for the peasants, for the state, and for humanity at large there was nothing more advantageous than serfdom and manorial labour; the only difference is that the faith of the landed proprietors is old and unmasked, while the faith of the progressists is still fresh and in full force.

The art of printing is another favourite and trite theme of the progressists. Its dissemination, and the dissemination of the rudiments which comes with it, has always been regarded as an undoubted good for the whole nation. Why is that so? The art of printing, reading, and that which is called culture, are the deep-rooted superstitions of the religion of progress, and so I will ask the reader in this matter most frankly to renounce all such faith and to ask himself: Why is it so, and why is that culture, which we, the minority, regard as a benefit, and as we, consequently, do the art of printing and of reading, which latter we wish to disseminate so,— why are that art of printing, that reading, and that culture a benefit to the majority,— to the masses?

We have said before, in several articles of ours, why that culture, which we possess, by its essence cannot be a good for the masses. We shall now speak exclusively of the art of printing.

It is evident to me that the distribution of periodicals and books, the uninterrupted and immense progress of the art of printing, have been very advantageous to writers, editors, publishers, proof-readers, and compositors. Immense sums have in this manner passed by indirect ways from the people into the hands of these men. The art of printing is so advantageous for these people that all kinds of means are thought out in order to increase the number of readers: poetry, stories, scandals, obloquy, gossips, polemics, presents, premiums, societies for the encouragement of reading, distribution of books, and schools for the increase of the number of those who can read. No labour is so well paid as literature. No interest is so great as on the literary capital. The number of literary workers grows with every day. The pettiness and insignificance of literature increases in proportion with the increase of its organs.

"But if the number of books and periodicals increases, if literature pays so well, it must be necessary," naïve people will tell me. "Consequently the farming out of the monopolies is necessary, if they pay so well," I will reply.

The success of literature would appear as satisfying a want of the people, only if the whole nation were in sympathy with it; but that condition does not exist, just as it did not exist when the monopolies were farmed out. Literature, just like the monopolies, is only an artful exploitation, advantageous only for those who take part in it, and disadvantageous for the masses.

There is the *Contemporary*, and the *Contemporary Word*, and the *Contemporary Chronicle*, and the *Russian Word*, the *Russian Messenger*, and the *Time*, and *Our Time*, and the *Eagle*, and the *Little Star*, the *Garland*, and the *Reader*, the *Popular Reading*, and *Reading for the People*; and there are certain words in certain combinations and permutations, as titles of periodicals and newspapers, and all these periodicals believe firmly that they represent certain thoughts and tendencies. And there are the works of Púshkin, of Gógol, of Turgénev, of Derzhávin. And all these periodicals and works, in spite of their long existence, are unknown and unnecessary to the people and are of no advantage to it.

I have already spoken of the efforts which I have made to inoculate the masses with our social literature. I became convinced, as any one else would, that in order that a Russian from the masses should take a liking to Púshkin's "Borís Godunóv," or Solovév's history, this man must cease being what he is, that is, an independent man, who satisfies all his human wants. Our literature has taken no hold on the masses — I hope that those who know the people and the literature will not doubt it.

What benefit do the masses derive from literature? The people have as yet no cheap Bibles and saints' almanacs. Other books, which fall into their hands, to their thinking, betray only the stupidity and insignificance of their authors; their money and work are wasted, and the advantage from printing to the masses — see how much time has passed — is nil. The masses have not learned from books to plough, to make kvas, to weave bast shoes, to build huts, to sing songs, or even to pray. Every conscientious judge, who is not enthralled by his faith in progress, will admit that there have been no advantages to the masses from printing. But the disadvantages are many.

Mr. Dal, a conscientious observer, has published his observations on the influence exerted by the knowledge of the rudiments on the masses. He proclaimed that the rudiments corrupt the masses. Incontinent accusations and curses were heaped on the observer by all the believers in progress; it was decided that the knowledge of reading was injurious when it was an exception, and that this danger would disappear when it became the general rule. This may be an ingenious supposition, but it is only a supposition. The fact remains, and it has been confirmed by my own observations, and will be confirmed by all people who have direct relations with the masses, such as merchants, burghers, captains of rural police, priests, and peasants themselves.

But I shall probably be told by those who accept my deductions as just, that the progress of the art of printing, without bringing any direct advantage to the people, still works in the direction of their well-being by softening the manners of society; that, for example, the solution of the serf question is only the product of the progress of the art of printing.

To this I will reply that the softening of the manners of society has to be proved and that I personally do not see it and that I do not consider it necessary to take it on faith. I do not find, for example, that the relations of the manufacturer to the workman are any humaner than were the relations of the landed proprietor to the serf. But that is my personal view, which cannot serve as a proof. The chief objection that I have against such an argument is that, even taking as an example the emancipation from serfdom, I do not see that the art of printing has cooperated in its progressive solution. If the government had not said its decisive word in the matter, the press would certainly have decided it quite differently. We saw that the greater part of the organs of the press would have demanded emancipation without land, and would have adduced proofs which would have appeared just as reasonable, ingenious, and sarcastic.

The progress of the art of printing, like the progress of the electric telegraphs, is the monopoly of a certain class of society, advantageous only for the people of that class, who by the word "progress" understand their personal advantage, which thus is always contrary to the advantage of the masses.

It gives me pleasure to read the periodicals when I have nothing else to do, and I am even interested in Otho, the King of Greece. It gives me pleasure to write or edit an article, and to get money and fame from it. It gives me pleasure to receive a despatch about my sister's health and to know for certain what price I may expect for my wheat. In all these cases there is nothing prejudicial in the pleasures which I experience, and in the desires which I have that the conveniences giving rise to these pleasures may be increased; but it will be quite incorrect to suppose that my pleasures coincide with the increase of the well-being of humanity at large. It would be as incorrect to suppose this, as to suppose with the monopolist or landed proprietor that, by getting a great income without labour, he makes all humanity happy by encouraging art and giving many people work to do to supply his luxuries. I beg the reader to observe that Homer, Socrates, Aristotle, the German fairy-tales and songs, and, finally, the Russian epos, did not need the art of printing in order to be eternal.

Steam, the railways, and the much lauded steamboats locomotives, and engines in general, — we shall not speak of what may be in the future, of the results that arise from these inventions according to the contradictory theories of political economy, but will examine only those advantages which steam has brought to the masses.

I see a Túla peasant, a good friend of mine, who is in no need of rapid transit from Túla to Moscow, to the Rhine, to Paris, and back again. The possibility of such migrations does not in the least increase his well-being. He satisfies all his wants from his own labour, and, beginning with his food and ending with his wearing apparel, everything is produced by him alone: money is not wealth to him. This is so true that when he has money, he buries it in the ground and finds no need of making use of it. Thus, if the railways make the objects of manufactures and commerce more accessible to him he remains quite indifferent to this greater accessibility. He needs no tricot, no velvets, no watches, no French wines, no sardines. Everything which he needs, and which to his thinking forms wealth and increase of well-being, is acquired by his labour on his land.

Macaulay says that the best measure of the well-being of the labouring people is the amount of wages they receive. Is it possible that we, Russians, are to such an extent unacquainted with the condition of our people, and do not want to know it, that we repeat such a senseless and false proposition, so far as we are concerned? Is it not evident to every Russian that the earnings are to a common Russian an accident, a luxury, upon which nothing can be based?

The whole nation, every Russian without exception, will doubtless call rich a peasant of the steppe with his old ricks of grain on his threshing-floor, who never in his life has seen such a thing as wages, just as he will certainly regard as poor a suburban Moscow peasant, who always commands high wages. Not only is it impossible in Russia to determine the wealth by the amount of the wages, but one may boldly assert that for Russia the appearance of wages is a sign of the decline of wealth and well-being. This rule we, Russians, who know our people, can verify throughout Russia, and therefore, without discussing the wealth of the nations and the wealth of the whole of Europe, we may and must say that for Russia, that is, for the great majority of the Russian people, the scale of wages not only does not serve as a measure of their well-being, but that the very appearance of wages indicates the decline of the national wealth.

It is obvious that we must look for different first principles than those which exist in the rest of Europe; in the meantime European political economy wants to prescribe its laws for us. For the great majority of the Russian people money constitutes no wealth, and the cheapening of articles of manufacture does not increase their well-being. For this reason, the railways bring no advantages to the great mass of the population. (I beg the reader to observe that I am speaking of the advantages according to the conception of the masses themselves, and not of those advantages which the progress of civilization wants to enforce upon them.)

According to the ideas of the Russian people, the

increase of their well-being consists in the increase of the powers of the soil, in the increase of the amount of live stock, in the increase of the quantity of grain and, consequently, in its cheapening (I beg you to observe that no peasant ever complains of the cheapness of grain; it is only the European political economists who console him with the idea that the price of grain will be higher so that he will be able to purchase manufactured articles, — in which he is not interested), in the increase of working powers (a peasant never complains that there are too many people in his village), in the increase of forest land and pastures, in the absence of city temptations.

Which of these benefits do the railways offer the peasant? They increase the temptations; they destroy the forests; they take away labourers; they raise the price of bread. Maybe I am mistaken when I speak of the causes which lead the spirit of the people always to assume a hostile attitude toward the introduction of railways; I may have omitted some causes, but the undoubted fact of the permanent resistance of the popular spirit to the introduction of railways exists in its full force. The masses get accustomed to them only in the measure in which they succumb to the temptations of the railways and themselves become participants in the exploitation. The real people, that is, all those who work and live directly by the fruits of their work, — the preeminently agricultural masses, nine-tenths of the nation, without whom no progress could be thought of, are always inimical to them. Thus, those who believe in progress, a small part of society, say that the railways are an increase of the people's well-being, while the great majority of society says that it is a decrease.

We could easily verify and explain such a resistance to progress on the side of the people in every aspect of progress, but we shall confine ourselves to the above mentioned examples, and shall attempt to reply to the question which naturally arises: "Is there any need of trusting this counteraction of the masses? You say," we shall be told, "that those who are dissatisfied with the railways are the agricultural peasants, who pass their lives on the hanging beds, in a smoky hut, or behind the plough; who mend their own bast shoes and weave their own shirts; who have never read a book; who once every two weeks take off their vermin-ridden shirts; who tell the time by the sun and by cockcrows, and who have no other needs than slave labour, sleeping, eating, and intoxication. They are not men, but beasts," the progressists will say and think, "and therefore we think we are right not to pay any attention to their opinion, and to do for them what we have found to be good for us."

Such an opinion, though it be not expressed, is always at the basis of the reflections of the progressists; but I presume that these people, who are called savages, and whole generations of these savages, are just such people and just the same kind of humanity as your Palmerstons, Othos, and Bonapartes. I presume that generations of workmen have in them the same human characteristics, and especially the characteristic of finding a better place, — as a fish looks for a greater depth, — as your generations of lords, barons, professors, bankers, and so forth.

In this idea I am confirmed by my personal, no doubt insignificant, conviction, which is, that in the generations of workmen there lies more force and a greater consciousness of truth and goodness than in generations of barons, bankers, and professors; I am, above all, confirmed in this idea by the simple observation that a peasant just as sarcastically and cleverly condemns the master and makes fun of him, because he does not know what a plough is, or a drag, or buckwheat, or grits; and when to sow oats, when buckwheat; how to tell one track from another; how to find out whether a cow is with calf, or not: and because the master passes all his life in idleness, and so forth, — just as the master condemns the peasant because he mispronounces words, and because on a holiday he drinks like a fish, and because he does not know how to indicate a road.

I am also struck by the observation that two men, quarrelling, quite sincerely call each other fools and rascals. I am still more struck by this observation in the conflicts of Eastern nations with Europeans. Hindoos regard the English as barbarians and scoundrels, and thus the English look upon the Hindoos; the Japanese look thus upon the Europeans, and the Europeans upon the Japanese; even the most progressive nation, the French, regards the Germans as dullards, while the Germans think that the French are brainless.

From all these observations I come to the conclusion that if the progressists look upon the masses as having no right to consider their well-being, and the masses look upon the progressists as occupied with their own selfish ends, it is impossible from these contradictory views to conclude as to the justice of the one side or the other. For this reason I am constrained to side with the masses, on the ground that, first, the masses are more numerous than society, and because it must be assumed that a greater measure of truth is on the side of the masses, and, secondly and chiefly, because the masses could well get along without the society of the progressists, and could satisfy all their human wants, such as working, enjoying themselves, loving, thinking, and producing works of art (the Iliad, the Russian songs), whereas the progressists could not exist without the masses.

We lately read the history of the civilization of England by Buckle. This book had a great success in Europe (which is quite natural) and an immense success in the literary and learned circles of Russia, — and that is incomprehensible to me. Buckle analyzes the laws of civilization in a very entertaining manner; but this whole interest is lost for me and, it seems to me, for all Russians, who have no foundation whatever to suppose that we, Russians, must of necessity be subject to the same law of the progress of civilization to which the European nations are subject, and that the progress of civilization is a good. It is necessary first to prove both to us Russians.

We personally, for example, regard the progress of civilization as one of the greatest violent evils, to which a certain part of humanity is subject, nor do we regard this progress as inevitable. The author, who so strongly contends against propositions which are based on no proof, himself does not prove to us why the whole interest in history for him lies in the progress of civilization. For us this interest lies in the progress of the common well-being. The progress of well-being, according to our conviction, not only does not spring from the progress of civilization, but for the most part is opposed to it. If there are people who think differently, this statement must be proved. We have found these proofs neither in the direct observations of the phenomena of life, nor in the pages of historians, philosophers, and publicists. We see, on the contrary, that these people, and Mr. Márkov with them, in their arguments against us, without any foundation recognize as proved the question of the identity of the well-being and the civilization.

We have made a very long digression, which may appear to be irrelevant, only to say that we do not believe in progress as increasing well-being; that we have no grounds whatever for believing in it; and that we have been looking in our first article for a different measure of what is good and bad than the recognition of progress as good and that which is not progress as bad. Having elucidated this chief hidden point of our disagreement with Mr. Márkov, we presume, with the majority of the so-called cultivated society, that the answers to the points of the article in the *Russian Messenger* will become easy and simple for us.

(1) The article in the *Russian Messenger* recognizes the right of one generation to interfere in the education of another, on the ground that it is natural and that each generation casts its handful on the heap of progress. We do not recognize this right because, not regarding progress as an unconditional good, we seek other foundations for such a right, and we assume that we have found them. If it were proved that our suppositions are erroneous, we still should not be able to recognize the belief in progress as well founded any more than the belief in Mohammed or in the Dalai-Lama.

(2) The article in the *Russian Messenger* recognizes the right of the upper classes to interfere in the popular education. We think we have shown sufficiently in the previous pages why interference in the education of the masses by those who believe in progress is unjust, but advantageous for the upper classes, and why their injustice seems to them a right, just as serfdom seemed to be a right.

(3) The author of the article in the *Russian Messenger* thinks that the schools cannot and must not be exempted from historical conditions. We think that these words make no sense, because, first, it is impossible, either in fact or in thought, to exempt anything from historical conditions; secondly, because, if the discovery of the laws upon which the school has been built and ought to be built is, in Mr. Márkov's opinion, an exemption from historical conditions, we assume that our thought, which has discovered certain laws, also acts within historical conditions, and that it is necessary to condemn or approve the thought itself by means of reason, in order to make it clear, and not to answer by the truth that we are living under historical conditions.

(4) The author of the article in the *Russian Messenger* thinks that our modern schools more nearly correspond to the demands of the time than the mediæval ones. We are sorry that we have given Mr. Márkov an occasion to prove this to us, and we gladly confess that, in proving the opposite, we fell into the common habit of subordinating historical facts to a preconceived idea. Mr. Márkov has done the same, probably more successfully and more eloquently than we. We do not wish to discuss this, sincerely confessing our error. It is so easy to talk a great deal in this field, without convincing anybody!

(5) The author of the article in the *Russian Messenger* regards our education as not injurious, but as useful, because our education trains men for progress, in which they believe. But we do not believe in progress and therefore continue to regard our education as injurious.

(6) The author of the article in the *Russian Messenger* thinks that full liberty of education is injurious and impossible. It is injurious, because we need men of progress, and not merely men, and impossible, because we have ready-made programmes for the education of men of progress, but we have no programmes for the education of mere men.

(7) The author thinks that the structure of the school at Yásnaya Polyána contradicts the editor's convictions. We admit that, as a personal matter, the more so, since the author himself knows how strong the influence of historical conditions is, and, therefore, ought to know that the school at Yásnaya Polyána is subject to the action of two forces, to what the author calls an extreme conviction and to historical conditions, that is, to the education of the teachers, the means, and so forth; besides, the school could gain but a very small degree of freedom and, consequently, of advantage over other schools. What would have happened if these convictions had not been extreme, as the author thinks they are? The author says that

the success of the school depends on love. But love is not accidental. Love can exist only with freedom. In all the schools founded on the convictions of the school at Yásnaya Polyána the same phenomenon has been repeated: the teacher fell in love with his school; and I am sure that the same teacher, with all the idealization possible, could not fall in love with a school where the children sit on benches, walk by the ringing of bells, and are whipped on Saturdays.

And (8) finally, the author does not agree with the Yásnaya Polyána definition of education. It is here that we shall have to make our meaning clearer. It seems to me that it would have been juster on the side of the author, if he, without entering into any further discussion, had taken the trouble to overthrow our definition. But he did not do that; he did not even look at it; called it trite, and gave his own definition: progress,— and, therefore, to teach in accordance with the demands of the time. Everything which we wrote about progress was written for the purpose of eliciting people's retorts. Instead of it, they do not dispute with us, but only say: What is the use of instinct, of the necessity of equality, and all that baggage of words, when there is a growing heap?

But we do not believe in progress, and so cannot be satisfied with the heap. Even if we did believe, we should say: Very well, the aim is to teach in accordance with the demands of the time, to add to the heap; we should admit that the mother teaches the child, with the intention of transmitting her knowledge to him, as Mr. Márkov says. But why? I should ask, and I should have a right to get an answer. A man breathes. Why? I ask. And I receive a reply, not that he breathes because he breathes, but in order to get the necessary supply of oxygen and to cast off the useless gases. And again I ask: Why the oxygen? And a physiologist sees the meaning of such a question and answers: In order to get heat. Why the heat? I ask. And here he answers, or tries to answer, and he seeks and knows that the more general such an answer will be, the richer it will be in deductions.

Now we ask: Why does one teach another? It seems to me there can be no question which lies nearer to a pedagogue than this. And we answer it, maybe irregularly, without proofs, but the question and the answer are categorical. Mr. Márkov (I do not attack Mr. Márkov, — every one who believes in progress will make the same reply) not only does not answer our question, he is not even able to see it. For him this question does not exist: it is nothing but a trite commonplace, to which, as to something funny, he directs the reader's especial attention. And yet, in this question and answer lies the essence of everything I have said, written, and thought about pedagogy.

Mr. Márkov and the public who agree with Mr. Márkov are intelligent, cultivated men, accustomed to reasoning; whence comes that sudden dulness of comprehension? *Progress.* The word "progress" is said, — and nonsense becomes clear, and what is clear looks like nonsense. I do not recognize the benefit of progress so long as it is not proved to me, and, therefore, as I observe the phenomenon of education, I need a definition of education, and I again repeat and explain what I have said: *Education is the activity of man which has for its base the need of equality and the invariable law of educational progress.*

As said before, to the study of the laws of education we apply not the metaphysical method, but the method of deductions from observations. We observe the phenomena of education in its most general sense, including the bringing up.

In every phenomenon of education we see two factors,

the educator and the one who is being educated. In order to study the phenomena of education, as we understand it, and to find its definition and criterion, we necessarily must study both activities and find the cause which unites the two activities into one phenomenon, called education.

Let us first examine the activity of the person under education, and its causes. The activity of the person who is being educated, whatever, wherever, and in whatever way he may learn (even if he reads books by himself), consists in assimilating the manner, the form, or the contents of the idea of the man, or men, whom he regards as knowing more than he knows. The moment he reaches the level of his educators, the moment he no longer considers the educators higher in knowledge than he is, the activity of education, on the side of the person under education, involuntarily stops, and no conditions whatever can make him continue it. A man cannot learn from another, if the man who learns knows as much as the man who teaches. A teacher of arithmetic, who does not know algebra, involuntarily stops his teaching of arithmetic the moment the pupil has made the knowledge of arithmetic completely his own.

It would seem useless to prove that, as soon as the knowledge of the teacher and the pupil is equalized, the activity of teaching, of education in the larger sense, inevitably stops between the pupil and the teacher, and there begins a new activity, which consists in the teacher's opening to the pupil a new perspective of knowledge, familiar to him, but unknown to the pupil, in this or that branch of science, and the education continues until the pupil's knowledge is equalized with that of the teacher; or having reached the teacher's level in his knowledge of arithmetic, the pupil gives up his teacher and takes up a book, from which he learns algebra. In this case, the book, or the author of the book, appears as the new teacher, and the activity of education lasts only so long as the pupil has not reached the level of the book, or of the author of the book. Again the activity of education comes to a close immediately upon having reached a point of equality in knowledge.

It seems useless to prove this truth, which may be verified in all imaginable cases of education. From these observations and considerations we conclude that the activity of education, considered only from the side of him who is being educated, has for its foundation the tendency of the pupil to become equal in knowledge with his educator. This truth is proved by the simple observation that the moment the equality has been reached, the activity immediately and inevitably comes to an end, and by this other, more simple observation, that in every education may be observed this greater or lesser approach to equality. A good or a bad education is always and everywhere, in the whole human race, determined only by the rapidity with which this equality between teacher and pupil takes place: the slower, the worse; the faster, the better.

This truth is so simple and self-evident that there is no need of proving it. But it behoves us to prove why this simple truth never occurs to anybody, is not expressed by anybody, or meets with enraged resistance when it is expressed.

The following are the causes: Outside of the chief foundation of every education, which springs from the very essence of the activity of education, — the tendency toward an equalization of knowledge, — there have arisen other causes in civil society, which urge on toward education. These causes seem so persistent that the pedagogues keep only these in view, losing sight of the chief foundation. Considering now only the activity of him who is being educated, we shall discover many seeming foundations of education, besides the essential one which we have enunciated. The impossibility of admitting these foundations can easily be proved.

These false, but active, foundations are the following: The first and most operative, — the child learns in order not to be punished; the second, — the child learns in order to be rewarded; the third, — the child learns in order to be better than the rest; the fourth, — the child, or young man, learns, in order to obtain an advantageous position in life.

These foundations, acknowledged by all, may be classified under three heads: (1) Learning on the basis of obedience; (2) learning on the basis of egotism; and (3) learning on the basis of material advantages and ambition. Indeed, on the basis of these three divisions the various pedagogical schools have been built up: the Protestant schools, on obedience; the Catholic schools of the Jesuits, on the basis of rivalry and egotism; our Russian schools, on the basis of material advantages, civil privileges, and ambition.

The groundlessness of these incentive causes is apparent, in the first place, in actual life, on account of the universal dissatisfaction with the educational institutions based on these foundations; in the second place, for the reason, which I have expressed ten times, and will keep expressing until I get an answer to it, that under such conditions (obedience, egotism, and material advantages) there is no common criterion of pedagogy, and the theologian and the natural scientist at once regard their schools as impeccable, and all the other schools as positively harmful; finally, in the third place, because, taking obedience, egotism, and the material advantages for the basis of the activity of the learner, the definition of education becomes impossible.

By admitting that the equality of knowledge is the aim of the learner's activity, I see that upon reaching this aim the activity itself stops; but by assuming obedience, egotism, and material advantages as the aim, I see, on the contrary, that however obedient the learner may become, however he may surpass all the others in worth, no matter what material advantages and civil rights he may have obtained, his aim is not reached, and the possibility of the activity of education does not stop. I see, in reality, that the aim of education, by admitting such false bases, is never attained, that is, that the equality of knowledge is not acquired, but there is obtained, independently of education, a habit of obedience, an irritable egotism, and material advantages. The adoption of these false foundations of education explains to me all the errors of pedagogy and the incompatibility of the results of education with the demands, inherent in man, made upon it, to which these errors lead.

Let us now analyze the activity of the educator. Just as in the first case, we shall find, by observing this phenomenon in civil society, many various causes of this activity. These causes may be brought under the following heads: the first and foremost, — the desire of making people useful to us (landed proprietors who had their manorial servants instructed in music; the government which trains officers, officials, and engineers for itself); the second, — also obedience and material advantages, which cause a student of the university, for a certain remuneration, to teach children according to a given programme; the third, — egotism, which urges a man on to teach in order to display his knowledge; and the fourth, — the desire to make others participants in one's interests, to transmit one's convictions to them, and, for that reason, to impart one's knowledge to them.

It seems to me that every activity of the educator comes under one of these four heads, from the activity of the mother, who teaches her child to speak, and the tutor, who, for a set remuneration, teaches the French language, to the professor and author.

By applying the same measure to these subdivisions that we have applied to the bases of the learner's activity, we shall find:

Firstly, that the activity which has for its aim the training of useful people, such as the former landed proprietors and the government trained, does not come to an end when the aim is reached, — consequently, it is not its final end. The government and the landed proprietors could proceed still farther in their activity of education. Very frequently the attainment of the aim of usefulness has nothing in common with education, so that I cannot recognize usefulness as the measure of the activity of the educator.

Secondly, if we are to assume as the basis of the activity of a teacher of a gymnasium, or of a tutor, obedience to him who has entrusted him with the education, and the material advantages accruing to him from this activity, — I again see that with the acquisition of the greatest quantity of material advantages the education does not stop. On the contrary, I see that the acquisition of greater material advantages, as a reward for the education, is frequently independent of the degree of the education furnished.

Thirdly, if we are to admit that egotism and the desire to display one's knowledge serve as the aim of education, then I again see that the attainment of the highest praise for one's lectures or book does not stop the activity of education, for the praise bestowed upon the educator may be independent of the amount of education acquired by the student; I see, on the contrary, that the praise may be squandered by people who are not acquiring education.

Fourthly, at last, by examining this last aim of education, I see that if the activity of the educator is directed toward equalizing the knowledge of the learner with his own, this activity comes to an end the moment this aim has been attained.

Indeed, by applying this definition to reality, I see that all the other causes are only external, vital phenomena, which cloud the fundamental aim of every educator. The direct aim of a teacher of arithmetic consists only in having his pupil assimilate all the laws of mathematical thinking which he himself possesses. The aim of a teacher of French, the aim of a teacher of chemistry and philosophy, are one and the same; and the moment that aim is attained, the activity comes to an end.

Only that instruction has everywhere and in all ages been regarded as good, in which the pupil becomes completely equal to the teacher, — and the more so, the better, and the less the worse. Precisely the same phenomenon may be observed in literature, in this mediate means of education. We regard only those books as good, in which the author, or educator, transmits all his knowledge to the reader or the learner.

Thus, by considering the phenomena of education as a mutual activity of educator and learner, we see that this activity in either case has for its basis one and the same thing, — the tendency of man toward equalized knowledge.

In the definition which we made before, we expressed precisely this, except that we did not make it clear that by equality we meant the equality of knowledge. We added, however: "The tendency toward equality and the invariable law of educational progress." Mr. Márkov understood neither the one nor the other, and was very much startled to find there the invariable law of educational progress.

The law of educational progress means only that inasmuch as education is the tendency of people toward an equality of knowledge, this equality cannot be obtained on a lower stage of knowledge, but may be obtained only on a higher stage, for the simple reason that a child may find out what I know, while I cannot forget what I know; and also, because I may be acquainted with the mode of thought of past generations, while past generations cannot know my mode of thought. This I call the invariable law of educational progress.

Thus I answer to all of Mr. Márkov's points as follows: First, that it is not right to prove anything by the fact that everything is growing better, — it is necessary first to prove whether really everything is growing better, or not; secondly, that education is only that activity of man which has for its base man's need of equality and the invariable law of educational progress.

I have only tried to lead Mr. Márkov out of the waste of useless historical considerations and to explain to him that which he did not understand.

# ARE THE PEASANT CHILDREN TO LEARN TO WRITE FROM US?

## Or, Are We to Learn from the Peasant Children?

---

IN the fourth number of *Yásnaya Polyána*, in the department of children's compositions, there was printed by the editor's mistake "A Story of How a Boy Was Frightened in Túla." This story was not composed by a boy, but by the teacher from a boy's dream as related to him. Some of the readers, who follow the numbers of *Yásnaya Polyána*, have expressed their doubts as regards the authorship of this story. I hasten to beg the readers' indulgence for this oversight, and to remark that in such matters a falsification is impossible. This story was recognized, not because it was better, but because it was worse, infinitely worse, than all children's compositions. All the other stories belong to the children themselves. Two of them, "He Feeds with the Spoon, and Pricks the Eye with the Handle," and "A Soldier's Life," were composed in the following manner.

The chief art of the teacher, in the study of language, and the chief exercise with the aim in view of guiding children to write compositions consist in giving them themes, and not so much in furnishing them as in presenting a large choice, in pointing out the extent of the composition, and in indicating the initial steps. Many clever and talented pupils wrote nonsense; they wrote: "It began to burn, they began to drag out things, and I went into the street," and nothing came of it, although the subject was rich, and that which was described left a deep impression on the child. They did not understand, above all, why they should write, and what good there was in writing. They did not understand the art of expressing life by means of words, nor the charm of this art.

As I have already mentioned in the second number, I tried many different methods of giving them themes to write. I gave them, according to their inclinations, exact, artistic, touching, funny, epic themes, — all to no purpose. Here is how I unexpectedly hit upon the present method.

The reading of the collection of Snegirév's proverbs has long formed one of my favourite occupations, — nay, enjoyments. To every proverb I imagine individuals from among the people and their conflicts in the sense of the proverb. Among the number of unrealizable dreams, I always imagine a series of pictures, or stories, written to fit the proverbs. Once, last winter, I forgot everything after dinner in the reading of Snegirév's book, and even returned to the school with the book. It was the lesson in the Russian language.

"Well, write something on a proverb!" I said.

The best pupils, Fédka, Sémka, and others, pricked up their ears.

"What do you mean by 'on a proverb'? What is it? Tell us!" the questions ran.

I happened to open to the proverb: "He feeds with the spoon, and pricks the eye with the handle."

"Now, imagine," I said, "that a peasant has taken a beggar to his house, and then begins to rebuke him for

*Peasant children.*

the good he has done him, and you will get that 'he feeds with the spoon, and pricks the eye with the handle.'"

"But how are you going to write it up?" said Fédka and all the rest who had pricked up their ears. They retreated, having convinced themselves that this matter was above their strength, and betook themselves to the work which they had begun.

"Write it yourself," one of them said to me.

Everybody was busy with his work; I took a pen and inkstand, and began to write.

"Well," said I, "who will write it best? I am with you."

I began the story, printed in the fourth number of the *Yásnaya Polyána*, and wrote down the first page. Every unbiassed man, who has the artistic sense and feels with the people, will, upon reading this first page, written by me, and the following pages of the story, written by the pupils themselves, separate this page from the rest, as he will take a fly out of the milk: it is so false, so artificial, and written in such a bad language. I must remark that in the original form it was even more monstrous, since much has been corrected, thanks to the indications of the pupils.

Fédka kept looking up from his copy-book to me, and, upon meeting my eyes, smiled, winked, and repeated: "Write, write, or I'll give it to you!" He was evidently amused to see a grown person write a theme.

Having finished his theme worse and faster than usual, he climbed on the back of my chair and began to read over my shoulders. I could not proceed; others came up to us, and I read to them what I had written.

They did not like it, and nobody praised it. I felt ashamed, and, to soothe my literary ambition, I began to tell them the plan of what was to follow. In the proportion as I advanced in my story, I became enthusiastic, corrected myself, and they kept helping me out. One would say that the old man should be a magician; another would remark: "No, that won't do,—he will be just a soldier; the best thing will be if he steals from him; no, that won't go with the proverb," and so forth.

All were exceedingly interested. It was evidently a new and exciting sensation for them to be present at the process of creation, and to take part in it. Their judgments were all, for the most part, of the same kind, and they were just, both as to the very structure of the story and as to the details and characterizations of the persons. Nearly all of them took part in the composition; but, from the start, there distinguished themselves positive Sémka, by his clearly defined artistic quality of description, and Fédka, by the correctness of his poetical conceptions, and especially by the glow and rapidity of his imagination.

Their demands had so little of the accidental in them and were so definite, that more than once I debated with them, only to give way to them. I was strongly possessed by the demands of a regular structure and of an exact correspondence of the idea of the proverb to the story; while they, on the contrary, were only concerned about the demands of artistic truth. I, for example, wanted that the peasant, who had taken the old man to his house, should himself repent of his good deed,—while they regarded this as impossible and created a cross old woman.

I said: "The peasant was at first sorry for the old man, and later he hated to give away the bread."

Fédka replied that that would be improbable: "He did not obey the old woman from the start and would not submit later."

"What kind of a man is he, according to you?" I asked.

"He is like Uncle Timoféy," said Fédka, smiling. "He has a scanty beard, goes to church, and he has bees."

"Is he good, but stubborn?" I asked.

"Yes," said Fédka, "he will not obey the old woman."

From the time that the old man was brought into the hut, the work became animated. They evidently for the first time felt the charm of clothing artistic details in words. Sémka distinguished himself more than the rest in this respect: the correctest details were poured forth one after the other. The only reproach that could be made to him was that these details sketched only minutes of the present, without connection with the general feeling of the story. I hardly could write as fast as they told me the incidents, and only asked them to wait and not forget what they had told me.

Sémka seemed to see and describe that which was before his eyes: the stiff, frozen bast shoes, and the dirt oozing from them, as they melted out, and the toast into which they were changed when the old woman threw them into the oven.

Fédka, on the contrary, saw only such details as evoked in him the particular feeling with which he looked upon a certain person. Fédka saw the snow drifting behind the peasant's leg-rags, and the feeling of compassion with which the peasant said: "Lord, how it snows!" (Fédka's face even showed how the peasant said it, and he swung his hands and shook his head.) He saw the overcoat, a mass of rags and patches, and the torn shirt, behind which could be seen the haggard body of the old man, wet from the thawing snow. He created the old woman, who growled as, at the command of her husband, she took off his bast shoes, and the pitiful groan of the old man as he muttered through his teeth: "Softly, motherkin, I have sores here."

Sémka needed mainly objective pictures: bast shoes, an overcoat, an old man, a woman, almost without any connection between them; but Fédka had to evoke the feeling of pity with which he himself was permeated. He ran ahead of the story, telling how he would feed the old man, how he would fall down at night, and how he would later teach a boy in the field to read, so that I was obliged to ask him not to be in such a hurry and not to forget what he had said. His eyes sparkled to the point of tears; his swarthy, thin little hands were cramped convulsively; he was angry with me, and kept urging me on: "Have you written it, have you written it?" he kept asking me.

He treated all the rest despotically; he wanted to talk all the time, not as a story is told, but as it is written, that is, artistically to clothe in words the sensuous pictures. Thus, for example, he would not allow words to be transposed; if he once said, "I have sores on my feet," he would not permit me to say, "On my feet I have sores." His soul, now softened and irritated by the sentiment of pity, that is, of love, clothed every image in an artistic form, and denied everything that did not correspond to the idea of eternal beauty and harmony.

The moment Sémka was carried away by the expression of disproportionable details about the lambs in the doorbench, and so forth, Fédka grew angry and said, "What a lot of bosh!" I only needed to suggest what the peasant was doing, while his wife went to the gossip, when in Fédka's imagination there would immediately arise a picture with lambs, bleating in the door-bench, with the sighs of the old man and the delirium of the boy Serézhka; I only needed to suggest an artificial and false picture, when he immediately would angrily remark that that was not necessary.

For example, I suggested the description of the peasant's looks, to which he agreed; but to my proposition to describe what the peasant was thinking while his wife had run over to the gossip, there immediately rose before him the very form of the thought: "If you got in the way of Savóska the corpse, he would pull all your locks out!" He said this in such a fatigued and calmly serious and habitual and, at the same time, good-natured voice, leaning his head on his hand, that the boys rolled in laughter.

The chief quality in every art, the feeling of measure, was developed in him to an extraordinary degree. He writhed at the suggestion of any superfluous feature, made by some one of the boys.

He directed the structure of the story so despotically, and with such right to this despotism, that the boys soon went home, and only he and Sémka, who would not give in to him, though working in another direction, were left. We worked from seven to eleven o'clock; they felt neither hunger nor fatigue, and even got angry at me when I stopped writing; they undertook to relieve me in writing, but they soon gave that up as matters would not go well.

It was then for the first time that Fédka asked my name. We laughed because he did not know.

"I know," he said, "how to call you; but how do they call you in the manor? We have such names as Fokanýchev, Zyábrev, Ermílin."

I told him.

"Are we going to print it?" he asked.

"Yes."

"Then we shall have to print: Work by Makárov, Morózov, and Tolstóy."

He was agitated for a long time and could not fall asleep, and I cannot express that feeling of agitation, joy, fear, and almost regret, which I experienced during that evening. I felt that with that day a new world of enjoyment and suffering was opened up to him, — the world of art; I thought that I had received an insight in what no one has a right to see, — the germination of the mysterious flower of poetry.

I felt both dread and joy, like the seeker after the treasure who suddenly sees the flower of the fern, — I felt joy, because suddenly and quite unexpectedly there was revealed to me that stone of the philosophers, which I had vainly been trying to find for two years, — the art of teaching the expression of thoughts; and dread, because this art called for new demands, a whole world of desires, which stood in no relation to the surroundings of the pupils, as I thought in the first moment. There was no mistaking. It was not an accident, but a conscious creation.

I beg the reader to read the first chapter of the story and to notice that wealth of features of true creative talent scattered through it; for example, the feature when the woman in anger complains about her husband to the gossip, and yet weeps, although the author has an apparent dislike for her, when the gossip reminds her of the ruin of her house. For the author, who writes by reasoning out and from memory, the cross woman represents only the opposite of the peasant, — she had to invite the gossip for no other reason than the desire to annoy her husband; but with Fédka the artistic feeling extends also to the woman, and she, too, weeps, fears, and suffers, — she is not guilty, to his manner of thinking. Then the accessory feature when the gossip puts on a woman's fur coat. I remember how struck I was by this and how I asked: "Why a woman's fur coat?" None of us had led Fédka up to the idea that the gossip had put on a fur coat.

He said: "It is more like it!"

When I asked him whether it would do to say that he put on a man's fur coat, he said:

"No, a woman's fur coat is better."

Indeed, this feature is extraordinary. At first it does not occur to one why it should be a woman's fur coat, and yet one feels that it is excellent and cannot be otherwise.

Every artistic word, whether it belongs to Göthe or to Fédka, differs from the inartistic in that it evokes an endless mass of thoughts, images, and explanations.

The gossip in a woman's fur coat involuntarily presents himself to us as a sickly, narrow-chested peasant, just such as he apparently ought to be. The woman's fur coat, carelessly thrown on the bench and the first to fall into his hands, in addition, presents to us a winter evening scene in the life of the peasant. The fur coat leads you to imagine the late evening, during which the peasant is sitting without his wraps near a torch, and the women, coming in and out to fetch water and attend to the cattle, and all that external disorder of the peasant life, where not a person has his clearly defined clothes, and no one thing a definite place. With this one sentence, " He put on a woman's fur coat," the whole character of the surroundings, in which the action takes place, is clearly outlined, and this phrase is not used by accident, but consciously.

I remember vividly how in his imagination arose the words used by the peasant when he found the paper which he could not read.

" Now, if my Serézhka knew how to read, he would have come running to me, and would have grabbed the paper out of my hands, and would have read it all, and would have told me who the old man is."

One almost can see the relation of the peasant to the book which he is holding in his sunburnt hands; the kind man with his patriarchal and pious inclinations rises before you in his whole stature. You feel that the author has taken a deep liking to him and, therefore, has fully comprehended him, so that soon after he lets him make a digression about there being such times nowadays that, before one knows it, one's soul is perished.

The idea about the dream was suggested by me, but it was Fédka's idea to let the goat have sores on its legs, and this conception gave him much pleasure. The reflection of the peasant, while his back is itching, and the picture of the nocturnal quiet, — all that is far from being accidental, and in all these features one feels so strongly the conscious power of the artist!

I also remember how, when the peasant was to fall asleep, I proposed to make him reflect on the future of his son and on the future relations of his son with the old man, and to let the old man teach Serézhka reading, and so forth.

Fédka frowned and said: "Yes, yes, that is good," but it was obvious that he did not like that suggestion, and twice he forgot it.

His feeling of measure was stronger in him than in any of the authors I am acquainted with, — the feeling of measure, which but few artists acquire at the cost of immense labour and study, lived in its primitive force in his uncorrupted childish soul.

I gave up the lesson, because I was too much agitated.

"What is the matter with you? You are so pale, — are you ill?" my companion asked me. Indeed, only two or three times in my life have I experienced such a strong sensation as on that evening, and for a long time I was unable to render an account to myself of what I was experiencing. I dimly felt that I had criminally looked through a glass hive at the work of the bees, concealed from the gaze of mortal man; it seemed to me that I had debauched the pure, primitive soul of a peasant boy. I dimly felt something like repentance for an act of sacrilege. I thought of the children, whom idle and debauched old men allow to contort themselves and represent lascivious pictures in order to fan their wearied, worn-out imaginations, and, at the same time, I was happy, as must be happy the man who beholds that which no one beheld before.

For a long time I was unable to render an account to myself of the impression which it had produced on me, though I felt that this impression was one of those which at a mature age educate a man and lead him to a new stage of life, making him renounce the old and fully devote himself to the new. Even on the following day I could not make myself believe that which I had experienced the day before. It seemed so strange to me that a peasant boy, with the bare knowledge of reading, should suddenly manifest a conscious artistic power, such as Göthe, in all his immeasurable height of development, had been unable to equal. It seemed so strange and offensive to me that I, the author of "Childhood," who had had certain success and had earned recognition for artistic talent from a cultivated Russian public, — that I, in the matter of art, not only should be unable to teach anything to eleven-year-old Sémka or Fédka or to help them, but that I only with difficulty and in a happy moment of excitement should be able to follow and understand them. All that seemed so strange to me that I could not believe that which had happened the day before.

The next day we took up the continuation of the story. When I asked Fédka whether he had thought out the continuation, he only swayed his hands and said: "I know, I know! Who will write?"

We went to work, and again the children displayed the same feeling of artistic truth, measure, and enthusiasm.

In the middle of the lesson I was obliged to leave them.

They continued to write without me and finished two pages just as well done, just as well felt, and just as correctly, as the first. The only thing about these pages was that they were paler in details, that these details were not aptly disposed, and that there were two or three repetitions. All that apparently was due to the fact that the mechanism of writing hampered them.

The same took place on the third day. During these lessons other boys frequently joined us, and, as they knew the tenor and the contents of the story, they often helped us out by adding their correct features. Sémka now kept up with us, and now stayed away. Fédka alone carried the story from beginning to end and passed upon all the proposed changes.

There could no longer be any doubt or thought that this success was a matter of accident: we had apparently struck the method which was more natural and a greater incentive than everything tried before. But it was all so unusual that I did not believe that which took place before our eyes. It looked as though a special incident were necessary in order to destroy all my doubts.

I had to leave for a few days, and the story remained unfinished. The manuscript, three large sheets, closely covered with writing, was left in the room of the teacher, to whom I had shown it.

Even before my departure, while I was busy composing, a newly entered pupil had shown our boys the art of making paper flaps, and, as is generally the case, the whole school entered upon a period of flaps, which had supplanted a period of snow-balls, as these again had supplanted a period of whittling sticks. The period of the flaps lasted during my absence.

Sémka and Fédka, who were among the singers, used to come to the teacher's room for singing exercises, and they remained there whole evenings, and even nights. Between the singing and during the singing, the flaps, of course, did their business, and all kinds of paper, which fell into their hands, was transformed into flaps.

The teacher went to get his supper, having forgotten to mention that the papers on the table were important, and so the work of Makárov, Morózov, and Tolstóy was changed into flaps. On the following day, before the lessons, the clacking of the flaps so very much annoyed the pupils that they themselves instituted a persecution against the flaps: they were confiscated with shouts and screams, and solemnly stuck into the fire of the oven.

The period of the flaps came to an end, but with it perished our manuscript. Never had any loss been so hard to bear as the loss of these three sheets of writing. I was in despair, I wanted to give it all up and begin a new story, but I could not forget the loss, and so involuntarily every minute kept nagging at the teacher and at the makers of the flaps.

(I must remark here, upon this occasion, that just by means of the external disorder and full freedom of the pupils, which Mr. Márkov takes so charmingly to task in the *Russian Messenger*, and Mr. Glyébov in No. 4 of the periodical *Education*, I, without the least trouble, threats, or cunning, learned all the details of the complicated story of the transformation of the manuscript into flaps, and of its consignment to the flames.)

Sémka and Fédka saw that I was aggrieved, not understanding by what, and they sympathized with me. Fédka finally timidly proposed to me to begin another such a story.

"By yourselves?" I asked. "I shall not help you now."

"Sémka and I will stay here overnight," said Fédka.

And so they did. At nine o'clock, when the lessons were over, they came to the house, locked themselves up in my cabinet, which afforded me much pleasure, laughed awhile, and grew quiet. Until midnight I could hear them, every time I came up to the door, talking with each other in low tones and scratching their pens. Once only they debated about what came first and what later, and they came to me to settle the dispute, whether he looked for the wallet before the woman went to the gossip, or after. I told them that it made no difference which.

At midnight I knocked and asked to be let in. Fédka in a new white fur coat, with black trimming, was sitting deep in the armchair, with one leg over the other, leaning his shaggy little head on his hand, and fumbling the scissors in the other hand. His large black eyes, gleaming with an unnatural, but serious sparkle, like that of a grown person, were looking somewhere into the distance; his irregular lips, compressed as though for a whistle, apparently held back the word which he, having coined it in his imagination, was about to express.

Sémka, standing at the large writing-table, with a large white patch of sheepskin over his back (the tailors had but lately been in the village), with ungirt belt, and dishevelled hair, was writing crooked lines, constantly sticking his pen into the inkstand.

I tossed Sémka's hair, and his fat face with protruding cheekbones and matted hair, as he, with surprised and sleepy eyes, looked in fright at me, was so funny, that I burst out into a laugh, but the children did not laugh with me.

Without changing the expression of his face, Fédka touched Sémka's sleeve and told him to go on. "Thou must wait," he said, "we shall be through soon." (Fédka says "thou" to me whenever he is carried away by something and agitated.) He continued to dictate.

I took away their copy-book, and five minutes later, when they, seating themselves near a small safe, were getting away with potatoes and kvas, and, looking at the silver spoons, which they thought so funny, laughing their sonorous, childish laugh, without any cause whatever, — the old woman, hearing them up-stairs, also burst out laughing, without knowing why.

"Don't tip so!" said Sémka. "Sit straight, or you will eat on one side only."

They took off their fur coats, and, spreading them under the writing-table, lay down on them to sleep, all the time rolling out their healthy, charming, childish, peasant laugh.

I read over what they had written. It was a new variant of the same thing. A few things were left out, and a few new, artistic beauties were added. Again there was the same feeling of beauty, truth, and measure. Later on one sheet of the lost manuscript was found. In the printed story I combined both variants from memory, and from the sheet which was recovered.

The writing of this story took place early in spring, before the end of our scholastic year. For various reasons I was unable to make new experiments. On given proverbs only one story was written by two very mediocre and spoilt children, being the sons of manorial servants. "He who is fond of a holiday gets drunk before daybreak," was printed in the third number. The same phenomena were repeated with these boys and with this story as had been observed with Sémka and Fédka and the first story, only with a difference in the degree of talent and in the enthusiasm and the cooperation on my part.

In the summer we have never had school and never will have. We shall devote a separate article to the cause why teaching is impossible in the summer in our school.

One part of the summer Fédka and some other boys lived with me. Having had a swim, and being tired of playing, they took it into their heads to work. I proposed to them to write a composition, and so told them several themes. I told them a very entertaining story about the theft of some money, the story of a murder, the story of a marvellous conversion of a Milker to Orthodoxy, and I also proposed to them to write in the form of an autobiography the history of a boy whose poor and dissolute father is sent to the army, and to whom the father later returns a reformed, good man.

I said: "I should write it like this. I remember that when I was a child I had a father, a mother, and some other relatives, and who they were. Then I should write that I remember how my father was all the time out on sprees, while my mother wept, and he beat her; then, how he was sent to the army; how she wept; how our life grew harder; how father returned, and he did not seem to recognize me, but asked me whether Matréna — that is, his wife — was alive; and how all were happy, and we began to live well."

That was all which I said in the beginning. Fédka took a great liking to this theme. He immediately took the pen and paper, and began to write. During his writing, I only hinted to him about the sister and about the mother's death. The rest he wrote himself and did not even show it to me, except the first chapter, until it was all done.

When he showed me the first chapter, and I began to read, I felt that he was greatly agitated and that, holding his breath, he kept looking now at the manuscript and watching my reading, and now at my face, wishing to divine upon it an expression of approbation or disapproval.

When I told him that it was very good, he flamed up, without saying anything to me, with agitated, though slow, steps walked with the copy-book up to the table, put it down, and slowly walked out into the yard. Outside he was madly wanton with the boys during the day, and, whenever our eyes met, looked at me with a grateful and kindly glance. The next day he forgot entirely about what he had written

I only wrote out the title, divided the story into chapters, and here and there corrected the mistakes, which were due to carelessness. This story, in its primitive form, is being printed in a book under the title of "A Soldier's Life."

I do not speak of the first chapter, although there are some inimitable beauties even there, and although heedless Gordyéy is there represented exceedingly true to life and vividly, — Gordyéy, who seems to be ashamed to confess his repentance, and who regards it as proper to beg the meeting of the Commune only about his son; still, this chapter is incomparably weaker than all the following.

The fault is all my own, for I could not keep, during the writing of this chapter, from suggesting to him and telling him how I should have written. If there is a certain triteness in the introduction, when describing persons and dwellings, I am exclusively to blame for it. If I had left him alone, I am sure he would have described the same in action, imperceptibly, much more artistically, without the accepted and really impossible manner of logically distributed descriptions, which consists in first describing the *dramatis personæ*, even their biographies, then the locality and the surroundings, and then only the action itself.

Strange to say, all these descriptions, sometimes on dozens of pages, acquaint the reader much less with the persons than a carelessly dropped artistic feature during an action which has already begun among persons totally unfamiliar to the reader. Even thus in this first chapter, the one phrase of Gordyéy's, "That is all I need," when he, renouncing everything, acquiesces in his fate to become a soldier, and only asks the Commune not to abandon his son, — this phrase acquaints the reader much better with the person than the description of his attire, his figure, and his habit of frequenting the tavern, several times repeated and urged upon him by me. The same effect is produced by the words of the old woman, who always scolded her son, when, during her grief, she enviously remarks to her daughter-in-law,: "Stop, Matréna! What is to be done? Evidently God has willed it so! You are young yet, — maybe God will grant you to see him again. But see how old I am — I am ill — before you know it, I shall be dead!"

In the second chapter there may still be noted my influence of triteness and tampering, but here again the profoundly artistic features in the description of pictures and of the boy's death redeem the whole matter. I suggested to him that the boy had thin legs, I also suggested the sentimental details about Uncle Nefédya, who digs the little grave; but the lamentation of the mother, expressed in one clause, "O Lord, when will this slavery end!" presents to the reader the whole essence of the situation; and thereupon that night, when the elder brother is wakened by his mother's tears, and her answer to the grandmother's inquiry what the matter was, with the simple words, "My son has died," and the grandmother, getting up and making a fire and washing the little body, — all that is strictly his own; all this is so compressed, so simple, so strong, — not one word may be omitted, not one word changed, nor added. There are in all five lines, and in these five lines there is painted for the reader the whole picture of that sad night, — a picture reflected in the imagination of a boy six or seven years old.

"At midnight the mother for some reason began to weep. Grandmother arose and said : ' What is the matter ? Christ be with you !' The mother said : ' My son has died.' Grandmother made a fire, washed the boy, put a shirt on him, girded him, and placed him beneath the images. When day broke — "

You see the boy himself, awakened by the familiar tears of his mother, half-sleepy, under a caftan somewhere on the hanging bed, with frightened and sparkling eyes watching the proceedings in the hut; you see the haggard soldier's widow, who but the day before had said, "How soon will this slavery come to an end?" repentant and crushed by the thought of the end of this slavery, to such an extent that she only says, "My son has died," and knows not what to do, and calls for the grandmother to help her; and you see the old woman, worn out by the sufferings of life, bent down, emaciated, with bony limbs, as she calmly takes hold of the work with her hands that are accustomed to labour; she lights a torch, brings the water, and washes the boy; she places everything in the right place, and sets the boy, washed and girt, under the images. And you see those images, and all that night without sleep, until daybreak, as though you yourself were living through it, as that boy lived through it, gazing at it from underneath the caftan; that night arises before you with all its details and remains in your imagination.

In the third chapter there is less of my influence. The whole personality of the nurse belongs to him. Even in the first chapter, he characterized the relations of the nurse with the family in one sentence: "She was working for her own dowry, to get ready for marriage."

This one feature paints the girl as she is: she cannot take part, and she really does not take part, in the joys and sorrows of her family. She has her lawful interests, her only aim, decreed by Providence, — her future marriage, her future family.

An author of our kind, especially one who wants to instruct the people by presenting to them models of morality worthy of imitation, would certainly have treated the nurse with reference to the interest she took in the common want and sorrow of the family. He would have made her a disgraceful example of indifference, or a model of love and self-sacrifice, and there would have been an idea, but not a living person, the nurse. Only a man who has profoundly studied and learned life could understand that for the nurse the question of the family's bereavement, and of the father's military service, was lawfully a secondary question, for she has her marriage ahead.

This very thing, in the simplicity of his heart, sees the artist, though but a child. If we had described the nurse as a most sympathetic, self-sacrificing girl, we should not be able at all to present her to our imagination, and we should not love her, as we love her now. Now there stands before me the dear, living form of the fat-cheeked, ruddy-faced girl, running in the evening to take part in the round dance, in shoes and red cotton kerchief bought with the money earned by her, loving her family though distressed by that poverty and gloom which form such a contrast to her own mood.

I feel that she is a good girl, if for no other reason than because her mother never complained about her nor was aggrieved by her. On the contrary, I feel that she, with the cares about her attire, with the snatches of tunable songs, with the village gossips, brought from the summer field work or from the wintry street, was the only representative of mirth, youth, and hope during the sad time of the soldier woman's loneliness. He says with good reason that the only joy there was, was when the nurse-girl was married. It is, therefore, with good reason that he describes the wedding-feast at such length and with so much love; it is with good reason that he makes the mother say after the wedding, "Now we are completely ruined." It is evident that, by giving up the nurse, they lost that joy and merriment which she had brought with her into the house.

All that description of the wedding is uncommonly good. There are some details there which simply stagger you, and, remembering that it is an eleven-year-old boy who wrote it, you ask yourself, "Is it possible it is not merest accident?" Back of this compressed and strong description you just see the eleven-year-old boy, not taller than the table, with his bright and intelligent eyes, to whom nobody pays any attention, but who remembers and notices everything.

When, for example, he wanted some bread, he did not say that he asked his mother for it, but that he bent his mother down. This is not said by accident, but because he remembers his relation to his mother at that stage of his growth, and because he remembers how timid that relation was in the presence of others, and how familiar in their absence. There is one other thing out of a mass of observations which he could have made during the wedding ceremony which seemed to have impressed him, and which he noted down, because to him and to each of us it pictures the whole character of these ceremonies. When they said that it was bitter, the nurse took Kondráshka by his ears, and they began to kiss each other. Then the death of the grandmother, her thought of her son before her death, and the peculiar character of the mother's grief, — all that is so firm and so compressed, and all that is strictly his own.

I told him most about the father's return when I gave him the plot of the story. I liked that scene, and I told it to him with trite sentimentality. He, too, liked the scene, and he asked me: "Don't tell me anything! I know it all myself, I do," and sat down to write, after which he finished the story at one sitting.

It will be very interesting for me to know the opinion of other judges, but I consider it my duty frankly to express my opinion. I have not come across anything like these pages in Russian literature. In the whole meeting there is not one reference to its having been touching; all that there is told is how it happened, and only so much of what took place is told as is necessary for the reader to understand the situation of all the persons.

The soldier said only three sentences in his house. At first he braced himself and said, "Good morning!" When he began to forget the part he was to play, he said, "Is that all there is of your family?" And everything was said in the words, "Where is my mother?"

What simple and natural words they all are, and not one person is forgotten! The boy was happy, and even wept; but he was a child, and so he, in spite of his father's tears, kept examining his wallet and pockets. Nor is the nurse forgotten. You almost see that ruddy woman, who, in shoes and fine attire, timidly enters the room, and, without saying anything, kisses her father. You almost see the embarrassed and happy father, who kisses all in succession, without knowing whom, and who, upon learning that the young woman is his daughter, calls her up once more and now kisses her, not as any young woman, but as a daughter, whom he had once left behind, without taking any thought of her.

The father is reformed. How many false and inept phrases we should have used upon that occasion! But Fédka simply told how the nurse brought some liquor, and he did not drink it. You just seem to see the woman, who, taking out of her pouch the last twenty-three kopeks, breathing heavily, in a whisper orders the young woman in the vestibule to bring some liquor, and deposits the copper money in her open hand.

You see the young woman, who, raising her apron with her hand, with the bottle underneath it, thumping with her shoes and swinging her elbows, runs down to the tavern. You see her enter the room with flushed face, taking the bottle out from underneath the apron, and you see her mother place it on the table with an expression of self-contentment and joy, and how she feels both annoyed and happy because her husband has stopped drinking. And you see that if he has given up drinking at such an occasion, he certainly has reformed. You feel that the members of the family have become different people.

"My father said a prayer and sat down at the table. I sat down by his side; the nurse sat down on the doorbench, and mother stood at the table, and looked at him, and said: 'See how much younger you look! You have no beard now!' All laughed."

Only when all the others left, the real family conversation began. Only then it was revealed that the soldier had grown rich. He had become enriched in the simplest and most natural manner, as nearly all people in the world grow rich, that is, money which did not belong to him, the Crown's money, by a lucky accident came into his hands. Some of the readers of the story remarked that this detail was immoral, and that the conception of the Crown as a milch-cow ought to be eradicated, and not strengthened in the masses. But to me this feature, leaving alone its artistic truth, is particularly pleasing. The Crown's money always remains somewhere,— why, then, is it not to remain in the hands of some homeless soldier Gordyéy?

We frequently meet with diametrically opposite conceptions of honesty in the masses and in the upper classes. The demands of the masses are peculiarly serious and severe in respect to honesty in the nearest relations, for example, in relation to the family, the village, the Commune. In relation to outsiders,— the public, the government, especially the foreigner, the treasury,— the application of the common rules of honesty presents itself but dimly. A peasant who will never tell a lie to his brother, who will endure all kinds of privations for his family, who will not take a superfluous or unearned kopek from his fellow villager or neighbour,— the same peasant will strip a foreigner or townsman like a linden switch, and will at every word tell a man of the gentry or an official a lie; if he be a soldier, he will without the slightest compunction stab a captive Frenchman, and, if Crown money falls into his hands, he will not regard it a crime before his family to take advantage of it.

In the upper classes, on the contrary, the very opposite takes place. A man of our kind will much sooner deceive a wife, a brother, a merchant, with whom he has had dealings for dozens of years, his servants, his peasants, his neighbour,— and this same man abroad is all the time consumed by fear lest he should cheat somebody, and begs all the time to have pointed out to him any one he may be owing money to. This same gentleman of our class will stint his company and regiment, to obtain money for his champagne and gloves, and will bubble up with civilities before a captive Frenchman. The same man regards it as the greatest crime to make use of the Crown's money, when he is penniless, — he only regards it so, for generally he will not stand his ground when the opportunity offers itself, but will commit that which he himself regards as a piece of rascality.

I am not saying which is better, — I am only telling what is, as it appears to me. I will, however, remark that honesty is not a conviction and that the expression "honest convictions" is nonsense. Honesty is a moral habit; in order to acquire it, it is impossible to go by any other part than to begin with the nearest relations. The expression "honest convictions" is, in my opinion, absolutely meaningless: there are honest habits, but not honest convictions.

The words "honest convictions" are an empty phrase; for this reason those reputed honest convictions, which refer to the most remote vital conditions, to the Crown's money, to the government, to Europe, to humanity, and which are not based on habits of honesty and not educated on the nearest vital relations, — for this reason those honest convictions, or, more correctly, those empty phrases of honesty, prove inadequate in relation to life.

I return to the story. The mention of the money taken from the Crown, which in the first moment may appear immoral, in our opinion, on the contrary, is a charming, touching characteristic. How often a *littérateur* of our class, wishing, in the simplicity of his soul, to represent his hero as an ideal of honesty, shows us all the dirty and corrupt interior of his imagination! Here, on the contrary, the author must make his hero happy: for happiness, his return to his family would suffice, but he had to abolish the poverty which had been weighing so heavily on the family for so many years; where was he to get the wealth from? From the impersonal Crown. To give wealth, one has to get it first, — and it could not have been got in a more lawful and clever manner.

In the very scene when the money is mentioned there is a tiny detail, one word, which seems to strike me anew, every time I read it. It illumines the whole picture, paints all the persons and their relations, and only one word, and an incorrectly, syntactically incorrectly, used word at that, — the word "hastened." A teacher of syntax must say that it is irregular. Hastened demands some modification, — hastened to do what? the teacher ought to ask. And here it is simply said: "Mother took the money and hastened and carried it away to bury it," and it is charming. I wish I myself had used such a word, and I wish that teachers, who teach language, might say or write such a sentence.

"When we had eaten, the nurse kissed father again and went home. Then father began to rummage through his wallet, and mother and I just looked on. Mother saw a little book there, so she says: 'Oh, you have learned to read?' Says father: 'I have.'

"Then father took out a kerchief tied in a large knot and gave it to mother.

"Says mother: 'What is this?'

"Says father: 'Money.'

"Mother was happy and hastened and carried it away to bury it. Then mother came back, and says she:

"'Where did you get it?'

"Says father: 'I was an under-officer and had Crown money: I gave it to the soldiers, and what was left in my hands, I kept.'

"My mother was so happy and ran around like a mad person. The day had passed, and the evening came. They lighted a fire. My father took the book and began to read. I sat down near him and listened, and mother held the torch. Father read the book for a long time. Then we lay down to sleep. I lay down on the back bench with father, and mother lay down at our feet, and they talked for a long time, almost until midnight. Then we fell asleep."

Here again we have a scarcely perceptible detail, which does not startle us in the least, but which leaves a deep impression, — the detail of their going to bed: the father lay down with his son, the mother lay at their feet, and they did not get tired talking for a long time. How tightly, I think, the son must have hugged to his father's breast, and what a joy and happiness it was for him, falling asleep and waking again, to hear the two voices, one of which he had not heard for so long a time.

One would think all is ended: the father has returned, and there is no more poverty. But Fédka was not satisfied with that (his imaginary people apparently made a deep impression upon his imagination); he had to form a picture of their changed life, to present to himself vividly that now the woman was no longer alone, a saddened soldier's wife with small babies, but that there was a strong man in the house, who would take off the wearied shoulders of his wife all the burden of the crushing sorrow and want, and would independently, firmly, and merrily begin a new life.

For this purpose he paints us only one scene: the powerful soldier with a notched axe chops some wood and brings it into the house. You see the keen-eyed boy, used to the groans of his feeble mother and grandmother, with wonderment, respect, and pride admiring the bared muscular arms of his father, the energetic swinging of the axe, coinciding with the pectoral sigh of masculine labour, and the block, which, like a piece of kindling-wood, is split under the notched axe. You look at it, and your mind is eased about the future life of the soldier's wife. Now she will not be lost, the dear one, I think.

"In the morning mother got up, walked over to father, and says she: 'Gordyéy, get up! I need some wood to make a fire in the oven.'

"Father got up, dressed himself, put on his cap, and says he: 'Have you an axe?'

## HOW PEASANT CHILDREN WRITE 217

"Says mother: 'I have, — it is notched; maybe it won't cut.'

"My father took the axe firmly with both his hands, walked over to the block, put it up standing, swung the axe with all his might, and split the block; he chopped up some wood and brought it to the house. Mother made a fire in the oven, and it burned, and soon it grew daylight."

But the artist is not satisfied with that. He wants to show us another side of their lives, the poetry of the happy family life, and so he paints the following picture for us:

"When it was all daylight, my father said: 'Matréna!'

"My mother came up, and says she: 'Well, what?'

"Says father: 'I am thinking of buying a cow, five sheep, two little horses, and a hut, — this one is falling to pieces, — well, that will take about one hundred and fifty roubles.'

"Mother thought awhile, then says she: 'Well, we shall spend all the money.'

"Says father: 'We will begin to work.'

"Says mother: 'All right, we will buy it all, but where shall we get the timber?'

"Says father: 'Hasn't Kiryúkha any?'

"Says mother: 'That's where the trouble is: the Fokanýchevs have taken it away.'

"Father thought awhile, and says he: 'Well, we shall get it from Brántsev.'

"Says mother: 'I doubt whether he has any.'

"Says father: 'Why should he not have? He has a forest.'

"Says mother: 'I am afraid he will ask too much, — he is such a beast.'

"Says father: 'I will take some brandy to him, and maybe we shall come to some understanding; and you bake an egg in the ashes for dinner.'

"Mother got the dinner ready, — she borrowed from her friends. Then father took the brandy and went to Brántsev's, and we stayed at home, waiting for a long time. I felt lonely without father. I began to ask mother to let me go there where father was.

"Says mother: 'You will lose your way.'

"I began to cry and wanted to go, but mother slapped me, and I sat down on the oven and cried more than before. Then I saw father coming into the room. Says he: 'Why are you crying?'

"Says mother: 'Fédka wanted to run after you, and I gave him a beating.'

"Father walked over to me, and says he: 'What are you crying about?'

"I began to complain of mother. Father went up to mother and began to beat her, in jest, saying: 'Don't beat Fédka! Don't beat Fédka!'

"Mother pretended to be crying. I sat down on father's knees and was happy. Then father sat down at the table, and put me by his side, and shouted: 'Mother, give Fédka and me something to eat, — we are hungry!'

"And mother gave us some beef, and we began to eat. When we were through dinner, says mother: 'What about the timber?'

"Says father: 'Fifty roubles in silver.'

"Says mother: 'That is not bad.'

"Says father: 'I must say, it is fine timber.'"

It seems so simple: so little is said, and you see the perspective of their whole domestic life. You see that the boy is still a child, who will cry and a minute later will be happy; you see that the boy is not able to appreciate his mother's love, and that he has exchanged her for the virile father who was chopping the block; you see that the mother knows that it must be so, and she is not jealous; you see that splendid Gordyéy, whose heart is brimful of happiness.

You notice that they ate beef, and that is a charming

comedy, which they all play, and all know that it is a comedy, which they play from excess of happiness. "Don't beat Fédka! Don't beat Fédka!" says the father, raising his hand against her. And the mother, who is used to unfeigned tears, pretends to be crying, with a smile of happiness at the father and the son, and the boy, who climbed on his father's knees, was proud and happy, not knowing why, — proud and happy, no doubt, because now they were all happy.

"Then father sat down at the table, and put me by his side, and shouted: 'Mother, give Fédka and me something to eat, — we are hungry!'"

"We are hungry," and he placed him by his side. What love and happy pride of love breathes in these words! There is nothing more charming and heartfelt in the whole charming story than this last chapter.

But what do we mean to say by all that? What import does this story, written, probably, by an exceptional boy, have pedagogically? We shall be told: "You, the teacher, may unconsciously, to yourself, have helped in the composition of these stories, and it would be too difficult to find the limits of that which belongs to you, and of that which is original."

We shall be told: "We shall admit that the story is good, but that is only one kind of literature."

We shall be told: "Fédka and the other boys, whose compositions you have printed, are happy exceptions."

We shall be told: "You are yourself a writer, and, without knowing it, you have been helping the pupils along paths which cannot be prescribed as a rule to other teachers who are not authors themselves."

We shall be told: "From all that it is impossible to deduce a common rule or theory. It is partially an interesting phenomenon, and nothing else."

I shall try to give my deductions in such a manner as to serve as answers to all the retorts imagined by me.

The feelings of truth, beauty, and goodness are independent of the degree of development. Beauty, truth, and goodness are conceptions which express only the harmony of relations in the sense of truth, beauty, and goodness. Lie is only a non-correspondence of relations in the sense of truth; there is no absolute truth. I am not lying when I say that the tables whirl about under the touch of my fingers, if I believe it to be so, even though it is an untruth; but I am lying when I say that I have no money when, according to my ideas, I have money. No immense nose is monstrous, but it is monstrous on a small face. Monstrosity is only a disharmony in relation to beauty. To give away my dinner to a mendicant, or to eat it up myself has nothing of badness in it; but to give it away, or eat it up myself, while my mother is starving is a disharmony of relations in the sense of goodness.

In bringing up, educating, developing, or in any way you please influencing the child, we ought to have and unconsciously do have one aim in view, — to attain the greatest harmony possible in the sense of truth, beauty, and goodness. If time did not run, if the child did not live with every side of himself, we should be able quietly to attain this harmony by supplementing there where there seems to be a lack, and by reducing where there seems to be a superfluity. But the child lives; every side of his existence strives after development, trying to outstrip every other side, and, for the most part, we mistake the progress of these sides of his being for the aim, and coöperate in this development only, instead of aiding the harmony of the development. In this lies the eternal mistake of all pedagogical theories.

We see our ideal before us, whereas it is behind us. The necessary development of man is far from being a means of attaining that ideal of harmony which we bear within us; it is, on the contrary, a hindrance, put in our way by the Creator, in the attainment of the highest ideal of harmony. In this necessary law of forward motion lies the meaning of that fruit of that tree of the knowledge of good and evil, which our first ancestor tasted.

A healthy child is born into the world, completely satisfying all the demands of unconditional harmony in relation to truth, beauty, and goodness, which we bear within us; he is near to inanimate beings, — to the plant, to the animal, to Nature, which always represents to us that truth, beauty, and goodness, which we are seeking and wishing for. In all the ages and with all men, the child has been represented as a model of innocence, sinlessness, goodness, truth, and beauty. "Man is born perfect" is a great word enunciated by Rousseau, and this word will remain firm and true, like a rock. At birth man represents the prototype of harmony, truth, beauty, and goodness. But every hour in life, every minute of time increases the extent, the quantity, and the duration of those relations which during his birth were in full harmony, and every step and every hour threaten the impairment of that harmony, and every successive step and every successive hour threaten a new impairment and give no hope of the restitution of the impaired harmony.

For the most part educators forget that the child's age is the prototype of harmony, and they assume the development of the child, which goes on independently according to immutable laws, as the aim. The development is erroneously taken for the aim because to the educators happens that which takes place with poor sculptors.

Instead of trying to arrest a local exaggerated development or the general development, instead of waiting for a new incident to destroy the irregularity which has arisen, just as a poor sculptor, instead of eradicating that which is superfluous, keeps pasting on more and more, —

even thus educators seem to be concerned only about not interrupting the process of development, and if they ever think of the harmony, they try to attain it by approaching an unknown prototype in the future, by departing from the prototype in the present and in the past.

No matter how irregular the development of a child may be, there are always left in him the primitive features of harmony. By moderating, at least by not pushing, the development, we may hope to get a certain approach to regularity and harmony. But we are so sure of ourselves, we are so visionarily devoted to the false ideal of manhood perfection, we are so impatient with irregularities which are near to us and so firmly believe in our ability to correct them, we are so little able to comprehend and value the primitive beauty of a child, that we, as fast as we can, magnify and paste up the irregularities that strike our vision,— we correct, we educate the child. Now one side has to be equalized with the other, now the other has to be equalized with the first. The child is developed more and more, and all the time departs more and more from the former shattered prototype, and the attainment of the imaginary prototype of the perfection of manhood becomes ever more impossible. Our ideal is behind us, not before us. Education spoils, it does not correct men. The more a child is spoiled, the less he ought to be educated, the more liberty he needs.

It is impossible and absurd to teach and educate a child, for the simple reason that the child stands nearer than I do, than any grown-up man does, to that ideal of harmony, truth, beauty, and goodness, to which I, in my pride, wish to raise him. The consciousness of this ideal is more powerful in him than in me. All he needs of me is the material, in order to fill out harmoniously and on all sides. The moment I gave him full liberty and stopped teaching him, he wrote a poetical production, the like of which cannot be found in Russian literature. Therefore, it is my conviction that we cannot teach children in general, and peasant children in particular, to write and compose. All that we can do is to teach them how to go about writing.

If what I did in order to obtain this result may be called method, this method consisted in the following:

(1) Give a great variety of themes, not inventing them specially for the children, but propose such as appear most serious and interesting to the teacher himself.

(2) Give the children children's compositions to read, and give them only children's compositions as models, for children's compositions are always more correct, more artistic, and more moral than the compositions of grown people.

(3) (Most important.) When looking through a pupil's composition, never make any remarks to him about the cleanliness of the copy-book, nor about penmanship, nor orthography, nor, above all, about the structure of the sentences and about logic.

(4) Since the difficulty of composition does not lie in the volume, nor the contents, nor the artistic quality of the theme, the sequence of the themes is not to be based on volume, nor on the contents, nor on the language, but in the mechanism of the work, which consists, first, in selecting one out of a large number of ideas and images presented; secondly, in choosing words for it and clothing it in words; thirdly, in remembering it and finding a place for it; fourthly, in not repeating nor leaving out anything, and in the ability of combining what follows with that which precedes, all the time keeping in mind what is already written down; fifthly, and finally, in thinking and writing at the same time, without having one of these acts interfere with the other. To obtain this end, I did as follows: A few of those sides of the labour I at first took upon myself, by degrees transferring them

to their care. At first I chose from the ideas and images that presented themselves to them such as I considered best, and retained them, and pointed out the place, and consulted what had already been written, keeping them from repetitions, and myself wrote, leaving to them only the clothing of the images and ideas in words; then I allowed them to make their own choice, and later to consult that which had been written down, until, at last, as in the case of "A Soldier's Life," they took the whole matter into their own hands.

# THE SCHOOL AT YÁSNAYA POLYÁNA

For the Months of November and December
1862

# THE SCHOOL AT YÁSNAYA POLYÁNA

For the Months of November and December, 1862

---

GENERAL SKETCH OF THE CHARACTER OF THE SCHOOL

WE have no beginners. The lowest class reads, writes solves problems in the first three arithmetical operations and reads sacred history, so that the subjects are divided in the programme in the following manner:

(1) Mechanical and graded reading, (2) writing, (3) penmanship, (4) grammar, (5) sacred history, (6) Russian history, (7) drawing, (8) mechanical drawing, (9) singing, (10) mathematics, (11) talks on the natural sciences, (12) religion.

Before saying anything about the instruction, I must give a short sketch of what the Yásnaya Polyána school is and of what stage of its growth it is in.

Like all living beings, the school not only becomes modified with every year, day, and hour, but also is subject to temporary crises, hardships, ailments, and evil moods. The Yásnaya Polyána school passed through such a crisis during this last summer. There were many causes for it: in the first place, as is always the case, all our best pupils left us, and we met them only occasionally at work in the field, or in the pastures; secondly, new teachers had come to the school, and new influences began to be brought to bear upon it; thirdly, every day of the summer brought new visiting teachers, who were taking advantage of the summer vacation. Nothing is more detrimental to the regular progress of the school than visitors. In one way or another the teacher adapts himself to the visitors.

We have four teachers. Two old ones, who have been teaching in the school for two years, and have become accustomed to the pupils, their work, the freedom and the external disorder of the school. The two new teachers — both themselves fresh from school — are lovers of external precision, programmes, bells, and so forth, and have not yet adapted themselves to the school so well as the first. What for the first seems reasonable, necessary, unavoidable, like the features of a beloved though homely child, that has grown up under one's eyes, to the new teachers sometime appears as a corrigible fault.

The school is held in a two-story stone building. Two rooms are given up to the school, one is a physical cabinet, and two are occupied by the teachers. Under the roof of the porch hangs a bell, with a rope attached to the clapper; in the vestibule down-stairs stand parallel and horizontal bars, while in the vestibule up-stairs there is a joiner's bench. The staircase and the floor of the vestibule are covered with snow or mud; here also hangs the programme.

The order of instruction is as follows: At about eight o'clock, the teacher living in the school, a lover of external order and the administrator of the school, sends one of the boys who nearly always stay overnight with him to ring the bell.

In the village, people rise with the fires. From the school the fires have long been observed in the windows, and half an hour after the ringing of the bell there appear,

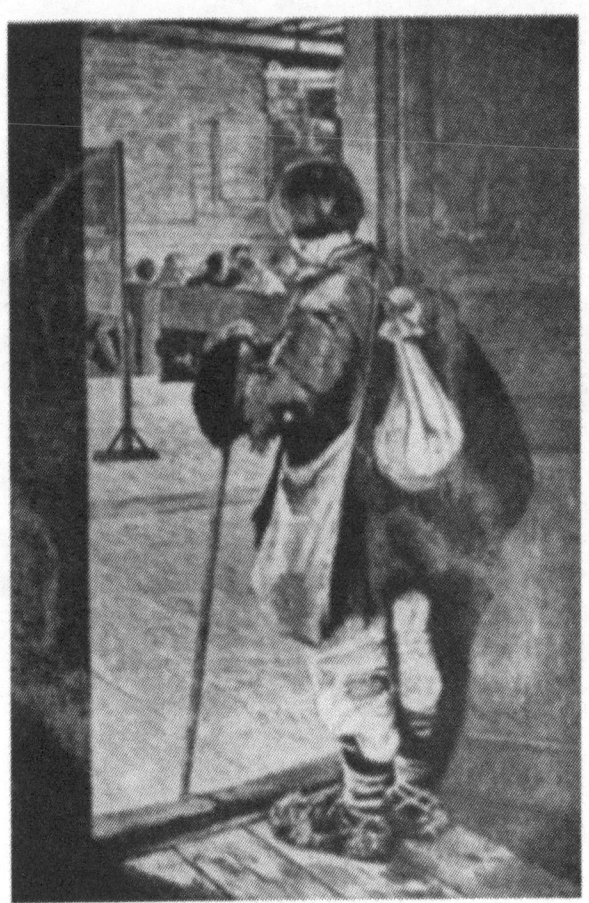

*At the door of the shool.*

in the mist, in the rain, or in the oblique rays of the autumnal sun, dark figures, by twos, by threes, or singly, on the mounds (the village is separated from the school by a ravine). The herding feeling has long disappeared in the pupils. A pupil no longer has the need of waiting and shouting: "O boys, let's to school! She has begun." He knows by this time that "school" is neuter, and he knows a few other things, and, strange to say, for that very reason has no longer any need of a crowd. When the time comes to go, he goes. It seems to me that the personalities are becoming more independent, their characters more sharply defined, with every day. I have never noticed the pupils playing on their way, unless it be a very young child, or a new pupil, who had begun his instruction in some other school. The children bring nothing with them, — neither books, nor copy-books. No lessons are given for home.

Not only do they carry nothing in their hands, but they have nothing to carry even in their heads. They are not obliged to remember any lesson, — nothing that they were doing the day before. They are not vexed by the thought of the impending lesson. They bring with them nothing but their impressionable natures and their convictions that to-day it will be as jolly in school as it was yesterday. They do not think of their classes until they have begun.

No one is ever rebuked for tardiness, and they never are tardy, except some of the older ones whose fathers now and then keep them back to do some work. In such cases they come running to school at full speed, and all out of breath.

So long as the teacher has not arrived, they gather near the porch, pushing each other off the steps, or skating on the frozen crust of the smooth road, while some go to the schoolrooms. If it is cold, they read. write, or play, waiting for the teacher.

The girls do not mingle with the boys. When the boys have anything to do with the girls, they never address any one in particular, but always all collectively: "O girls, why don't you skate?" or, "I guess the girls are frozen," or, "Now, girls, all of you against me!" There is only one girl, from the manor, with enormous, all-around ability, about ten years of age, who is beginning to stand out from the herd of girls. This girl alone the boys treat as their equal, as a boy, except for a delicate shade of politeness, condescension, and reserve.

Let us suppose, for example, that according to the programme there is in the first, the lowest, class, mechanical reading, in the second, graded reading, in the third, mathematics.

The teacher comes to the room, where on the floor lie screaming children, shouting, "The heap is not large enough!" or, "You are choking me, boys!" or, "That will do! Don't pull my hair!" and so forth.

"Peter Mikháylovich!" a voice at the bottom of the heap calls out to the teacher as he enters, "tell them to stop!"

"Good morning, Peter Mikháylovich!" shout the others, continuing their game.

The teacher takes the books and gives them to those who have gone with him up to the bookcase; those who are lying on top of the heap, without getting up, also ask for books. The heap becomes smaller by degrees. The moment the majority have books, the rest run to the bookcase and cry: "Me too, me too. Give me yesterday's book; and me the *Koltsóvian* book," and so forth. If there are two left who, excited from the struggle, still keep rolling on the floor, those who have the books cry out to them:

"Don't bother us! We can't hear a word! Stop now!"

The excited boys submit and, out of breath, take hold of their books, and only at first, while sitting at their books, keep swinging their legs from unallayed excitement. The martial spirit takes flight, and the reading spirit reigns in the room.

With the same enthusiasm with which he was pulling Mítka's hair, he is now reading the *Koltsóvian* book (so they call Koltsóv's works with us), almost clenching his teeth, his eyes aflame, and seeing nothing about him but his book. It will take as much effort to tear him away from the book as it took before to get him away from fighting.

They sit down wherever they please: on the benches, the tables, the window-sill, the floor, and in the armchair. The girls always sit down near each other. Friends, of the same village, especially the younger ones (they have greater comradeship), always sit together. The moment one such has decided to sit down in the corner, all his friends, pushing one another and diving under the benches, make for the same place, sit down near him, and, looking about them, express as much happiness and contentment in their faces as though their having taken up those seats would make them happy for the rest of their lives. The large armchair, which somehow found its way into the room, forms the object of envy for the more independent individuals, — for the manorial girl and for others. The moment one of them makes up his mind to sit down in the chair, another guesses his intentions from his looks, and there ensues a struggle. One boy pushes out another, and the victor spreads himself in it, with his head way below the back, and goes on reading like the rest, all absorbed in his work.

I have never noticed any one whispering, or pinching his neighbour, or giggling, or snorting into his hand, or complaining against another. When a pupil who has been studying with a sexton or in a county school comes to us with such a complaint, we say to him: "Why don't you pinch back?"

The two lower classes meet in one room, while the advanced class goes to the next. The teacher comes, and, in the lowest class, all surround him at the board, or on the benches, or sit or lie on the table about the teacher or one of the reading boys. If it is a writing lesson, they seat themselves in a more orderly way, but they keep getting up, in order to look at the copy-books of the others, and to show theirs to the teacher.

According to the programme, there are to be four lessons before noon, but there sometimes are only three or two, and sometimes there are entirely different subjects. The teacher may begin with arithmetic and pass over to geometry, or he may start on sacred history, and end up with grammar. At times the teacher and pupils are so carried away, that, instead of one hour, the class lasts three hours. Sometimes the pupils themselves cry: "More, more!" and scold those who are tired of the subject. "If you are tired, go to the babies," they will call out contemptuously.

All the pupils meet together for the class of religion, which is the only regular class we have, because the teacher lives two versts away and comes only twice a week; they also meet together for the drawing class. Before these classes there is animation, fighting, shouting, and the most pronounced external disorder: some drag the benches from one room into another; some fight; some of the children of the manorial servants run home for some bread, which they roast in the stove; one is taking something away from a boy; another is doing some gymnastics, and, just as in the disorder of the morning, it is much easier to allow them to quiet themselves and resume their natural order than forcibly to settle them. With the present spirit of the school it would be physically impossible to stop them. The louder the teacher calls, — this has actually happened, — the louder they shout: his loud voice only excites them. If you stop them, or, if you can do that, if you carry them away into another direction, this small sea begins to billow less and less until it finally grows calm. In the majority of cases there is no need to say anything. The drawing class, everybody's favourite class, is at noon when, after three hours' work, the children are beginning to be hungry, and the benches and tables have to be taken from one room to another, and there is a terrible hubbub; and yet, in spite of it, the moment the teacher is ready, the pupils are, too, and if one of them should keep them back from starting, he gets his punishment meted out to him by the children themselves.

I must explain myself. In presenting a description of the Yásnaya Polyána school, I do not mean to offer a model of what is needed and is good for a school, but simply to furnish an actual description of the school. I presume that such descriptions may have their use. If I shall succeed in the following numbers in presenting a clear account of the evolution of the school, it will become intelligible to the reader what it is that has led to the formation of the present character of the school, why I regard such an order as good, and why it would be absolutely impossible for me to change it, even if I wanted.

The school has evolved freely from the principles introduced into it by teacher and pupils. In spite of the preponderating influence of the teacher, the pupil has always had the right not to come to school, or, having come, not to listen to the teacher. The teacher has had the right not to admit a pupil, and has had the possibility of bringing to bear all the force of his influence on the majority of pupils, on the society, always composed of the school children.

The farther the pupils proceed, the more the instruction branches out and the more necessary does order become. For this reason, in the normal non-compulsory development of the school, the more the pupils become educated, the fitter they become for order, and the more strongly they themselves feel the need of order, and the greater is the teacher's influence in this respect. In the Yásnaya Polyána school this rule has always been observed, from the day of its foundation. At first it was impossible to subdivide into classes, or subjects, or recess, or lessons; everything naturally blended into one, and all the attempts at separation remained futile. Now we have pupils in the first class, who themselves demand that the programme be adhered to, who are dissatisfied when they are disturbed in their lessons, and who constantly drive out the little children who run in to them.

In my opinion, this external disorder is useful and not to be replaced by anything else, however strange and inconvenient it may seem for the teacher. I shall often have occasion to speak of the advantages of this system, and now I will say only this much about the reputed inconveniences: First, this disorder, or free order, is terrible to us only because we are accustomed to something quite different, in which we have been educated. Secondly, in this case, as in many similar cases, force is used only through haste and through insufficient respect for human nature. We think that the disorder is growing greater and greater, and that there are no limits to it, — we think that there is no other means of stopping it but by the use of force, — whereas we only need to wait a little, and the disorder (or animation) calms down naturally by itself, growing into a much better and more permanent order than what we have created.

School children, small men though they be, have the same needs as we, and they reason in the same manner; they all want to learn, coming to school for this only, and so they will naturally arrive at the conclusion that they must submit to certain conditions in order to acquire knowledge.

They are more than merely men, they are a company of men, united by one idea. And where three are gathered in My name, there will I be with them! When they submit only to natural laws, such as arise from their natures, they do not feel provoked and do not murmur; but when they submit to your predetermined interference, they do not believe in the legality of your bells, programmes, and regulations.

How often have I seen children fighting, when the teacher would rush up to take them apart, which would only make the separated enemies look awry at each other, and would not keep them, even in the presence of a stern teacher, from rushing later against each other in order to inflict a more painful kick! How often do I see every day some Kiryúshka, with set teeth, fly at Taráska, pull his hair, knock him down, and, if it costs him his life, try to maim his enemy, — and not a minute passes before Taráska laughs underneath Kiryúshka, — it is so much easier personally to square up accounts; in less than five minutes both become friends and sit down near each other.

The other day, between classes, two boys got into a hand-to-hand fight in the corner; one of them is a remarkable mathematician, about nine years of age, of the second class; the other, a close-cropped manorial servant's son, an intelligent, but revengeful, tiny, black-eyed boy, nicknamed Pussy. Pussy had grabbed the mathematician by his hair and jammed his head against the wall; the mathematician in vain tried to get hold of Pussy's cropped bristles. Pussy's black little eyes were triumphant. The mathematician with difficulty restrained his tears and kept saying: "Well, well! What? What?" He was evidently badly off, though he tried to brace himself.

This lasted quite awhile, and I was in a quandary what to do. "They are fighting, they are fighting!" cried the boys, crowding in the corner. The little boys laughed, while the big ones, without taking them apart, exchanged serious looks, which, together with the silence, did not escape Pussy. He saw that he was doing something bad, and began to smile criminally and to let go of the mathematician's hair by degrees.

The mathematician got away from Pussy, pushed him so that he fell with the back of his head against the wall, and walked away satisfied. Pussy burst out weeping, made for his enemy, and struck him with all his might, though not painfully, on his fur coat. The mathematician wanted to pay him back, but just then several disapproving voices were heard.

"I declare, he is fighting a little fellow!" cried the spectators. "Run, Pussy!"

This was the end of the matter, and it was as though it had never happened, except, I suppose, that the dim consciousness of both fighting is not a pleasant matter, because it causes both pain.

It seems to me I observed here the sentiment of justice, which guides a crowd. How often such matters are settled no one knows on the basis of what law, and yet satisfactorily to both sides. How arbitrary and unjust in comparison with it are all educational methods employed in such cases!

"You are both guilty, get down on your knees!" says the educator, and the educator is wrong, because only one of them is guilty, and that guilty one is now triumphant, as he is kneeling and ruminating his unspent rage, while the innocent boy is doubly punished.

Or, "You are guilty of having done this or that, and you will be punished," says the educator, and the punished boy hates his enemy so much the more, because the despotic power, the legality of which he does not acknowledge, is on his enemy's side.

Or, "Forgive him, as God orders you to, and be better than he," says the educator. You tell him to be better than he, and he only wants to be stronger, and does not, and cannot, understand anything better.

Or, "Both of you are wrong: ask each other's forgiveness and kiss each other, children!" That is worst of all, on account of the lie and the flimsiness of that kiss, and because the feeling which was being allayed only flames out anew.

Leave them alone, if you are not a father, or mother, and simply sorry for your child, and, therefore, always right when you pull away by the hair the one that has given your son a beating, — leave them alone and see how simply and naturally the whole matter will settle itself, and at the same time in what a complicated and varied manner, like all unconscious vital relations.

It may be that teachers who have had no experience in such disorder, or free order, will think that without the teacher's interference such a disorder may have physically injurious results, and so forth. In the Yásnaya Polyána school there have been only two cases of injuries since last spring. One boy was pushed down the porch and he skinned his leg to the bone (the wound healed up in two weeks), and they scorched another boy's cheek with burned rubber, from which he had a mark left for about two weeks. It happens not oftener than once a week that somebody cries, and then not from pain, but from anger or shame. With the exception of these two cases, we cannot recall any bruises or bumps for the whole summer among thirty to forty pupils left entirely to themselves.

I am convinced that the school ought not to interfere in that part of the education which belongs to the family; that the school has no right and ought not to reward and punish; that the best police and administration of a school consist in giving full liberty to the pupils to study and settle their disputes as they know best. I am convinced of it, and yet, in spite of it, the old habits of the educational schools are so strong in us that we frequently depart from that rule in the Yásnaya Polyána school. Last semester, namely in November, there happened two such cases of punishment.

During the class in drawing, the newly arrived teacher noticed a boy who kept shouting, without paying any attention to the teacher, and madly striking his neighbours without any cause. Finding it impossible to assuage him with words, the teacher led him out from his seat and took his slate away from him; that was his punishment. During the rest of the lesson the boy was bathed in tears. It was the very boy whom I had not received at the opening of the Yásnaya Polyána school, as I regarded him as a hopeless idiot. The main characteristics of the boy are dulness and meekness. His comrades never let him play with them, laugh at him, and ridicule him, and in surprise say of him: "What a funny boy Pétka is! If you strike him, — even the little fellows strike him, — he just picks himself up and goes away."

"He has not any heart at all," a boy said to me about him.

If such a boy was wrought up to such an extent that the teacher punished him, the punished boy was certainly not the one who was at fault.

Another case. In the summer, while the building was being repaired, a Leyden jar had disappeared from the physical cabinet; later, when there were no longer any carpenters or calciminers in the house, there disappeared on various occasions pencils and books. We asked the boys: the best pupils, those who had been with us the longest, our old friends, blushed, and looked so timid that any prosecuting magistrate would have taken their embarrassment for the surest proof of their guilt. But I knew them, and could answer for them as for myself. I understood that the mere thought of a suspicion offended them deeply and painfully: a boy whom I will call Fédor, a talented and tender nature, was all pale, and he trembled and wept. They promised to tell me if they found it out; but they refused to make a search.

A few days later the thief was found: he was a manorial boy from a distant village. He had influenced a peasant boy who came with him from the same village, and both together had hidden the stolen objects in a small chest. This discovery produced a strange effect on his schoolmates: something like relief, and even joy, and at the same time contempt and compassion for the thief.

We proposed to them to mete out a punishment to the thief: some demanded that he be flogged, but that they themselves should do the flogging; others said that a label with the inscription "thief" ought to be sewn on his coat. This punishment, to our shame be it said, had been used by us before, and the very boy who the year before had worn such a label, with the inscription "liar," was the most persistent in demanding that label for the thief. We agreed on the label, and while a girl was sewing it on, all the pupils, with malicious joy, looked at the punished boys, and made fun of them. They demanded that the punishment be increased: "Take them through the village! Let them keep on the labels until the holidays," said they.

The punished boys wept. The peasant child, who had been influenced by the manorial boy, a talented storyteller and joker, a white-skinned, plump little fellow, was crying his heart away at the top of his boyish voice. The other, the chief criminal, a hump-nosed boy, with fine features and an intelligent face, was pale; his lips quivered; his eyes looked wildly and angrily at the triumphant boys, and now and then his face twitched unnaturally as though getting ready to cry. His cap, with torn visor, was poised on the back of his head, his hair was dishevelled, and his clothes soiled with chalk.

All that struck me and everybody else forcibly, as though we saw it all for the first time. The hostile attention of all was directed upon him. And this he was painfully conscious of. When he, without looking around and with bent head, and with a peculiar criminal gait, as

I thought, walked home, and the children, running after him in a crowd, teased him in a peculiarly unnatural and strangely cruel manner, as though an evil spirit were guiding them against their will, something told me that it was not good. But the matter stood as it was, and the thief went with the label for a whole day. From that time on I thought he was studying with less zeal, and he no longer took part in the games and conversations of the boys outside the school.

Once I came to the classroom, when all the pupils with a certain terror informed me that the boy had again stolen. He had taken away twenty kopeks in copper from the teacher's room, and he had been caught hiding the money under the staircase. We again attached the label to him, — and the old monstrous scene was repeated. I began to admonish him, just as all educators admonish; a grown up boy, a good talker, who was present, began to admonish him, too, repeating the words which he, no doubt, had heard from his father, an innkeeper.

"You steal once, and you steal a second time," he spoke, solemnly declaiming his words, "and it becomes a habit, and leads to no good."

I began to feel vexed. I was almost enraged against the thief. I looked at the face of the punished boy, which now was even paler, more suffering, and more cruel than before; I for some reason thought of prisoners in jail, and I suddenly felt so ashamed and felt such loathing for myself that I tore off the stupid label, told him to go wherever he pleased, and suddenly convinced myself, not through reasoning, but with my whole being, that I had no right to torment the unfortunate boy, and that I could not make of him what I and the innkeeper's son would like to make of him. I convinced myself that there were secrets of the soul, hidden from us, upon which only life can act, and not moral precepts and punishments.

What nonsense! The boy has stolen a book. By a whole, complicated road of feelings, thoughts, faulty ratiocinations, he was led to take a book belonging to somebody else, which he for some reason locked up in a chest, — and I paste on him a piece of paper with the word "thief," which means something entirely different! What for? To punish him by shaming him, I shall be told. To punish him by shaming him? What for? What is shame? How do we know that shame destroys the inclination toward thieving? Maybe it only encourages it. Maybe that which was expressed in his face was not at all shame. Indeed, I know for sure that it was not shame, but something quite different, which might have slept for ever in his soul, and which it was not good to evoke. Maybe there, in the world, which is called real, in the world of the Palmerstons, Cayenne, — in the world where not that is reasonable which is reasonable, but that which is real, — let people, who themselves have been punished, invent rights and duties to punish. Our world of children — of simple, independent men — must remain pure from self-deception and the criminal faith in the legality of punishment, free from that self-deception and belief that the feeling of revenge becomes just the moment you call it punishment.

We will proceed with the description of the daily order of instruction. At about two o'clock the hungry children run home. In spite of their hunger, they lag behind a few minutes to find out their grades. The grades at the present time amuse them very much, though they give them no privileges.

"I have five plus, and Olgúshka has caught a whopper of a cipher! — And I got four!" they cry.

The grades serve to them as a measure of their work, and dissatisfaction with grades is expressed only when they are not just. There is trouble when a pupil has tried hard, and the teacher by oversight gives him less than he deserves. He will not give the teacher any rest and will weep bitter tears, if he cannot get him to change it. Bad marks, if they are deserved, remain without protest. However, marks are left with us from the old order and are beginning to fall into disuse.

At the first lesson after the dinner recess, the pupils gather just as in the morning, and wait for the teacher in the same manner. It is generally a lesson in sacred or Russian history, for which all the classes meet together. This lesson generally begins at close of day. The teacher stands or sits down in the middle of the room, and the crowd gathers around him in amphitheatrical order, on benches, on tables, on window-sills.

All the evening lessons, especially the first, have a peculiar character of calm, dreaminess, and poetry, differing in this from the morning classes. You come to the school at fall of day: no lights are seen in the windows; it is almost quiet, and only tracks of snow on the staircase, freshly carried in, a weak din and rustling beyond the door, and some urchin clattering on the staircase, by taking two steps at a time and holding on to the balustrade, prove that the pupils are at school.

Walk into the room! It is almost dark behind the frozen windows; the best pupils are jammed toward the teacher by the rest of the children, and, turning up their little heads, are looking straight into the teacher's mouth. The independent manorial girl is always sitting with a careworn face on the high table, and, it seems, is swallowing every word; the poorer pupils, the small fry, sit farther away: they listen attentively, even austerely; they behave just like the big boys, but, in spite of their attention, we know that they will not tell a thing, even though they may remember some.

Some press down on other people's shoulders, and others stand up on the table. Occasionally one pushes his way into the crowd, where he busies himself with drawing some figures with his nail on somebody's back. It is not often that one will look back at you. When a new story is being told, all listen in dead silence; when there is a repetition, ambitious voices are heard now and then, being unable to keep from helping the teacher out. Still, if there is an old story which they like, they ask the teacher to repeat it in his own words, and then they do not allow any one to interrupt him.

"What is the matter with you? Can't you hold in? Keep quiet!" they will call out to a forward boy.

It pains them to hear the character and the artistic quality of the teacher's story interrupted. Of late it has been the story of Christ's life. They every time asked to have it all told to them. If the whole story is not told to them, they themselves supply their favourite ending, — the history of Peter's denying Christ, and of the Saviour's passion.

You would think all are dead: there is no stir, — can they be asleep? You walk up to them in the semi-darkness and look into the face of some little fellow, — he is sitting, his eyes staring at the teacher, frowning from close attention, and for the tenth time brushing away the arm of his companion, which is pressing down on his shoulder. You tickle his neck, — he does not even smile; he only bends his head, as though to drive away a fly, and again abandons himself to the mysterious and poetical story, how the veil of the church was rent and it grew dark upon earth, — and he has a mingled sensation of dread and joy.

Now the teacher is through with his story, and all rise from their seats, and, crowding around their teacher, try to outcry each other in their attempt to tell what they have retained. There is a terrible hubbub, — the teacher barely can follow them all. Those who are forbidden to tell anything, the teacher being sure that they know it all, are not satisfied: they approach the other teacher;

and if he is not there, they importune a companion, a stranger, even the keeper of the fires, or walk from corner to corner by twos and by threes, begging everybody to listen to them. It is rare for one to tell at a time. They themselves divide up in groups, those of equal strength keeping together, and begin to tell, encouraging and correcting each other, and waiting for their turns. "Come, let us take it together," says one to another, but the one who is addressed knows that he can't keep up with him, and so he sends him to another. As soon as they have had their say and have quieted down, lights are brought, and a different mood comes over the boys.

In the evenings in general, and at the next lessons in particular, the hubbub is not so great, and the docility and the confidence in the teacher are greater. The pupils seem to evince an abhorrence for mathematics and analysis, and a liking for singing, reading, and especially for stories.

"What's the use in having mathematics all the time, and writing? Better tell us something, about the earth, or even history, and we will listen," say all.

At about eight o'clock the eyes begin to get heavy; they begin to yawn; the candles burn more dimly, — they are not trimmed so often; the elder children hold themselves up, but the younger, the poorer students, fall asleep, leaning on the table, under the pleasant sounds of the teacher's voice.

At times, when the classes are uninteresting, and there have been many of them (we often have seven long hours a day), and the children are tired, or before the holidays, when the ovens at home are prepared for a hot bath, two or three boys will suddenly rush into the room during the second or third afternoon class-hour, and will hurriedly pick out their caps.

"What's up?"

"Going home."

"And studies? There is to be singing yet!"

"The boys say they are going home," says one, slipping away with his cap.

"Who says so?"

"The boys are gone!"

"How is that?" asks the perplexed teacher who has prepared his lesson. "Stay!"

But another boy runs into the room, with an excited and perplexed face.

"What are you staying here for?" he angrily attacks the one held back, who, in indecision, pushes the cotton batting back into his cap. "The boys are way down there, — I guess as far as the smithy."

"Have they gone?"

"They have."

And both run away, calling from behind the door: "Good-bye, Iván Ivánovich!"

Who are the boys that decided to go home, and how did they decide it? God knows. You will never find out who decided it. They did not take counsel, did not conspire, but simply, some boys wanted to go home, "The boys are going!" — and their feet rattle down-stairs, and one rolls down the steps in catlike form, and, leaping and tumbling in the snow, running a race with each other along the narrow path, the children bolt for home.

Such occurrences take place once or twice a week. It is aggravating and disagreeable for the teacher, — who will not admit that? But who will not admit, at the same time, that, on account of one such an occurrence, the five, six, and even seven lessons a day for each class, which are, of their own accord and with pleasure, attended by the pupils, receive a so much greater significance? Only by the recurrence of such cases could one gain the certainty that the instruction, though insufficient and one-sided, was not entirely bad and not detrimental.

If the question were put like this: Which would be

better, that not one such occurrence should take place during the whole year, or that this should happen for more than half the lessons, — we should choose the latter. At least, I was always glad to see these things happen several times a month in the Yásnaya Polyána school. In spite of the frequently repeated statements to the boys that they may leave any time they wish, the influence of the teacher is so strong that, of late, I have been afraid that the discipline of the classes, programmes, and grades might, imperceptibly to them, so restrict their liberty that they would submit to the cunning of the nets of order set by us and that they would lose the possibility of choice and protest. Their continued willingness to come to school, in spite of the liberty granted them, does not, I think, by any means prove the especial qualities of the Yásnaya Polyána school, — I believe that the same would be repeated in the majority of schools, and that the desire to study is so strong in children that, in order to satisfy their desire, they will submit to many hard conditions and will forgive many defects. The possibility of such escapades is useful and necessary only as a means of securing the teacher against the most detrimental and coarsest errors and abuses.

In the evening we have singing, graded reading, talks, physical experiments, and writing of compositions. Of these, their favourite subjects are reading and experiments. During the reading the older children lie down on the large table in star-shaped form, — their heads together, their feet radiating out, and one reads, and all tell the contents to each other. The younger children locate themselves with their books by twos, and if the book is intelligible to them, they read it as we do, by getting close to the light and making themselves comfortable, and apparently they derive pleasure from it. Some, trying to unite two kinds of enjoyment, seat themselves opposite the burning stove, and warm themselves and read.

Not all are admitted to the class in experiments, only the oldest and best, and the more intelligent ones of the second class. This class has assumed, with us, a vespertine, most fantastic character, precisely fitting the mood produced by the reading of fairy-tales. Here the fairy-like element is materialized, — everything is personified by them: the pith-ball which is repelled by the sealing-wax, the deflecting magnetic needle, the iron filings scurrying over the sheet of paper underneath which the magnet is guided, present themselves to them as living objects. The most intelligent boys, who understand the cause of these phenomena, become excited and talk to the needle, the ball, the filings: "Come now! Hold on! Where are you going? Stop there! Ho there! Let her go!" and so forth.

Generally the classes end at between eight to nine o'clock, if the carpentry work does not keep the boys longer, and then the whole mass of them run shouting into the yard, from where they begin to scatter in groups in all the directions of the village, calling to each other from a distance. Sometimes they scheme to coast downhill into the village on a large sleigh standing outside the gate, by tying up the shafts: they crawl in and disappear with screaming in the snow-dust, leaving, here and there along the road, black spots of children tumbled out. Outside the school, in the open air, there establish themselves, despite all the liberty granted there, new relations between pupils and teachers, of greater liberty, greater simplicity, and greater confidence, — those very relations, which, to us, appear as the ideal of what the school is to strive after.

The other day we read Gógol's "The Elf-king" with the first class. The last scenes powerfully affected them and excited their imagination: some tried to look like witches and kept mentioning the last night.

It was not cold outside, — a moonless winter night

with clouds in the sky. We stopped at the cross-road; the older, third-year pupils stopped near me, asking me to accompany them farther; the younger ones looked awhile at me and then coasted down-hill. The younger ones had begun to study with a new teacher and there is no longer that confidence between them and me, as between the older boys and me.

"Come, let us go to the preserve" (a small forest within two hundred steps of the house), said one of them. Fédka, a small boy of ten, of a tender, impressionable, poetical, and dashing nature, was the most persistent in his demands. Danger seems to form his chief condition for enjoyment. In the summer it always made me shudder to see him, with two other boys, swim out into the very middle of the pond, which was something like three hundred and fifty feet wide, and now and then disappear in the hot reflections of the summer sun, and then swim over the depth, while turning on his back, spurting up the water, and calling out in a thin voice to his companions on the shore, that they might see what a dashing fellow he was.

He knew that there were wolves in the forest now, and so he wanted to go to the preserve. All chimed in, and so we went, four of us, into the wood. Another boy, I shall call him Sémka, a physically and morally sound lad of about twelve, nicknamed Vavílo, walked ahead and kept exchanging calls with somebody in his ringing voice. Prónka, a sickly, meek, and uncommonly talented boy, the son of a poor family, — sickly, I think, mainly on account of insufficient food, — was walking by my side.

Fédka was walking between me and Sémka, talking all the time in his extremely soft voice, telling us how he had herded horses here in the summer, or saying that he was not afraid of anything, or asking, "Suppose one should jump out!" and insisting on my answering him. We did not go into the forest itself, — that would have been too terrible, — but even near the forest it was getting darker: we could hardly see the path, and the fires of the village were hidden from view.

Sémka stopped and began to listen.

"Stop, boys! What is that?" he suddenly said.

We grew silent, but we could hear nothing; still it added terror to our fear.

"Well, what should we do, if one should jump out and make straight for us?" Fédka asked.

We began to talk about robbers in the Caucasus. They recalled a story of the Caucasus I had told them long ago, and I told them again about abréks, about Cossacks, about Khádzhi-Murát. Sémka was strutting ahead of us, stepping broadly in his big boots, and evenly swaying his strong back. Prónka tried to walk by my side, but Fédka pushed him off the path, and Prónka, who apparently always submitted to such treatment on account of his poverty, rushed up to my side only during the most interesting passages, though sinking knee-deep in the snow.

Everybody who knows anything about peasant children has noticed that they are not accustomed to any kind of caresses, — tender words, kisses, being touched with a hand, and so forth, — and that they cannot bear these caresses. I have observed ladies in peasant schools, who, wishing to show their favours to a boy, say, "Come, my darling, I will kiss you!" and actually kiss him, whereat the boy so kissed is embarrassed and feels offended and wonders why that was done to him. A boy of five years of age stands above these caresses, — he is a lad. It was for this reason that I was startled when Fédka, who was walking by my side, in the most terrible part of the story suddenly touched me at first lightly with his sleeve and then clasped two of my fingers with his whole hand, and did not let them out of his grasp.

The moment I grew silent, Fédka demanded that I

should proceed, and he did that in such an imploring and agitated voice that I could not refuse his request.

"Don't get in my way!" he once angrily called out to Prónka, who had run ahead; he was carried away to the point of cruelty,—he had such a mingled feeling of terror and joy, as he was holding on to my finger, and no one should dare to interrupt his pleasure.

"More, more! That's fine!"

We passed the forest and were approaching the village from the other end.

"Let us go there again,' all cried, when the lights became visible. "Let us take another walk!"

We walked in silence, now and then sinking in the loose, untrodden path; the white darkness seemed to be swaying before our eyes; the clouds hung low, as though piling upon us, — there was no end to that whiteness over which we alone crunched through the snow; the wind rustled through the bare tops of the aspens, but we were protected from the wind behind the forest.

I finished my story by telling them that, the abrék being surrounded, he began to sing songs, and then threw himself on his dagger. All were silent.

"Why did he sing a song when he was surrounded?" asked Sémka.

"Didn't you hear? He was getting ready to die!" Fédka replied, sorrowfully.

"I think he sang a prayer," added Prónka.

All agreed. Fédka suddenly stopped.

"How was it when they cut the throat of your aunt?" he asked, — he had not had enough terrors. "Tell us! Tell us!"

I told them once more that terrible story of the murder of Countess Tolstóy, and they stood silently about me, gazing at my face.

"The fellow got caught!" said Sémka.

"It did frighten him to walk through the night, while she

lay with her throat cut," said Fédka. "I should have run away myself!" and he moved up his hand on my two fingers.

We stopped in the grove, beyond the threshing-floors, at the very end of the village. Sémka picked up a stick from the snow and began to strike the frozen trunk of a linden-tree. The hoarfrost fell from the branches upon his cap, and the lonely sound of his beating was borne through the forest.

"Lev Nikoláevich," Fédka said (I thought he wanted to say something again about the countess), "why do people learn singing? I often wonder why they really do?"

God knows what made him jump from the terrors of the murder to this question; but by everything, — by the sound of his voice, by the seriousness with which he requested an answer, by the silence which the other two preserved, — I could feel a vivid and lawful connection of this question and the preceding conversation. Whatever the connection may have consisted in, whether in my explaining the possibility of crime from ignorance (I had told them so), or in his verifying himself, by transferring himself into the soul of the murderer and recalling his favourite occupation (he has a charming voice and immense talent for music), or whether the connection consisted in his feeling that now was the time for intimate conversation, and that now in his soul had arisen all the questions demanding a solution, — the question did not surprise any of us.

"What is drawing for? And why is it good to write?" I said, positively not knowing how to explain to him what art was for.

"What is drawing for?" he repeated, thoughtfully. What he was asking me was what art was for, and I did not dare and did not know how to explain to him.

"What is drawing for?" said Sémka. "You draw everything, and then you know how to make things from the drawing."

"No, that is mechanical drawing," said Fédka, "but why do you draw figures?"

Sémka's healthy nature was not at a loss:

"What is a stick for? What is a linden for?" he said, still striking the linden.

"Yes, what is the linden for?" I asked.

"To make rafters with," replied Sémka.

"What is it for in summer, when it has not yet been cut down?"

"For nothing."

"Really," Fédka kept stubbornly at it, "why does a linden grow?"

And we began to speak of there not being only a usefulness of things, but also a beauty, and that art was beauty, and we understood each other, and Fédka comprehended well why a linden grew and what singing was for.

Prónka agreed with us, but he had mostly in mind moral beauty, — goodness.

Sémka understood it rightly with his big brain, but he did not recognize beauty without usefulness. He doubted, as people of great intelligence doubt, feeling that art is a force, but feeling in their souls no need of that force; he wanted, like them, to reach out for that art by means of reason, and tried to start that fire in himself.

"Let us sing 'He who' to-morrow, — I remember my voice."

He has a correct ear, but no taste, no artistic quality in singing.

Fédka comprehended completely that the linden was nice with its leafage and that it was nice to look at it in summer, — and nothing else was needed.

Prónka understood that it was a pity to cut it down, because it, too, had life: "When we drink the sap of the linden, it is just the same as though we were drinking blood."

Sémka did not say much, but it was evident that he did not think there was much use in a linden when it was rotten.

It feels strange to me to repeat what we spoke on that evening, but I remember we said everything, I think, that there was to be said on utility and on plastic and moral beauty.

We went to the village. Fédka still clung to my hand, — this time, I thought, from gratitude. We were all so near to each other on that night, as we had not been for a long time. Prónka walked by our side over the broad village street.

"I declare, there is light still in Mazánov's house!" he said. "As I was going this morning to school, Gavryúkha was coming from the tavern," he added, "drunk, oh, so drunk! The horse was all in a lather, and he kept warming him up — I always feel sorry for such things. Really I do! What does he strike him for?"

"The other day father gave his horse the reins, coming from Túla," said Sémka, "and the horse took him into a snowdrift, but he was drunk and asleep."

"Gavryúkha kept switching him over the eyes — and I felt so sorry for him," Prónka repeated once more. "What did he strike him for? He got down and just switched him."

Sémka suddenly stopped.

"They are asleep," he said, looking through the windows of his black, crooked hut. "Won't you walk a little more?"

"No."

"Goo-ood-bye, Lev Nikoláevich," he suddenly shouted, and, as though tearing himself away from us, darted for his house, raised the latch and disappeared.

"So you will take us home? First one, and then another?" asked Fédka.

We walked ahead. In Prónka's house there was a

light. We looked through the window: his mother, a tall, handsome, but emaciated woman, with black eyebrows and eyes, was sitting at the table and cleaning potatoes; in the middle of the room hung a cradle; Prónka's other brother, the mathematician of the second class, was standing at the table and eating potatoes with salt. It was a tiny, dirty, black house.

"What is the matter with you?" the mother cried to Prónka. "Where have you been?"

Prónka smiled a meek, sickly smile, looking at the window. His mother guessed that he was not alone, and immediately assumed an insincere, feigned expression.

There was now Fédka left.

"The tailors are at our house, so there is a light there," he said in the mollified voice of that evening. "Good-bye, Lev Nikoláevich!" he added, softly and tenderly, and began to knock the closed door with the ring.

"Let me in!" his thin voice rang out through the winter stillness of the village.

Quite a time passed before he was admitted. I looked through the window: it was a large room; on the oven and on the benches feet could be seen; his father was playing cards with the tailors, — a few copper coins were lying on the table. A woman, the boy's stepmother, was sitting near the torch-holder, eagerly looking at the money. One tailor, an arrant knave, still a young peasant, was holding his cards on the table, bending them like bark, and triumphantly looking at his partner. Fédka's father, the collar of his shirt being all unbuttoned, scowling from mental strain and annoyance, was fumbling his cards in indecision, waving his heavy peasant hand over them.

"Let me in!"

The woman got up and went to open the door.

"Good-bye!" Fédka repeated. "Let us walk often that way!"

I see honest, good, liberal men, members of charitable

societies, who are ready to give and who do give one-hundredth part of their possessions to the poor, who have established schools, and who, reading this, will say, "It is not good!" and will shake their heads.

"Why develop them forcibly? Why give them sentiments and conceptions which will make them hostile to their surroundings? Why take them out of their existence?" they will say.

Of course, it is even worse with those who regard themselves as leaders, and who will say: "A fine state it will be, where all want to be thinkers and artists, and where nobody will be working!"

These say without ambiguity that they do not like to work, and that, therefore, there have to be people who are not merely unfit for any other activity, but simply slaves, who must work for others.

Is it good, is it bad, is it necessary to take them out of their surroundings, and so forth? Who knows? And who can take them out of their surroundings? That is not done by a mere mechanical contrivance. Is it good or bad to add sugar to flour, or pepper to beer?

Fédka is not vexed by his tattered caftan, but moral questions and doubts torment him, and you want to give him three roubles, a catechism, and a tract about the usefulness of labour, and about meekness which you yourselves cannot bear. He does not need three roubles: he will find and take them when he needs them, and he will learn to work without your aid, just as he has learned to breathe; he needs that to which life has brought you, your own life and that of ten generations not crushed by work. You have had leisure to seek, think, suffer, — so give him that which you have gained by suffering, — that is what he wants; but you, like an Egyptian priest, veil yourselves from him in a mysterious mantle and bury in the ground the talent given you by history. Fear not: nothing human is injurious to man. Are you in doubt? Abandon yourselves to your feelings, and they will not deceive you. Have faith in his nature, and you will convince yourselves that he will take only as much as history has enjoined you to give to him, as much as has been worked in you by means of suffering.

The school is free, and the first pupils to enter were those from the village of Yásnaya Polyána. Many of these pupils have left the school because their parents did not regard the instruction as good; many, having learned to read and write, stopped coming and hired themselves out at the railroad, — the chief occupation at our village. At first they brought the children from the near-by poorer villages, but because of the inconvenience of the distance or of boarding them out (in our village the cheapest board is two roubles in silver a month), they were soon taken out of school. From the distant villages the well-to-do peasants, pleased to hear that the school was free and that, as it was rumoured among the people, they taught well at the Yásnaya Polyána school, began to send their children, but this winter, when schools were opened in the villages, they took them out again and put them into the village pay schools. There were then left in the Yásnaya Polyána school the children of the Yásnaya Polyána peasants, who attend school in the winter, but in the summer, from April to the middle of October, work in the fields, and the children of innkeepers, clerks, soldiers, manorial servants, dramshop-keepers, sextons, and rich peasants, who are brought there from a distance of thirty and even fifty versts.

There are in all about forty pupils, but rarely more than thirty at a time. The girls form ten or only six per cent. of the whole, being from three to five in number. Boys from the age of seven to thirteen are the normal age with us. In addition to these we have every year three or four grown people who come to us for a month, and sometimes the whole winter, and then leave us.

For the grown people, who come to school singly, the order of the school is very inconvenient: on account of their age and their feeling of dignity they cannot take part in the animation of the school, nor can they free themselves from their contempt for the youngsters, and so they remain entirely alone. The animation of the school is only an obstacle to them. They generally come to finish the instruction begun before, having some little knowledge, and with the conviction that instruction consists in making them learn the book, of which they have heard before, or in which they have had experience. In order to come to the school, they had to overcome their own fear and embarrassment and to endure a domestic storm and the ridicule of their companions. "Look at the stallion that is going to study!" Besides, they constantly feel that every day lost at school is a day lost at labour, which forms their only capital, and so all the time that they are at school they are in an irritable state of hurry and zeal, which more than anything else is detrimental to study.

During the time which I am describing now we had three such grown people, one of whom is studying even now. A grown pupil acts as at a fire: no sooner has he finished writing than he grabs a book with one hand, while he puts down the pen held in the other, and begins to read standing; take the book away from him, and he takes hold of the slate; take that away from him, and he is completely at a loss.

There was one labourer this fall, who studied with us and at the same time made the fires in the school. He learned to read and write in two weeks, but that was not learning, but a disease, something like a protracted spree. Passing with an armful of wood through the classroom, he would stop, with the wood still in his arms, and, bending over a boy's head, would spell *s, k, a — ska*, and then go to his place. If he did not succeed in doing so, he looked with envy, almost with malice, at the children; when he was at liberty, we could not do anything with him: he gazed steadfastly at his book, repeating *b, a — ba, r, i — ri*, and so forth, and while in this state he lost all ability to understand anything else.

When the grown men had to sing or draw, or to listen to a history recitation, or to look at experiments, it became apparent that they submitted to cruel necessity, and, like hungry people who are torn away from their food, they waited only for the moment when they could again bury themselves in their spelling-books. Remaining true to the rule, I have not compelled boys to study the A B C when they do not want to do so, and so I do not insist on a grown person's learning mechanics or drawing, when he wants the A B C. Everybody takes what he wants.

In general, the grown persons, who started their instruction elsewhere, have not yet found a place for themselves in the Yásnaya Polyána school, and their instruction proceeds poorly : there is something unnatural and morbid in their relation to the school. The Sunday schools which I have seen present the same phenomenon in regard to grown persons, and so any information in respect to a successful free education of grown-up people would be a very precious acquisition for us.

The view of the masses as regards our school has much changed from the beginning of its existence. Of the former view we shall have to speak in the history of the Yásnaya Polyána school; but now the people say that in the Yásnaya Polyána school " they teach everything and all the sciences, and there are some awfully smart teachers there, — they say they can make thunder and lightning! And the boys comprehend well, — they have begun to read and write."

Some of them — the rich innkeepers — send their children to school out of vanity, " to promote them into the full science, so that they may know division" (division is the highest conception they have of scholastic wisdom); other fathers assume that science is very profitable; but the most send their children to school unconsciously, submitting to the spirit of the time.

Out of these boys, who form the majority, the most encouraging to us are those who were *just* sent to school and who have become so fond of study that their parents now submit to the desire of the children, and themselves feel unconsciously that something good is being done to their children and have not the heart to take the children out of school.

One father told me that he once used up a whole candle, holding it over his boy's book, and praised both his son and the book. It was the Gospel.

"My father," another pupil told me, "now and then listens to a fairy-tale, and laughs, and goes away; and if it is something divine, he sits and listens until midnight, holding the candle for me."

I called with the new teacher at the house of a pupil, and, in order to show him off, had the boy solve an algebraic equation for the teacher. The mother was busy at the oven, and we forgot all about her; while listening to her son, as he briskly and earnestly transformed the equation, saying, "$2ab - c - d$, divided by 3," and so forth she all the time kept her face covered with her hand, with difficulty restraining herself, and finally burst out into laughter and was unable to explain to us what it was she was laughing about.

Another father, a soldier, once came after his son; he found him in the drawing class, and when he saw his son's art, he began to say "you" instead of "thou" to him and did not have the heart to give him the water chestnuts which he had brought him as a present.

The common opinion is, I think, as follows: They teach everything there (just as to gentlemen's children), many useless things, but they also teach them to read and write in a short time, — and so it is all right to send the children there.

There are also ill-wishing rumours current among people, but they now have little weight. Two fine boys lately left school for the alleged reason that we did not teach writing at school. Another, a soldier, wanted to send his boy, but, upon examining one of our pupils and finding that he read the psalter with hesitation, he decided that our instruction was *bad*, and that only the fame of the school was *good*.

A few of the Yásnaya Polyána peasants have not stopped fearing lest the old rumours should prove true; they imagine that there is some ulterior purpose in teaching the children and that at an unforeseen hour somebody will slip a cart under their boys and haul them off to Moscow.

The dissatisfaction with the absence of corporal punishment and order at school has now almost entirely disappeared. I have often had occasion to observe the perplexity of a father, when, coming to the school for his boy, he saw the pupils running about, making a hubbub, and tussling with each other. He is convinced that naughtiness is detrimental, and yet he believes that we teach well, and he is at a loss to combine the two.

Gymnastics now and then cause them to reassert their conviction that it somehow is hard on the stomach, and that "it does not go through." Soon after fasting, or in the fall, when the vegetables get ripe, gymnastics do the most harm, and the old women cover up the pots and explain that the cause of it all is the naughtiness and the twisting.

For some, though only a small number, even the spirit of equality in the school serves as a subject of dissatisfaction. In November we had two girls, the daughters of a rich innkeeper, in cloaks and caps, who at first kept themselves aloof, but later got used to the rest and forgot their tea and the cleaning of their teeth with tobacco, and began to study well. Their father, dressed in a Crimean sheepskin fur coat, all unbuttoned, entered the school and found them standing in a crowd of dirty bast shoe boys, who, leaning with their hands on the head-gear of the girls, were listening to what the teacher was saying; the father was offended and took his girls out of the school, though he did not confess the cause of his dissatisfaction.

Finally, there are some children who leave school because their parents, who have sent their children to school in order to gain somebody's favour by it, take them out again, when the need of gaining somebody's favour has passed.

And thus, there are twelve subjects, three classes, forty pupils in all, four teachers, and from five to seven recitations a day. The teachers keep diaries of their occupations, which they communicate to each other on Sundays, and in conformity with which they arrange their plans for the following week. These plans are not carried out each week, but are modified in conformity with the needs of the pupils.

## MECHANICAL READING

Reading forms part of language instruction. The problem of language instruction consists, in our opinion, in guiding people to understand the contents of books written in the literary language. The knowledge of the literary language is necessary because the good books are all in that language.

At first, soon after the foundation of the school, there was no subdivision of reading into mechanical and graded, for the pupils read only that which they could understand, — their own compositions, words and sentences written on the blackboard with chalk, and then Khudyakóv's and Afanásev's fairy-tales. I then supposed that for the children to learn to read, they had to like reading, and in order to like reading it was necessary that the reading matter be intelligible and interesting. That seemed so rational and clear, and yet the idea was false.

In the first place, in order to pass from the reading on the walls to the reading in books, it became necessary to devote special attention to mechanical reading with each pupil according to any book whatsoever. As long as the number of pupils was inconsiderable and subjects were not subdivided, that was possible, and I could, without much labour, transfer the children from reading on the wall to reading in a book; but with the arrival of new pupils that became impossible. The younger pupils were not able to read a fairy-tale and understand it: the labour of putting together the words and at the same time of understanding their meaning was too much for them.

Another inconvenience was that the graded reading came to an end with the fairy-tales, and whatever book we took, — whether "The Popular Reading," "The Soldier's Reading," Púshkin, Gógol, Karamzín, — it turned out that the older pupils experienced the same difficulty in reading Púshkin as the younger ones experienced in the reading of the fables: they could not combine the labour of reading and comprehending what they read, though they understood a little when we read to them.

We first thought that the difficulty was in the imperfect mechanism of the pupils' reading, and we invented mechanical reading, reading for the process of reading, — the teacher read alternately with the pupils, — but matters did not improve, and the same perplexity arose in reading "Robinson Crusoe."

In the summer, during the transitional stage of our schools, we hoped to be able to vanquish this difficulty in the simplest and most approved manner possible. Why not confess it, — we succumbed to false shame before our visitors. (Our pupils read much worse than those who had studied the same length of time with a sexton.) The new teacher proposed to introduce reading aloud from the same books, and we agreed to it. Having once become possessed of the false idea that the pupils must by all means read fluently during this very year, we put down on the programme mechanical and graded reading, and we made them read about two hours a day out of the same books, and that was very convenient for us.

But this one departure from the rule of the pupils' freedom led to lies and to one blunder after another. We bought some booklets, — the fairy-tales by Púshkin and by Ershóv, — we placed the boys on benches, and one had to read aloud while the others followed his reading. To find out whether they were really following, the teacher asked now one, now another, a question.

At first we thought that everything was well. You come to the school, — all sit in orderly fashion on benches; one reads, the rest follow. The one who reads says: "Marcy, my Queen Fish!" and the others, or the teacher, correct him: "Mercy, my Queen Fish!" Ivánov hunts for the place and goes on reading. All are busy; you may hear the teacher; every word is correctly pronounced, and they read quite fluently.

You would think all is well; but examine it closely, — the one who is reading is reading the same thing for the thirtieth or fortieth time. (A printed sheet will not last longer than a week, and it is terribly expensive to buy new books all the time, while there are only two comprehensible books for peasant children, — the fairy-tales by Khudyakóv and by Afanásev. Besides, a book which has once been read by a class and is known by heart by some is not only familiar to all the pupils, but even the home people are tired of it.) The reader becomes timid, listening to his lonely voice amid the silence of the room; all his effort is directed toward observing all the punctuation marks and the accents, and he acquires the habit of reading without understanding the meaning, for he is burdened with other demands. The hearers do the same, and, hoping always to strike the right place when they are asked, evenly guide their fingers along the lines and are distracted by other things. The meaning of what is read involuntarily lodges in their heads at times, or it does not stay there at all, being a secondary consideration.

The chief harm lies in that eternal battle of cunning and of tricks between the pupils and the teacher, which is developed with such an order, and which had not existed in our school heretofore; whereas the only advantage of this method of reading, consisting in the correct pronunciation of words, had no meaning whatsoever for our pupils. Our pupils had been learning to read the sentences written and pronounced by them on the board, and all knew that you write *kogo* and pronounce it *kavo;* but I consider it useless to teach stops and changes of voice from the punctuation marks, because every five-year-old boy makes correct use of the punctuation marks in his voice, if he understands what he is saying. Therefore it is easier to teach him to understand that which he speaks from the book (which he must attain sooner or later) than to teach him to sing, as though from music, the punctuation marks. And yet, how convenient that is for the teacher!

*The teacher always involuntarily strives after selecting that method of instruction which is most convenient for himself. The more convenient the method is for the teacher, the more it is inconvenient for the pupils. Only that manner of instruction is correct with which the pupils are satisfied.*

These three laws of instruction were most palpably reflected by the mechanical reading in the school at Yásnaya Polyána.

Thanks to the vitality of the spirit of the school, especially when the old pupils returned to it from their field labours, this reading of itself fell into disuse: the pupils grew tired, and began to play and became slack in their work. Above all, the reading with stories, which was to verify the success of the mechanical reading, proved that there was no such progress, that in five weeks we had not advanced one step in reading, while many had fallen behind. The best mathematician of the first class, R——, who mentally extracted square roots, had forgotten how to read to such an extent that we had to read with him by syllables.

We abandoned the reading from the booklets, and racked our brains to discover a means of mechanical reading. The simple idea that the time had not yet come for good mechanical reading, that there was no urgent need for it at the present time, and that the pupils themselves would find the best method, when that need should arise, burst upon us only within a short time. During that search the following processes established themselves of their own accord:

During the reading lessons, now divided in name only into graded and mechanical, the worst readers come in twos and take some book (sometimes fairy-tales, or the Gospel, and at times a song collection or a number of the *Popular Reading*) and read by twos for the process of reading only, and when that book is an intelligible fairy-tale, they read it with comprehension, after which they demand of the teacher that he should ask them questions, although the class is called mechanical. At times the pupils, generally the poorest, take the same book several times in succession, open it at the same page, read one and the same tale, and memorize it, not only without the teacher's order, but even in spite of his explicit prohibition; sometimes these poor pupils come to the teacher, or to an older boy, and ask him to read with them. Those who can read better, pupils of the second class, are not so fond of reading in company, less often read for the process of reading, and if they memorize anything, it is some poem, but not a prose tale.

With the oldest boys the same phenomenon is repeated, with this one difference which has struck me during the last month. In their class of graded reading they get some one book, which they read in turn, and then all together tell its contents. They were joined this fall by a very talented boy, Ch——, who had studied for two years with a sexton and who therefore is ahead of them all in reading, — he reads as well as we do, and so the pupils understand the graded reading, at least a little of it, only when Ch—— reads, and yet each of them wants to read himself. But the moment a bad reader begins to read, all express their dissatisfaction, — especially when the story is interesting, — they laugh and are angry, and the poor reader is ashamed, and there begin endless disputes. Last month one of these declared that, cost what it might, he would read as well as Ch—— within a week; others made the same declaration, and suddenly mechanical reading became the favourite subject. They would sit an hour or an hour and a half at a time, without tearing themselves away from the book, which they did not understand; they began to take their books home, and really made in three weeks such progress as could hardly have been expected.

There happened to them the direct opposite of what generally takes place with those who learn the rudiments. Generally a man learns to read, but there is nothing for him to read or understand; here it turned out that the pupils convinced themselves that there was something to read and understand, but that they did not read well enough, and so they tried to become more proficient in reading.

We have now abandoned mechanical reading entirely, and matters are carried on as described above; each pupil is permitted to use whatever method is most convenient for him, and, strange to say, they have made use of all the methods I am acquainted with: (1) Reading with the teacher, (2) reading for the process of reading, (3) reading with memorizing, (4) reading in general, and (5) reading with the comprehension of what is being read.

The *first*, in use by the mothers of the whole world, is not a scholastic, but a domestic method. It consists in the pupil's coming and asking to read with the teacher, whereupon the teacher reads, guiding his every syllable and the combination of syllables, — the very first rational and immutable method, which the pupil is the first to demand, and upon which the teacher involuntarily hits. In spite of all means which are supposed to mechanize instruction and presumably facilitate the work of the teacher with a large number of pupils, this method will always remain the best and the only one for teaching people to read, and to read fluently.

The *second* method of teaching to read, also a favourite one, through which every one has passed who has learned to read fluently, consists in giving the pupil a book and leaving it entirely to him to spell and understand as well as he can. The pupil, who has learned to read by syllables so fluently that he does not feel the need of asking the sexton to read with him, but depends upon himself, always acquires that passion for the process of reading which is so ridiculed in Gógol's "Petrúshka," and on account of that passion advances. God knows in what manner that kind of reading assumes any definite shape in his mind, but he thus gets used to the forms of the letters, to the process of syllable combinations, to the pronunciation of words, and even to understanding what he reads, and I have had occasion to convince myself by actual experience that our insistence that the pupil should understand what he reads only retards the result. There are many autodidacts who have learned to read well in this way, although the defects of this system must be apparent to everybody.

The *third* method of teaching reading consists in learning by heart prayers, poems, in general anything printed, and in pronouncing that which has so been memorized, looking at the book all the time.

The *fourth* method consists in that which has proved so detrimental in the Yásnaya Polyána school,— in the reading from a few books only. It arose unpremeditatedly in our school. At first we did not have enough books, and two pupils had to read together; later, they themselves became fond of this, and when the order is given to read, pupils of precisely the same ability pair off, or sometimes assemble three at a time, around one book, and one reads, while the others watch and correct him. You will only disturb them if you rearrange them, for they are quite sure who their matches are, and Taráska will certainly ask for Dúnka.

"You come here to read, and you go to your partner!"

Some of them do not like such collective reading, because they do not need it. The advantage of such reading in common lies in the greater precision of pronunciation and in the greater freedom of comprehension left to him who is not reading, but watching; but the whole advantage, thus produced, becomes harmful the moment this method, or, for that, any other method, is extended to the whole school.

In fine, another favourite method of ours, the *fifth*, is the graded reading, that is, the reading of books with ever growing interest and comprehension.

All these methods, as mentioned above, quite naturally came into use in our school, and in one month we made considerable progress.

The business of the teacher is to afford a choice of all known and unknown methods that may make the matter of learning easier for the pupil. It is true, with a certain method, — say with reading out of one book, — the instruction becomes easy and convenient for the teacher, and has the aspect of seriousness and regularity; but with our order it seems not only difficult, but to many appears even impossible. How, they say, is one to guess what is needed for each pupil, and how is one to decide whether the demand of each is justified? How can one help being lost in this heterogeneous crowd which is subject to no rule?

To this I will reply that we cannot get rid of our old view of the school as a disciplined company of soldiers, commanded to-day by one lieutenant, and to-morrow by another. For the teacher who has adapted himself to the liberty of the school, each pupil represents a separate character, putting forth separate demands, which only the freedom of choice can satisfy.

If it had not been for the freedom and for the external disorder, which seems so strange and impossible to some, we not only should never have struck these five methods of reading, but should never have been able to employ and apportion them according to the exigencies of the pupils, and therefore should never have attained those brilliant results which we have of late attained in reading.

How often have we had occasion to observe the perplexity of the visitors to our school, who in two hours' time wanted to study the method of instruction, which we do not have, and in the course of the same two hours told us all about their own method! How frequently we listened to the advice of these same visitors to introduce the very method which, unknown to them, was being used in their presence in the school, only that it was not generalized as a despotic rule!

GRADED READING

Although, as we said, the mechanical and graded readings in reality blended into one, — these two subjects are still subdivided for us according to their aims. It seems to us that the aim of the first is the art of fluently forming words out of certain signs, while the aim of the second is the knowledge of the literary language.

For the study of the literary language we, naturally, thought of a means which seemed exceedingly simple, but which, in reality, was most difficult. It seemed to us that after the pupils had learned to read sentences written on the board by pupils themselves, we ought to give them Khudyakóv's and Afanásev's fairy-tales, then something more difficult and more complicated as regards language, then something more difficult still, and so on, up to the language of Karamzín, Púshkin, and the Code of Laws; but this supposition, like the majority of our, and in general of any, suppositions, was not realized.

From the language which they themselves employed in their writing on the boards, I succeeded in transferring them to the language of the fairy-tales, but in order to take them from the language of the fairy-tales to a higher level, we did not find that transitional "something" in our literature. We tried "Robinson Crusoe," — the thing did not work: some of the boys wept from vexation, because they could not understand and tell it; I began to tell it to them in my own words, and they began to believe in the possibility of grasping that wisdom, made out the meaning of it, and in a month finished "Robinson Crusoe," but with tedium and, in the end, almost in disgust.

The labour was too great for them. They got at things mostly through memory, and they remembered parts of it, if they told them each evening soon after the reading; but not one of them could make the whole his own. They remembered, unfortunately, only certain incomprehensible words, and began to use them without rhyme or reason, as is generally the case with half-educated people.

I saw that something was wrong, but did not know

how to help the matter. To justify myself and clear my conscience, I began to give them to read all kinds of popular imitations, such as "Uncle Naúm" and "Aunt Natálya," though I knew in advance that they would not like them, — and my supposition came true. These books were the most tiresome for the pupils, if they were expected to tell their contents.

After "Robinson Crusoe" I tried Púshkin, namely, his "The Gravedigger;" but without my aid they were still less able to tell it than "Robinson Crusoe," and "The Gravedigger" seemed much duller to them. The author's apostrophes to the reader, his frivolous relation to his persons, his jocular characterizations, his incompleteness of detail, — all that is so incompatible with their needs, that I definitely gave up Púshkin, whose stories I had assumed to be most regularly constructed, simple, and, therefore, intelligible to the masses.

I then tried Gógol's "The Night Before Christmas." With my reading, it at first pleased them, especially the grown pupils, but the moment I left them alone, they could not comprehend anything and felt ennui. Even with my reading they did not ask to have it repeated. The wealth of colours, the fantasticalness and capriciousness of the structure are contrary to their needs.

Then again I tried to read Gnyédich's translation of the Iliad to them, and the reading produced only a strange perplexity in them; they supposed that it was written in French, and did not understand a thing so long as I did not tell the contents to them in my own words, but even then the plot of the poem made no impression on their minds. Skeptic Sémka, a sound, logical nature, was struck by the picture of Phœbus, with the clanking arrows at his back, flying down from Olympus, but he apparently did not know where to lodge the image.

"But why did he not smash to pieces as he flew down from the mountain?" he kept asking me.

"According to their idea he was a god," I answered him.

"A god? But were there not many of them? Then he was not the real God. It is no joke to fly down from such a mountain: he must have been smashed all to pieces," he tried to prove to me, swaying his arms.

I tried George Sand's "Gribouille," "Popular Reading," and "Soldier's Reading," — all in vain. We try everything we can find and everything they send to us, but we now try everything almost without any hope.

I am sitting at school and break the seal of a package containing a book purporting to be popular, fresh from the post-office.

"Uncle, let me read it, me!" cry several children, stretching out their hands, "so I can understand it."

I open the book and read:

"The life of the great Saint Alexis presents to us an example of the flaming faith of piety, untiring activity, and warm love of his country, for which this holy man did such important service;" or, "Three hundred years have passed since Bohemia became dependent on Germany;" or, "The village of Karachárovo, spreading out at the foot of a mountain, lies in one of the most fertile Governments of Russia;" or, "Broadly lay and stretched the road, the path;" or a popular exposition of some natural science on one sheet, half of which is filled with the author's address to the peasant and his taking him into his confidence.

If I give such a book to one of the boys, — his eyes grow dim, and he begins to yawn.

"No, I can't understand it, Lev Nikoláevich," he will say, returning the book.

It is a mystery to us for whom and by whom these popular books are written. Out of all the books of this kind, read by us, nothing was left but "The Grandfather," by the story-teller Zolotóv, which had a great success both in the school and at home.

Some of these are simply poor compositions, written in a bad literary language and finding no readers with the public at large, and so dedicated to the masses; others, worse still, written not in Russian, but in some newly invented language which is supposed to be the people's language, something like the language in Krylóv's fables; others again are remodellings of foreign books intended for the people, but not popular. The only books that are comprehensible to the people and according to their taste are not such as are written for the people, but such as have their origin in the people, namely, fairy-tales, proverbs, collections of songs, legends, of verses, of riddles, and of late the collection made by Vodovózov, and so on.

One who has not had the experience could hardly believe with what ever new pleasure all similar books, not excepting any, are read, — even the sayings of the Russian people, the bylínas, and the song-books, Snegirév's proverbs, the chronicles, and all the monuments of ancient literature without exception. I have observed that children have a greater liking for the reading of such books than grown persons have; they read them several times over, memorize them, joyfully take them home, and in their games and talks give each other names taken from the ancient bylínas and songs. Grown-up persons, either because they are not so natural, or because they have grown to make a show of their knowledge of the book language, or because they unconsciously feel the necessity of the knowledge of the book language, are less addicted to the reading of such books, and prefer those in which the words, images, and thoughts are half-unintelligible to them.

And yet, no matter how books of this kind are liked by the pupils, the aim, which we probably erroneously put to ourselves, is not attained by them: there still remains the same abyss between these books and the literary language. So far we have found no means of coming out of this false circle, although we are all the time making new experiments and new suppositions, trying to discover our error. We beg all those who have this matter at heart to communicate to us their propositions, experiments, and solutions of the question. The insoluble question for us consists in the following: For the education of the people the possibility and the desire to read good books are peremptory, but the good books are written in a language which the masses do not comprehend. In order to learn to understand, one must read a great deal; in order to read with pleasure, one must comprehend. Where is here the error, and how can we escape this situation?

Maybe there is a transitional literature, which we do not recognize for lack of knowledge; maybe the study of the books current among the people, and the people's view of these books, will reveal to us those paths by which the men of the people obtain the comprehension of the literary language.

We devote a special department in the periodical to the study of this question, and we ask all who understand the importance of this matter to send us their articles upon this subject.

Maybe the cause of it lies in our aloofness from the masses, in the forced education of the upper classes, and matters will be mended only by time, which creates not a chrestomathy, but a whole transitional literature, composed of all books now appearing and organically arranging itself into a course of graded reading. Maybe, too, the masses do not understand and do not wish to understand our literary language because there is nothing for them to understand, because our whole literature is not good for them, and they are themselves evolving a literature for themselves.

Finally, the last proposition, which seems to us the most likely, is that the seeming defect does not lie in

the essence of the case, but in our prepossession with
the thought that the aim of language instruction is to
raise the pupils to the level of the knowledge of the
literary language and, above all, in the rapid acquisition
of that knowledge. It is very likely that the graded
reading, the subject of our dreams, will appear of itself,
and that the knowledge of the literary language will of
its own accord come to each pupil, just as we constantly
see in the case of people who, without understanding, read
indiscriminately the psalter, novels, judicial documents,
and in that way acquire the knowledge of the literary
language.

Supposing this to be so, it is incomprehensible to us
why all the books published are so bad and not to the
people's taste, and we wonder what the schools must do
while waiting for that time to come; for there is one
proposition which we cannot admit, and that is, that,
having convinced ourselves in our mind that the knowledge of the literary language is useful, we should allow
ourselves by forced explanations, memorizing, and repetitions to teach the masses the literary language against
their will, as one teaches French. We must confess that
we have more than once tried to do so within the last two
months, when we invariably ran up against an insuperable loathing in the pupils, proving the falseness of the
measures accepted by us. During these experiments I
convinced myself that explanations of the meaning of
words and of speech in general are quite impossible even
for a talented teacher, not to mention even such favourite
explanations, employed by incapable teachers, as that
"assembly is a certain small synedrion," and so forth.
When explaining any one word, for example, the word
"impression," you either substitute another unintelligible
word in place of the one in question, or you give a whole
series of words, the connection of which is as unintelligible
as the word itself.

Nearly always it is not the word which is unintelligible, but the pupil lacks the very conception expressed by the word. The world is nearly always ready when the idea is present. Besides, the relation of the word to the idea and the formation of new ideas are such a complicated, mysterious, and tender process of the soul that every interference appears as a rude, clumsy force which retards the process of the development.

It is easy enough to say that the pupil must understand, but cannot everybody see what a number of different things may be understood while reading one and the same book? Though missing two or three words in the sentence, the pupil may grasp a fine shade of thought, or its relation to what precedes. You, the teacher, insist on one side of the comprehension, but the pupil does not at all need that which you want to explain to him. At times he may understand you, without being able to prove to you that he has comprehended, all the while dimly guessing and imbibing something quite different, and something very useful and important for him. You exact an explanation from him, and as he is to explain to you in words what impression the words have made upon him, he is silent, or begins to speak nonsense, or lies and deceives; he tries to discover that which you want of him and to adapt himself to your wishes, and so he invents an unexisting difficulty and labours over it; but the general impression produced by the book, the poetical feeling, which has helped him to divine the meaning, is intimidated and beats a retreat.

We read Gógol's "The Elf-king," repeating each period in our own words. Everything went well to the third page, where the following period is to be found: "All those learned people, both of the seminary and of the 'búrsa,' who fostered a certain traditional hatred against each other, were exceedingly poor as regards their means of subsistence and, at the same time, uncommonly voracious, so that it would have been an absolutely impossible matter to ascertain what number of flour and suet dumplings each of them got away with in the course of a supper, and therefore the voluntary contributions of the well-to-do proprietors could not be sufficient."

*Teacher.* Well, what have you read? (Nearly all the children are very well developed.)

*Best pupil.* In the búrsa the people were all big eaters, poor, and at supper got away with a lot of dumplings.

*Teacher.* What else?

*Pupil (a rogue, and having a good memory, says anything that occurs to him).* An impossible matter, the voluntary contributions.

*Teacher (angrily).* You must think. It is not that. What is an impossible matter?

Silence.

*Teacher.* Read it once more.

They read it. Another boy, with a good memory, added a few more words which he happened to recall: "The seminary, the feeding of the well-to-do proprietors could not be sufficient." Not one had understood anything. They began to talk the merest nonsense. The teacher became insistent.

*Teacher.* What is an impossible matter?

He wanted them to say: "It was impossible to ascertain."

*A pupil.* The búrsa is an impossible thing.

*Another pupil.* Very poor impossible.

They read it once more. They hunted for the word which the teacher needed, as for a needle, and they struck every word but the word "ascertain," and they became utterly discouraged. I — that same teacher I am speaking of — did not give in and had them take the whole period to pieces, but now they understood much less than when the first pupil told me the contents. After all there was not much to understand. The carelessly connected and drawn out period gave nothing to the reader; its essence was simple enough: the poor and voracious people got away with dumplings, — that and nothing more the author had intended to convey. I made all the fuss about the form, which was faulty, and by endeavouring to get at it, I only spoiled the whole class for the rest of the afternoon, and had crushed and ruined a mass of budding flowers of a many-sided comprehension.

Upon another occasion I in the same sinful and monstrous manner wasted my time on explaining the meaning of the word "instrument," and with the same disastrous result. On that same day, in the class of drawing, pupil Ch—— protested against his teacher, who demanded that the drawing-books should have "Romáshka's drawings" written upon them. He said that they had themselves drawn in the books, and that Romáshka had only invented the figure and that, therefore, they ought to write "Romáshka's composition," and not "Romáshka's drawing." In what way the distinction of these ideas had found its way into his head — just as now and then, though rarely, participles and introductory clauses appear in their compositions — will remain a mystery to me, into which it will be best not to penetrate.

The pupil must be given an opportunity to acquire new ideas and words from the general context. When he hears or reads an unintelligible word in an intelligible sentence, and then meets it in another sentence, he dimly begins to grasp a new idea, and he finally will come to feel the need of using the word by accident; once used, the word and the idea become his property. And there are a thousand other ways. But consciously to give the pupil new ideas and forms of a word is, in my opinion, as impossible and fruitless as to teach a child to walk by the law of equilibrium.

Every such attempt does not advance the pupil, but only removes him from the aim toward which he is to

tend, like the rude hand of a man, which, wishing to help
the flower to open, crushes everything all around and
violently opens the flower by its petals.

### WRITING, GRAMMAR, AND PENMANSHIP

Writing was taught in the following manner: The
pupils were taught simultaneously to recognize and draw
the letters, to spell and write the words, and to understand what they had read, and to write it down. They
stood at the wall, marking off spaces for themselves with
chalk on the board; one of them dictated whatever
occurred to him, and the others wrote. If there were
many of them, they were divided into several groups.
Then the others, in succession, dictated, and all read each
other's writing.

They wrote printed letters, and at first corrected the
mistakes of the incorrectly formed syllables and the separation of the words, then the mistakes $o - a$, and then
$ye - e$,[1] and so forth. This class formed itself quite
naturally. Every pupil who has learned to make the
letters is possessed by the passion of writing, and, at
first, the doors, the outer walls of the schoolhouse
and of the huts, where the pupils live, are covered with
letters and words, and it affords them the greatest pleasure to be able to write out whole sentences, such as
" Marfútka has had a fight with Olgúshka to-day."

In order to organize this class, the teacher had only to
show the children how to carry on the affair by themselves, just as a grown-up person teaches children any
kind of a game. Indeed, this class has been conducted
without change for two years, and every time as merrily
and as interestingly as a good game. Here we have reading, and pronunciation, and writing, and grammar. With
such writing we obtain in a natural manner the most diffi-

[1] The chie difficulties of Russian orthography.

cult thing for the initial study of language, — the faith in the stability of the form of the word, not only the printed word, but also the oral, — one's own word. I think that every teacher who has taught language, in addition to the use of Vostókov's grammar, has come across this difficulty.

Suppose you want to direct the pupil's attention to some word, say " me." You catch his sentence: " Mikíshka pushed me down the porch," he said.

" Whom did he push down?" you say, asking him to repeat the sentence, and hoping to get " me."

" Us," he replies.

" No, how did you say it?" you ask him.

" We fell down the porch on account of Mikíshka," or " When he pushed us, Praskútka flew down, and I after her," he replies.

Try to find the accusative singular and its ending in that. But he does not see any difference in the words which he employed. And if you take a book or if you repeat his words, he will be analyzing, not the living word, but something quite different. When he dictates, every word of his is caught on the wing by the other pupils and is written down.

" What did you say? How?" and he will not be permitted to change a single letter. Then there are the endless debates about one having written so and another so, and soon the dictating pupil begins to reflect about what he is to say, and he begins to understand that there are two things in speech, — form and contents. He says a certain sentence, thinking only of its meaning, and it escapes his lips like one word. They begin to question him, " How? What?" and he, repeating it several times to himself, becomes sure of the form and of the component parts, and fixes them by means of words.

Thus they write in the third, that is, the lowest, class, some writing in script, and others in printed letters

We not only do not insist on writing in script, but if there were anything which we should permit ourselves to prohibit the pupils, it would be their writing in script, which ruins their handwriting and is illegible. They get used to script in a natural manner: one learns one or two letters from an older boy; others learn from them, and frequently write like this: *uncle*; and before a week has passed, they all write in script.

With penmanship there happened this summer the same that had happened with the mechanical reading. The pupils wrote very wretchedly, and the new teacher introduced writing from copy (again a comfortable and easy method for the teacher). The pupils lost interest, and we were compelled to abandon penmanship and were unable to discover a means for improving the handwriting. The oldest class found that means by itself. Having finished the writing of sacred history, the pupils began to ask to be allowed to take their copy-books home. These copy-books were soiled, torn, and horribly scribbled over. The precise mathematician R—— asked for some scraps of paper, and began to rewrite his history. They all took a liking for that. "Let me have paper! Let me have the copy-book!" and there was started the fashion of penmanship which has continued up to the present in the higher class.

They took their copy-books, placed before them the model alphabet, copied each letter, and contended with each other. In two weeks they made great progress.

Nearly all of us were as children made to eat bread with our other food, though we did not like it, and yet now we do not eat otherwise than with bread. Nearly all of us were compelled to hold the pen with out-stretched fingers, but we held it with bent fingers because they were short, — and now we stretch our fingers. The question then is: Why did they torment us so when what is necessary comes later quite naturally? Will not the desire and the necessity of knowledge of anything else come in the same way?

In the second class compositions are written on slates from oral stories taken from sacred history, and these are later copied on paper. In the lowest, the third class, they write anything they can think of. In addition to that, the youngest in the evening write single sentences, composed by all together. One writes and the others whisper among themselves, noticing his mistakes, and wait only for the end, when they may catch him on a wrong *ye* instead of an *e*, or in an incorrectly placed preposition, and sometimes, in order to make some blunders themselves. It affords them great pleasure to write correctly and to correct the mistakes of others. The older ones get hold of any letter they can find, exercise themselves in the correction of mistakes, and use their utmost endeavour to write well; but they cannot endure grammar and the analysis of the language, and, in spite of our former bias for analysis, admit it only in very small proportions, and fall asleep orve ade the classes.

We have made all kinds of experiments in the instruction of grammar, and we must confess that not one of them has attained its end, — to make this instruction interesting. In the second and the first classes the new teacher made this summer an attempt at explaining the parts of the sentence, and a few of the children at first took interest in them as in charades and riddles. After lessons they frequently hit upon the idea of proposing riddles to each other, and they amused themselves in propounding each other such questions as "Where is the predicate?" on a par with "What sits on the bed hanging down its feet?" Of applications to correct writing there were none, and if there were, they were more faulty than correct.

Just the same happens with the letter *o*, when used for *a*. You tell a pupil that it is pronounced *a* but written *o*, —

and he writes *robota, molina* (instead of *rabota, malina*);
you tell him that two predicates are separated by a comma,
and he writes *I want, to say,* and so forth. It is impossible
to demand of him that he should each time give himself
an account of what in each sentence is a modifier, and
what a predicate. And if he does render himself an
account, he, during the process of the search, loses all
feeling which he needs in order to write correctly the rest,
not to mention the fact that during the syntactic analysis
the teacher is constantly compelled to use cunning before
his pupils and to deceive them, which they are well aware
of. For example: we came across the sentence, "There
were no mountains upon earth."[1] One said that the
subject was "earth," another said that the subject was
"mountains," while we declared that it was an impersonal
sentence. We saw that the pupils acquiesced only out of
politeness, but that they knew full well that our answer
was more stupid than theirs, which we inwardly admitted
to be so.

Having convinced ourselves of the inconvenience of
syntactical analysis, we tried the etymological analysis, —
parts of speech, declensions, and conjugations, and we also
propounded to each other riddles about the dative, about
the infinitive, and about adverbs, and that resulted in the
same tedium, the same abuse of the influence gained by
us, and the same inapplicability. In the upper class they
always write correctly *ye* in the dative and prepositional
cases, but when they correct that mistake in the younger
pupils, they are never able to give any reason why they
do so, and they must be reminded of the cases, in order
to remember the rule: "*Ye* in the dative." The youngest,
who have not yet heard anything about the parts of
speech, frequently call out *sebye ye*, not knowing them-

[1] The difficulty in the Russian sentence is that the subject is put in
the genitive case after a negative copula, hence the sentence becomes
impersonal.

selves why they do so, and apparently happy to have guessed right.

I tried of late an exercise of my own invention with the second class; it was one I, like all inventors, was carried away with, and it appeared unusually convenient and rational to me until I convinced myself of its inconsistencies through practice. Without naming the parts of the sentence, I made them write anything, frequently giving them the theme, that is, the subject, and making them through questions expand the sentence, by adding modifiers, new predicates, subjects, and modifying clauses.

"The wolves are running." When? Where? How? What wolves are running? Who else is running? They are running, and what else are they doing? I thought that by getting used to questions demanding this or that part, they would acquire the distinction of the parts of the sentence and of the parts of speech. So they did, but they grew tired of this, and they inwardly asked themselves what it was for, so that I myself was compelled to ask myself the same question without finding any answer to it. Neither man nor child likes, without a struggle, to give up the living word to be mechanically dismembered and disfigured. There is a certain feeling of self-preservation in the living word. If it is to develop, it tends to develop independently and only in conformity with all vital conditions. The moment you want to catch that word, to tighten it in the vise, to plane it off, and to give it such adornments as this word ought to get, according to your ideas, this word and the live thought and meaning connected with it becomes compressed and conceals itself, and in your hands is left nothing but the shell, on which you may expend all your cunning without harming or helping that word which you wanted to form.

The syntactical and grammatical analyses, the exercises in the expansion of the sentences, have been carried on in the second class until now, but they proceed indolently and, I suppose, will soon entirely disappear of their own accord. In addition to these, we use the following as an exercise in language, although it is not at all of a grammatical character:

(1) We propose to form periods out of certain given words: *Nikoláy, wood, learn,* and they write, "If Nikoláy had not been chopping wood, he would have come to learn," or, "Nikoláy is a good wood chopper, — we must learn from him," and so forth.

(2) We compose verses on a given measure, which exercise amuses particularly the oldest pupils. The verses turn out something like this:

> At the window sits a man
> In a torn coat;
> In the street a peasant leads
> By a rope a goat.

(3) An exercise which is very successful in the lowest class: a certain word is given, at first a noun, then an adjective, an adverb, a preposition. One of the pupils goes outside, and of those who remain each must form a sentence, in which the word is to be contained. The one who went out must guess it.

All these exercises — the writing of sentences from given words, the versification, and the guessing of words — have one common aim: to convince the pupil that the word is one having its own immutable laws, changes, endings, and correlations between these endings, — a conviction which is late in entering their minds, and which is needed before grammar. All these exercises give them pleasure; all the grammatical exercises breed tedium. The strangest and most significant thing is that grammar is dull, although there is nothing easier.

The moment you do not teach grammar from a book, beginning with definitions, a six-year-old child in half an hour begins to decline, conjugate, distinguish genders numbers, tenses, subjects, and predicates, and you feel that he knows it all as well as you do. (In our locality, there is no neuter gender: gun, hay, butter, window, everything is *she*, and grammar is of no avail here. The oldest pupils have known grammar for three years, and yet they make blunders in gender, and they avoid them only to the extent of corrections made and in so far as reading helps them.) Why do I teach them all that, when it appears that they know it as well as I do? Whether I ask him what the genitive plural feminine gender of "great" is, or where the predicate, and where the modifiers are, or what the origin of such and such a word is, — he is in doubt only about the nomenclature, otherwise he will always use an adjective correctly in any case and number you please. Consequently he knows declension. He will never use a sentence without a predicate, and he does not mix it up with its complement. He naturally feels the radical relation of words, and he is more conscious than you of the laws by which words are formed, because no one more frequently invents new words than children. Why, then, this nomenclature, and the demand of philosophical definitions, which are above his strength?

The only explanation for the necessity of grammar, outside of the demand made at examinations, may be found in its application to the regular exposition of ideas. In my own experience I have not found this application, and I do not find it in the examples of the lives of people who do not know grammar and yet write correctly, and of candidates of philology, who write incorrectly, and I hardly find a hint of the fact that the knowledge of grammar is applied to anything whatever by the pupils of the Yásnaya Polyána school. It seems to me that grammar goes by itself as a useless mental gymnastic exercise, and that the language, — the ability to write, read, and understand, goes by itself. Geometry and mathematics in general also appear at first as nothing more than mental gymnastics, but with this difference, that every proposition in geometry, every mathematical definition, brings with it further endless deductions and applications; while in grammar, even if we should agree with those who see in it an application of logic to language, there is a very narrow limit to these deductions and applications. The moment a pupil in one way or other masters a language, all applications from grammar tear away and drop off as something dead and lifeless.

We personally are not yet able completely to renounce the tradition that grammar, in the sense of the laws of language, is necessary for the regular exposition of ideas; it even seems to us that the pupils have a need of grammar, and that in them unconsciously lie the laws of grammar; but we are convinced that the grammar, such as we know it, is not at all the one which the pupils need, and that in this habit of teaching grammar lies some great historical misunderstanding. The child learns that *ye* is to be written in the word *sebye* (self), not because it is in the dative, however frequently he may have been told so, and not merely because he blindly imitates that which he has seen written down a number of times, — he generalizes these examples, only not in the form of the dative, but in some other manner.

We have a pupil from another school, who knows grammar excellently and who is not able to distinguish the third person from the infinitive reflexive, and another pupil, Fédka, who has no conception of the infinitive, and who, nevertheless, makes no mistake, for he explains the difficulty to himself and to others by adding the word "will." [1]

In the Yásnaya Polyána school we regard all known methods for the study of language as legitimate, as in the

[1] The third person present and the infinitive differ only by a soft sign. Of necessity, a passage had to be omitted here, as being one comprehensible only to a Russian student.

case of the study of the rudiments, and we employ them to just such an extent as they are cheerfully accepted by the pupils and in accordance with our knowledge; at the same time we consider none of these methods exceptional, and we continually try to find new methods. We are as little in accord with Mr. Perevlyésski's method, which did not stand a two days' experiment at the Yásnaya Polyána school, as with the very prevalent opinion that the only method to learn language is through writing, although writing forms at the Yásnaya Polyána school the chief method of language instruction. We seek and we hope to find.

## COMPOSITIONS

In the first and second class the choice of compositions is left to the students themselves. A favourite subject for compositions for the first and the second class is the history of the Old Testament, which they write two months after the teacher has told it to them. The first class lately began to write the New Testament, but not approximately as well as the Old; they even made more orthographical mistakes, — they did not understand it so well.

In the first class we tried compositions on given themes The first themes that most naturally occurred to us were the descriptions of simple objects, such as grain, the house, the wood, and so forth; but, to our great surprise, these demands upon our pupils almost made them weep, and, in spite of the aid afforded them by the teacher, who divided the description of the grain into a description of its growth, its change into bread, its use, — they emphatically refused to write upon such themes, or, if they did write, they made the most incomprehensible and senseless mistakes in orthography, in the language and in the meaning.

We tried to give them the description of certain events.

and all were as happy as if a present had been given to them. That which forms the favourite description of the schools — the so-called simple objects, — pigs, pots, a table — turned out to be incomparably more difficult than whole stories taken from their memories. The same mistake was repeated here as in all the other subjects of instruction, — to the teacher the simplest and most general appears as the easiest, whereas for a pupil only the complicated and living appears easy.

All the text-books of the natural sciences begin with general laws, the text-books of language with definitions, history with the division into periods, and even geometry with the definition of the concept of space and the mathematical point. Nearly every teacher, being guided by the same manner of thinking, gives as a first composition the definition of a table or bench, without taking the trouble to consider that in order to define a table or bench one has to stand on a high level of a philosophicoldialectic development, and that the same pupil who weeps over the composition on a bench will excellently describe the feeling of love or anger, the meeting of Joseph with his brothers, or a fight with his companion. The subjects of the compositions were naturally chosen from among descriptions of incidents, relations to persons, and the repetition of stories told.

The writing of compositions is a favourite occupation. The moment the oldest pupils get hold of a pencil and paper outside of school, they do not write "Dear Sir," but some fairy-tale of their own composition. At first I was vexed by the clumsiness and disproportionateness of the structure of the compositions; I thought I had properly inspired them with what was necessary, but they misunderstood me, and everything went badly: they did not seem to recognize any other necessity than that of writing without mistakes. But now the time has come in the natural course of events, and frequently we hear an expression of dissatisfaction when the composition is unnecessarily drawn out, or when there are frequent repetitions and jumps from one subject to another. It is hard to define wherein their demands consist, but these demands are lawful. "It is clumsy!" some of them cry, listening to the composition of a companion; some of them will not read their own after they have found that the composition of a comrade, as read to them, is good; some tear their copy-books out of the hands of the teacher, dissatisfied to hear it sound differently from what they wanted, and read it themselves. The individual characters are beginning to express themselves so definitely that we have experimented on making the pupils guess whose composition we have been reading, and the first class they guess without a mistake.

Exigencies of space make us delay the description of the instruction in language and in other subjects, and the extracts from the diaries of the teachers; here we shall only quote specimens from the writings of two students of the first class without change of orthography and punctuation marks, as given by them.

Composition by B—— (an exceedingly poor pupil, but an original and lively boy) about Túla and about study. The composition about study was quite successful with the boys. B—— is eleven years old; this is his third winter at the Yásnaya Polyána school, but he has studied before.

"About Túla:

"On the following Sunday I again went to Túla. When we arrived, Vladímir Aleksándrovich says to us and Váska Zhdánov go to the Sunday school. We went, and went, and went, and barely found it, we come and we see that all the teachers set. And there I saw the teacher the one that taught us botany. So I say good morning gentlemen! They say good morning. Then I ascended into the class, stood near the table, and I felt so lonely,

that I took and went about Túla. I went and went and
I see a woman selling white-bread. I began to take my
money out of my pocket, when I took it out I began to
buy white-breads, I bought them and went away. And I
saw also a man walking on a tower and looking where it
is burning. I am through with Túla."

"Composition of how I have been studying:

"When I was eight years old, I was sent to the cattle-
yard at Grúmy. There I studied well. And then I felt
lonely, I began to weep. And the old woman took a
stick and began to beat me. And I cried worse than
ever. And a few days later I went home and told everything. And they took me away from there and gave me
to Dúnka's mother. I studied well there and they never
beat me there, and I learned the whole A B C there.
Then they sent me to Fóka Demídovich. He beat me
dreadfully. Once I run away from him, and he told
them to catch me. When they catched me they took
me to him. He took me, stretched me out on a bench
and took into his hands a bundle of rawds and began to
strike me. And I cried with all my might, and when he
had beat me he made me read. And he himself listens
and says: 'What? You son of a b——, just see how
badly you read! Ah, what a swine!'"

Now here are two specimens of Fédka's compositions:
one on the presented theme; the other, chosen by himself, on his travel to Túla. (Fédka is studying the third
winter. He is ten years old.)

"About grain:

"Grain grows from the ground. At first it is green
grain. When it grows up a little, there sprout from it
ears and the women reap it. There is also grain like
grass, that the cattle eat very well."

That was the end of it. He felt that it was not good,
and was aggrieved. About Túla he wrote the following
without corrections.

"About Túla:

"When I was small I was five years old; then I heard the people went to some kind of Túla and I myself did not know what kind of a Túla it was. So I asked father. Dad! to what kind of Túla do you travel, oh it must be fine? Father says: it is. So I say, Dad! take me with you, I will see Túla Father says well all right, let the Sunday come I will take you. I was happy began to run and jump over the bench. After those days came Sunday. I just got up in the morning and father was already hitching the horses in the yard, I began to dress myself quickly. The moment I was dressed and went out into the yard, father had already hitched the horses. I sat down in the sleigh and I started. We travelled, and travelled, and made fourteen versts. I saw a tall church and I cried: father! see what a tall church. Father says: there is a smaller church but more butiful, I began, to ask him, father let us go there, I will pray to God. Father went. When we came, they suddenly rang the bell, I was frightened and asked father what it was, whether they were beating drums. Father says: no, mass is beginning. Then we went to church to pray to God. When we were through praying, we went to the market. And so I walk, and walk and stumble all the time, I kept looking around me. So we came to the market, I saw they were selling white-breads and wanted to take without money. And father says to me, do not take, or they will take your cap away. I say why will they take it, and father says, do not take without money, I say well give me ten kopeks, I will buy me a small white-bread. Father gave me, I bought three white-breads and ate them up and I say: Father, what fine white-breads. When we bought everything, we went to the horses and gave them to drink, gave them hay, when they had eaten, we hitched up the horses and went home, went into the hut and undressed myself and began to tell everybody how

I was in Túla, and how father and I were in church, and prayed to God. Then I fell asleep and I see in my dream as though father was again going to Túla. I immediately awoke, and I saw all were asleep, I took and went to sleep."

### SACRED HISTORY

From the foundation of the school even up to the present time the instruction in sacred and Russian history has been carried on in this manner: The children gather about the teacher, and the teacher, being only guided by the Bible, and for Russian history by Pogódin's "Norman Period," and Vodovózov's collection, tells the story, and then asks questions, and all begin to speak at the same time. When there are too many voices speaking at the same time, the teacher stops them, making them speak one at a time; the moment one hesitates, he asks others. When the teacher notices that some have not understood anything, he makes one of the best pupils repeat it for the benefit of those who have not understood. This was not premeditated, but grew up naturally, and it has been found equally successful with five and with thirty pupils if the teacher follows all, does not allow them to cry and repeat what has once been said, and does not permit the shouts to become maddening, but regulates that stream of merry animation and rivalry to the extent to which he needs it.

In the summer, during the frequent visits and changes of teachers, this order was changed, and the teaching of history was much less successful. The general noise was incomprehensible to the new teacher; it seemed to him that those who were telling the story through the noise would not be able to tell it singly; it seemed to him that they holloaed only to make a noise, and, above all, he felt uncomfortably warm in the mass of those closely pressing on his back and to the very mouths of the boys. (In order to comprehend better, the children have to be close to the man who is speaking, to see every change of his facial expressions, every motion of his. I have observed more than once that those passages are best understood where the speaker makes a correct gesture or a correct intonation.)

The new teacher introduced the sitting on benches and single answers. The one called out was silent and embarrassed, and the teacher, looking aside, with a *sweet* expression of submission to fate, or with a meek smile, said, " Well, and then ? Well, very well! " and so forth, — in that teacher's manner which we all know so well.

Moreover, I have convinced myself in practice that there is nothing more injurious to the development of the child than that kind of single questioning and the authoritative relation of teacher to pupils, arising from it, and for me there is nothing more provoking than such a spectacle.

A big man torments a little fellow, having no right to do so. The teacher knows that the pupil is tormented, as he stands blushing and perspiring before him; he himself feels uncomfortable and tired, but he has a rule by which a pupil may be taught to speak alone.

Why one should be taught to speak singly, nobody knows. Perhaps in order to make the child read a fable in the presence of his or her Excellency. I shall probably be told that without it it is impossible to determine the degree of his knowledge. To which I shall answer that it is indeed impossible for an outsider to determine the knowledge of a pupil in an hour, while the teacher always feels the measure of that knowledge without the pupil's answer and without examinations. It seems to me that the method of this single asking is the reminiscence of an old superstition. Anciently the teacher, who made his pupil learn by heart everything, could not, in any other way, determine the knowledge of his pupil except by making him repeat everything word for word. Then it was found that the repetition of words learned by heart was not knowledge, and the pupils were made to repeat in their own words; but the method of calling out singly and the demand of answering at the teacher's request was not changed. They left out of consideration that one may expect at any time and under all conditions that the pupil will repeat the words of the psalter or of a fable, but that, in order to be able to catch the contents of speech and to render it in his own words, the pupil must be in a certain favourable mood for it.

Not only in the lower schools and in the gymnasia, but even in the universities, I do not understand examinations according to given questions otherwise than under a system of memorizing word for word, or sentence for sentence. In my day (I left the university in the year 1845), I studied before the examinations, not word for word, but sentence for sentence, and I received five only from those professors whose notes I had learned by heart.

The visitors, who were so detrimental to the instruction in the Yásnaya Polyána school, in one way were very useful to me. They completely convinced me that the recitation of lessons and the examinations were a remnant of the superstitions of the mediæval school, and that with the present order of things they were positively impossible and only injurious. Frequently I was carried away by a childish vanity, wishing in an hour's time to show to an honoured visitor the knowledge of the pupils, and it turned out either that the visitor convinced himself that the pupils knew that which they did not know (I entertained him by some hocus-pocus) or that the visitor supposed that they did not know that which they knew very well. Such a tangle of misunderstandings took place between me and the visitor — a clever, talented man and a specialist in his business — during a perfect freedom of relations! What, then, must take place during the inspections of directors, and so forth, — even if we leave out of consideration that disturbance in the progress of teaching and the indefiniteness of ideas produced in the pupils by such examinations?

At the present time I am convinced of this: to make a résumé of all the pupil's knowledge is as impossible for the teacher as it is for an outsider, just as it is impossible to make a résumé of my own knowledge and yours in respect to any science whatsoever. If a forty-year-old man were to be taken to an examination in geography, it would be as stupid and strange as when a ten-year-old child is led to the examination. Both of them have to answer by rote, and in an hour of time it is impossible to find out their actual knowledge. In order to find out the knowledge of either, it is necessary to live for months with them.

Where examinations are introduced (by examination I understand every demand for an answer to a question), there only arises a new subject, demanding special labour, special ability: that subject is called "preparation for examinations or lessons." A pupil in the gymnasium studies history, mathematics, and, the main subject, the art of answering questions at the examinations. I do not regard this art as a useful subject of instruction. I, the teacher, judge of the degree of my pupils' knowledge as correctly as I judge of the degree of my own knowledge, although neither the pupils nor I myself recite any lessons. If an outsider wants to judge of the degree of that knowledge, let him live awhile with us and let him study the results of our knowledge and their applications to life. There is no other means, and all attempts at examination are only a deception, a lie, and an obstacle to instruction. In matters of instruction there is but one independent judge, the teacher, and only the pupils can control him.

During the history lessons the pupils answer all at once, not in order that any one might verify their knowledge, but because they feel the need of strengthening by

means of words the impression which they have received.
In the summer neither the new teacher nor I understood
that; we saw in that only a verification of their knowledge, and so we found it more convenient to verify it
singly. I did not then as yet reflect on the reason for its
being tedious and bad, but my faith in the rule of the
pupils' freedom saved me. The majority began to feel
dull; three of the boldest boys always answered alone
three of the most timid were constantly silent and wept
and received zeros.

During the summer I neglected the classes of sacred
history, and the teacher, a lover of order, had full liberty
to seat the pupils on the benches, to torment them singly,
and to murmur about the stubbornness of the children.
I several times advised him to allow the children in the
history class to leave the benches, but my advice was
taken by the teacher as a sweet and pardonable originality
(just as I know in advance that my advice will be
regarded as such by the majority of readers), and the
former order prevailed so long as the old teacher did not
return, and it was only in the diary of that teacher that
such entries were made: "I cannot get anything out of
Sávin; Gríshin did not tell a thing; Pétka's stubbornness
is a surprise to me, — he has not spoken a word; Sávin is
even worse than before," and so forth.

Sávin is a ruddy, chubby boy, with gleaming eyes and
long lashes, the son of an innkeeper or a merchant, in a
tanned fur coat, in small boots that fit him well, as
they are not his father's, and in a red cotton shirt and
trousers. The sympathetic and handsome personality of
that boy struck me more especially because in the class
of arithmetic he was the first, on account of the force of
his imagination and merry animation. He also reads and
writes not at all badly. But the moment he is asked a
question he presses his pretty curly head sidewise, tears
appear on his long lashes, and he looks as though he

wanted to hide somewhere from everybody, and it is evident that he is suffering beyond endurance. If he is made to learn by heart, he will recite a piece, but he is not able, or has not the courage, to express anything in his own words. It is either some fear inspired by his former teacher (he had studied before with a teacher of the clerical profession), or lack of confidence in himself, or his awkward position among boys who, in his opinion, stand below him, or aristocratism or annoyance that in this alone he is behind the rest and because he once showed himself in a bad light, or his little soul was offended by some careless word escaped from the teacher, or all these causes acting together, — God knows which, — but his bashfulness, though not a good feature in itself, is certainly inseparably connected with everything that is best in his childish soul. It is possible to knock all that out with a physical or moral stick, but the danger is that all the precious qualities, without which the teacher would find it hard to lead him on, might be knocked out at the same time.

The new teacher listened to my advice, dismissed the pupils from the benches, permitted them to crawl whereever they pleased, even on his back, and that same day all began to recite incomparably better, so that the entry was made in the teacher's diary, "Stubborn Sávin said a few words."

There is in the school something indefinite, which almost does not submit to the guidance of the teacher, and that is the spirit of the school. This spirit is subject to certain laws and to the negative influence of the teacher, that is, the teacher must avoid certain things in order not to break up that spirit. The spirit of the school is, for example, always in inverse relation to the compulsion and order of the school, in inverse relation to the interference of the teacher in the pupils' manner of thinking, in direct relation to the number of pupils, in inverse relation to the duration of a lesson, and so on. This spirit of the school is something that is rapidly communicated from pupil to pupil, and even to the teacher, something that is palpably expressed in the sound of the voice, in the eyes, the movements, the tension of the rivalry, — something very tangible, necessary, and extremely precious, and therefore something that ought to be the aim of every teacher. Just as the saliva in the mouth is necessary for the digestion, but is disagreeable and superfluous without food, even so this spirit of strained animation, though tedious and disagreeable outside the class, is a necessary condition for the assimilation of mental food. It is impossible to invent and artificially to prepare this mood, nor is it necessary to do so because it always makes its appearance of its own accord.

In the beginning of the school I made mistakes. The moment a boy began to comprehend badly and unwillingly, when the so habitual dulness of the school came over him, I used to say, "Jump awhile!" The boy began to jump; others, and he with them, laughed; and after the jumping the pupil was a different boy. But, after having repeated this jumping several times, it turned out that when I told the boy to jump he was overcome by a greater tedium, and he began to weep. He saw that he was not in the mood in which he ought to be, and yet he was not able to control his own soul, and did not wish to allow anybody else to control it. A child and a man are receptive only when in an excited state, therefore it is a great blunder to look upon the happy spirit of a school as upon an enemy, an obstacle, though we are often inclined to regard it as such.

But when the animation in a large class is so strong that it interferes with a teacher in his attempt to guide the class, then one feels tempted to cry out against the children and to subdue that spirit. If that animation has the lesson for an object, then nothing better is to be desired. But if the animation has passed over to another object, the fault is with the teacher who did not manage that animation properly. The problem of a teacher, which nearly every one carries out unconsciously, consists in constantly giving food to this animation and giving it the reins. You ask one pupil, and another wants to answer: he knows it, — he is bending over to you and gazing at you with both his eyes; he is scarcely able to keep his words back; he eagerly follows the story-teller and will not forgive him a single mistake; ask him, and he will tell you impassionately, and that which he will tell you will for ever impress itself upon his mind. But keep him in this tension, without allowing him to talk for half an hour, and he will pass his time in pinching his neighbour.

Another example: Walk out of a class of the county school, or from a German school, where it has been quiet, leaving the order that they are to proceed with their work, and half an hour later listen at the door; the class is animated, but the subject of the animation is different, it is the so-called mischievousness. We have often made this experiment in our classes. Leaving the class in the middle, when the shouting was at the loudest, we would return to the door to listen, and we would find that the boys continued to tell their stories, correcting and verifying each other, and frequently they would entirely quiet down, instead of being naughty without us.

Just as with the order of seating the pupils on the benches and asking them questions singly, even so with this order there are simple rules which one must know and without which the first experiment may be a failure. One must watch the criers who repeat the last words said, only to increase the noise. It is necessary to see to it that the charm of the noise should not become their main purpose and problem. It is necessary to test some pupils, as to whether they are able to tell everything by themselves, and whether they have grasped the whole meaning. If there are too many pupils, they ought to be divided into a number of divisions, and the pupils ought to tell the respective story to each other by divisions.

There is no need of fearing because a newly arrived pupil does not open his mouth for a month. All that is necessary is to watch whether he is busy with the story or with something else. Generally a newly arrived pupil grasps only the material side of the matter, and is all rapt in observing how the pupils sit and lie, how the teacher's lips are moving, how they all cry out at once; if he is a quiet boy, he will sit down just as the others do; if he is bold, he will cry like the rest, without getting the meaning of what is said, and only repeating the words of his neighbour. The teacher and his companions stop him, and he understands that something else is meant. A little time will pass, and he will begin to tell a story. It is difficult to find out how and when the flower of comprehension will open up in him.

Lately I had occasion to watch such an opening of the bud of comprehension in a very timid girl who had kept silent for a month. Mr. U—— was telling something, and I was an outside spectator and made my observations. When all began to tell the story, I noticed that Marfútka climbed down from the bench with the gesture with which story-tellers change the position of hearer to that of narrator, and came nearer. When all began to shout, I looked at her: she barely moved her lips, and her eyes were full of thought and animation. Upon meeting my glance, she lowered hers. A minute later I again looked around, and she was again whispering something to herself. I asked her to tell the story, and she was completely lost. Two days later she told a whole story beautifully.

The best proof that the pupils of our school remember

what is told them is found in the stories which they themselves write down from memory, given here with the correction of the orthographical mistakes only.

Extract from the note-book of ten-year-old M——:

"God commanded Abraham to bring his son Isaac as an offering. Abraham took two servants with him. Isaac carried the wood and the fire, and Abraham carried the knife. When they came to Mount Hor, Abraham left his two servants there and himself went with Isaac up the mountain. Says Isaac: 'Father, we have everything, where, then, is the victim?'

"Says Abraham: 'God has commanded me to sacrifice thee.'

"So Abraham made a fire and put his son down.

"Says Isaac: 'Father, bind me, or else I will jump up and kill thee.'

"Abraham took and tied him. He just swung his arm, and an angel flew down from the heavens and held back his arm and said: 'Abraham, do not place thine hand on thy young son, God sees thy faith.'

"Then the angel says to him: 'Go into the bush, a wether is caught there, bring him in place of thy son,' and Abraham brought a sacrifice to God.

"Then came the time for Abraham to marry off his son. They had a servant Eliezer. Abraham called up the servant and says he: 'Swear to me that thou wilt not take a bride from our town, but that thou wilt go where I send thee.'

"Abraham sent him to Nahor in the land of Mesopotamia. Eliezer took the camels and went away. When he came to a well he began to speak: 'Lord, give me such a bride, as will come first, and will give to drink to me and also to my camels,— she shall be the bride of my master Isaac.'

"Eliezer had barely said these words, when a maiden came. Eliezer began to ask her to give him to drink.

She gave him to drink, and says she: 'Maybe thy camels want to drink.'

"Says Eliezer: 'All right, give them to drink.'

"She gave the camels to drink, then Eliezer gave her a necklace, and says he: 'May I not stay overnight in your house?'

"Says she: 'Thou mayest.'

"When they came to the house, her relatives were eating supper, and they put Eliezer down to eat supper.

"Says Eliezer: 'I will not eat until I have said a word.'

"Eliezer told it to them.

"Said they: 'We are willing, how is she?'

"They asked her, — she was willing. Then her father and mother blessed Rebecca, Eliezer sat down with her, and they rode away, and Isaac was walking over the field. Rebecca saw Isaac and she covered herself with a towel. Isaac went up to her, took her hand, and led her to his house, and they were married."

From the note-book of the boy I—— F——, about Jacob:

"Rebecca had been sterile for nineteen years, then she bore twins, — Esau and Jacob. Esau was a hunter, and Jacob helped his mother. One day Esau went to kill beasts and he killed none and came home angry; and Jacob was eating a mess of pottage. Esau came and says he: 'Let me have of that mess.'

"Says Jacob: 'Give me thy birthright.'

"Says Esau: 'Take it.'

"'Swear.'

"Esau swore. Then Jacob gave Esau of the mess of pottage.

"When Isaac grew blind, he said: 'Esau, go and kill me some venison!'

"Esau went, Rebecca heard it, and says she to Jacob: 'Go and kill two kids.'

"Jacob went and killed two kids and brought them to his mother. She roasted them and wrapped Jacob in a skin, and Jacob brought the food to his father, and says he: 'I have brought thee thy favourite dish.'

"Says Isaac: 'Come up nearer to me.'

"Jacob came nearer. Isaac began to touch his body, and says he: 'It is Jacob's voice and Esau's body.'

"Then he blessed Jacob. Jacob just came out of the door, and Esau came in through the door, and says he: 'Here, father, is thy favourite dish.'

"Says Isaac: 'Esau was here before.'

"'No, father, Jacob has deceived thee,' and he himself went through the door, and wept, and says he: 'Let father die, and then I will get even with thee.'

"Rebecca says to Jacob: 'Go and ask thy father's benediction and then go to thine uncle Laban.'

"Isaac blessed Jacob, and he went to his uncle Laban. Here night overtook him. He stayed overnight in the field; he found a rock, put it under his head, and fell asleep. Suddenly he saw something in his dream, as though a ladder were standing from earth to heaven, and the angels were going up and down it, and on the top the Lord himself was standing, and says he:

"'Jacob, the land on which thou liest I give to thee and to thy descendants.'

"Jacob arose, and says he: 'How terrible it is here, evidently this is God's house, I will come back from there, and will build a church here.' Then he lighted a lamp, and he went on,—he saw shepherds herding some cattle. Jacob began to ask of them where his uncle Laban was living.

"The shepherds said: 'There is his daughter, she is driving the sheep to water.'

"Jacob went up to her, she could not push away the stone from the well. Jacob pushed the stone away and he watered the sheep, and says he: 'Whose daughter art thou?'

"She replied: 'Laban's.'

"'I am thy cousin.'

"They kissed each other and went home. Uncle Laban received him, and says he: 'Jacob, stay with me, I will pay thee.'

"Says Jacob: 'I will not live with thee for pay, but give me thy younger daughter Rachel.'

"Says Laban: 'Live seven years with me, then will I give thee my younger daughter Rachel, for we have no right to give a younger daughter away sooner.'

"Jacob lived for seven years with his uncle, then Laban gave him Rachel."

From the note-book of eight-year-old T—— F——, about Joseph:

"Jacob had twelve sons. He loved Joseph best of all, and had made for him a many-coloured dress. Then Joseph saw two dreams, and he told them to his brothers: 'It was as though we were reaping rye in the field and we reaped twelve sheaves. My sheaf was standing straight, and the eleven sheaves were bowing before my sheaf.'

"Say the brothers: 'Is it really so that we shall bow to thee?'

"And he had another dream: 'It was as though there were eleven stars in heaven, and the sun and moon were bowing to my star.'

"Say father and mother: 'Is it possible we shall bow before thee?'

"His brothers went a long distance away to herd cattle, then the father sent Joseph to take some food to his brothers. His brothers saw him, and say they: 'There comes our reader of dreams. Let us put him down in a bottomless well.'

"Reuben was thinking to himself: 'The moment they turn away, I will pull him out.' And there merchants came by. Says Reuben: 'Let us sell him to the Egyptian merchants.'

"They sold Joseph, and the merchants sold him to Potiphar the courtier. Potiphar loved him, and his wife loved him. Potiphar was absent somewhere, and his wife says to Joseph:

"'Joseph, let us kill my husband, and I will marry thee.'

"Says Joseph: 'If thou sayest that a second time, I will tell thy husband.'

"She took him by his garment and cried out loud. The servants heard her and came rushing in. Then Potiphar arrived. His wife told him that Joseph had intended to kill him, and then to marry her. Potiphar ordered him to be put in jail. As Joseph was a good man, he deserved well there, and he was made to look after the prison. Once upon a time Joseph went through the jail and saw two men sitting in sorrow. Joseph went up to them, and says he:

"'Why are ye so saddened?'

"Say they: 'We have had two dreams in one night, and there is nobody to explain them to us.'

"Says Joseph: 'What is it?'

"The cupbearer began to tell him: 'I dreamt that I had picked three berries, squeezed the juice, and given it to the king.'

"Says Joseph: 'Thou wilt be in thy place in three days.'

"Then the steward began to tell: 'I dreamt that I carried twelve loaves in a basket, and the bird flew about and picked at the bread.'

"Joseph said: 'Thou wilt be hanged in three days, and the birds will fly about and will pick thy body.'

"And so it happened. Once Pharaoh had two visions in one night and he called together all his wise men, and they could not explain his dreams to him. The cupbearer remembered and said:

"'I have a certain man in mind.'

## THE SCHOOL AT YÁSNAYA POLYÁNA 307

"The king sent his carriage for him. When he was brought, the king began to say: 'I dreamt that I stood on the bank of a river and there came out seven fat kine, and seven lean ones; the lean ones threw themselves on the fat ones and ate them up and did not get fat.'

"And he had another vision: 'I dreamt that there were growing seven full ears on one stalk, and seven empty ones; the empty ones threw themselves on the full ones, ate them up, and did not grow full.'

"Joseph said: 'This means that there will be seven fruitful years and seven hungry years.'

"The king gave Joseph a gold chain over his shoulder and the ring from his right hand, and told him to build granaries."

All that has been said refers to the teaching of sacred and Russian and natural history, of geography, partly of physics, chemistry, zoology, in general of all subjects except singing, mathematics, and drawing. About the instruction in sacred history in particular at that time I must say as follows:

First, why the Old Testament is chosen before anything else. Not only was the knowledge of sacred history demanded by the pupils and their parents, but I also discovered that of all oral information, which I had tried in the period of three years, nothing so fitted the comprehension of the boys' minds as the Bible. The same thing was repeated in all the other schools which I had had occasion to examine in the beginning. I tried the New Testament, Russian history, and geography; I tried the favourite subject of our day, — the explanations of the phenomena of Nature, — but all that was easily forgotten and was not readily listened to. On the other hand, the Old Testament was remembered and gladly repeated, with enthusiasm, both at school and at home, and it left such an impression upon the children that, two months after it had been told to them, they wrote down sacred history from memory in their note-books, with but few omissions.

It seems to me that the book of the childhood of the race will always be the best book of the childhood of each man. It seems to me impossible to put another book in its place. It seems to me injurious to change and shorten the Bible, as is done in Sonntag's text-books, and so forth. Everything, every word in it, is true, as revelation and as art. Read about the creation of the world in the Bible and in the short Sacred History, and the transformation of the Bible in the Sacred History will appear quite unintelligible to you; from the Sacred History you cannot learn otherwise than by memorizing, while in the Bible there is presented to the child a majestic and living picture, which he will never forget. The omissions in the Sacred History are quite unintelligible and only impair the character and beauty of Holy Scripture. Why, for example, do all the sacred histories omit that when there was nothing, the Spirit of God was borne over the abyss, that God, having created, surveyed His creation and saw that all was well, and that then it was morning and evening of such and such a day? Why do they leave out that God breathed the soul through the nostrils, that, having taken out a rib from Adam, he filled up the place with flesh, and so forth? Let uncorrupted children read the Bible, and then you will understand to what extent that is necessary and true. It may be that spoiled young ladies must not get the Bible into their hands, but when I read to peasant children, I did not leave out a single word. And nobody giggled behind somebody's back, and all listened with trepidation and natural awe. The story of Lot and his daughters, the story of Judas, provoke horror, not laughter.

How comprehensible and clear, particularly for a child, everything is, and, at the same time, how stern and serious! I can't understand what kind of an education would be possible if it were not for that book. And yet it seems if we learn these stories only in childhood and then partly forget them,—what good are they to us? And would it not be the same if we did not know them at all?

This seems so only so long as you do not teach others, when you have a chance to watch all the elements of your own development in other children. It seems that it is possible to teach the children to write and read, to give them a conception of history, geography, and the phenomena of Nature, without the Bible and before the Bible; and yet that is not done anywhere,—everywhere the child first learns the Bible, stories and extracts from it. The first relation of the teacher to the pupil is based upon that book. Such a universal phenomenon is not accidental. My absolutely free relation to the pupils in the beginning of the Yásnaya Polyána school helped me to find an explanation for this phenomenon.

A child, or man, entering school (I make no distinction between one of ten, thirty, or seventy years of age), brings with him his familiar and favourite view of things, as taken away by him from life. In order that a man of any age whatsoever should begin to learn, it is necessary that he should like learning. In order that he should like learning, he must recognize the falseness and insufficiency of his view of things and he must divine the new world conception, which the instruction is to open to him. Not one man or child would be able to learn, if the future of his learning presented itself to him only as an art of reading, writing, and counting; not one teacher would be able to teach, if he did not have in his power a higher world conception than what the pupils have. In order that the pupil may entirely surrender himself to the teacher, there must be lifted for him one side of the shroud which has been concealing from him all the charm of that world of thought, knowledge, and poetry, to which instruction was to introduce him. Only by being under the spell of that brilliant world ahead of him is the pupil able to work over himself in the manner in which we want him to.

What means have we, then, to lift that edge of the curtain for the pupil? As I have said, I thought, just as many think, that, being myself in that world to which I am to introduce the pupils, I could easily do so, and I taught the rudiments, I explained the phenomena of Nature, I told them, as it says in the A B C's, that the fruits of learning are sweet, but the pupils did not believe me and kept aloof. I tried to read the Bible to them, and I completely took possession of them. The edge of the curtain was lifted, and they surrendered themselves to me unconditionally. They fell in love with the book, with the study, and with me. All I had now to do was to guide them on.

After the Old Testament I told them the New, and they loved studying and me more and more. Then I told them universal, Russian, and natural history, when we were through with the Bible; they listened to everything, believed everything, begged to go on and on, and ever new perspectives of thought, knowledge, and poetry were opened up to them.

It may be this was an accident. It may be that in some other school the same results were obtained by beginning in an entirely different manner. Maybe. But this accidentalness was repeated too invariably in all schools and in all families, and the explanation of this phenomenon is too apparent to me to permit of any assumption that it is accidental.

There is no book like the Bible to open up a new world to the pupil and to make him without knowledge love knowledge. I speak even of those who do not look upon the Bible as a revelation. At least, there is no production that I know of, which unites all the sides of human thought in such a compressed poetical form as is to be found in the Bible. All the questions from the phenomena of Nature are explained by this book; all the primitive relations of men with each other, of the family, of the state, of religion, are for the first time consciously recognized in this book. The generalizations of ideas, wisdom, in a childishly simple form, for the first time spell the pupil's mind. The lyricism of David's psalms acts not only upon the minds of grown pupils, but everybody for the first time learns from this book the whole charm of the epos in its inimitable simplicity and strength.

Who has not wept over the story of Joseph and his meeting with his brothers? Who has not narrated with a sinking heart the story of Samson bound and deprived of his hair, as he, taking vengeance on his enemies, himself perishes under the ruins of the fallen palace, and a hundred other impressions, on which we have been brought up as on our mothers' milk?

Let those who deny the educational value of the Bible, who say that the Bible has outlived its usefulness, invent such a book, such stories, which explain the phenomena of Nature, or the phenomena from universal history, or from their imagination, which will be as readily received as the Biblical accounts, and then we shall admit that the Bible has outlived its usefulness.

Pedagogy serves as a verification of very many vital phenomena, and of social and abstract questions.

Materialism will then only have the right to announce itself a victor when the Bible of materialism shall be written, and the children are educated by that Bible. Owen's attempt cannot be regarded as a proof of such a possibility, just as the growth of a lemon-tree in a Moscow hothouse is not a proof that trees can grow without the open sky and the sun.

I repeat my conviction, which, perhaps, is deduced from a one-sided experience. Without the Bible the development of a child or a man is unthinkable in our society, just as it was unthinkable in Greek society without Homer. The Bible is the only book for the first reading of children. The Bible, both as to its contents and to its form, ought to serve as a model of all manuals and readers for children. An idiomatic translation of the Bible would be the best popular book. The appearance of such a translation in our time would be an epoch in the history of the Russian nation.

Now as to the instruction in sacred history. All the short sacred histories in the Russian language I consider a double crime: against its holiness, and against poetry. All these rifacimentos, having in view the facility of the study of sacred history, only make it more difficult. The Bible is read as a pleasure, at home, leaning the head on the arm; the abbreviated stories are learned by heart with the aid of a pointer. Not only are these short stories dull and incomprehensible, they also spoil the ability to understand the poetry of the Bible. I have observed more than once that bad, unintelligible language impairs the receptiveness of the inner meaning of the Bible. Unintelligible words, however, such as occur in the Bible, are remembered together with the incidents; they arrest the attention of the pupils by their novelty, and, as it were, serve as guide-posts in their stories.

Very frequently a pupil speaks only in order to make use of a pretty phrase for which he has taken a liking, and then the simplicity of imbibing the contents only is gone. I have also observed that pupils from other schools always feel much less or not at all the charm of the Biblical stories, which is destroyed by the necessity of memorizing and by the rude methods of the teacher connected with it. These pupils have even spoiled the younger pupils and their brothers, in the manner of whose narration there were reflected certain trite methods of the abbreviated sacred histories. Such trite stories have, by means of these injurious books, found their way among the masses, and frequently the pupils bring with them from home peculiar legends of the creation of the world, of Adam, and of Joseph the Beautiful. These pupils do not experience that which the fresh pupils feel when they listen to the Bible and with trepidation catch each word and think that now, at last, all the wisdom of the world will be revealed to them.

I have always taught sacred history from the Bible, and I regard any other instruction as injurious.

The New Testament is similarly told according to the Gospel and is later written down in note-books. The New Testament is not comprehended so well, and therefore demands more frequent repetitions.

Here are a few specimens from the stories of the New Testament.

From the copy-book of the boy I—— M——, about the Lord's supper:

"Once upon a time Jesus Christ sent His disciples to the city of Jerusalem and said to them: 'If you come across a man with water, follow him and ask him: Master, show us a room where we can prepare the passover. He will show you, and you prepare it there.'

"They went and saw what He had told them, and they prepared it. In the evening Jesus Himself went there with His disciples. During the supper Jesus Christ took off His garment and girded Himself with a towel. Then he took the laver and filled it with water and went to each disciple and washed his feet. When He went up to Peter and wanted to wash his feet, Peter said:

"'Lord! Thou wilt never wash my feet.'

"And Jesus Christ said to him: 'If I am not going to wash thy feet, thou wilt not be with Me in the Kingdom of Heaven.'

"Then Peter was frightened and says he: 'Lord! Not only my feet, but even my head and my whole body.'

"And Jesus said to him: 'Only the pure one has to get his feet washed.'

"Then Jesus Christ dressed Himself and sat down at the table, took the bread, blessed it and broke it and began to give it to His disciples, and He said: 'Take it and eat it,—it is My body.'

"They took it and ate it. Then Jesus took a bowl of wine, blessed it, and began to carry it around to the disciples, and He said: 'Take it and drink it,—it is My blood of the New Testament.'

"They took it and drank it. Then Jesus Christ said: 'One of you will betray Me.'

"And the disciples began to say: 'Lord, is it I?'

"And says Jesus Christ: 'No.'

"Then Judas says: 'Lord, is it I!'

"And Jesus Christ said half-aloud: 'Yes.'

"After that Jesus Christ said to His disciples: 'He to whom I shall give a piece of bread will betray Me.'

"Then Jesus Christ gave Judas a piece of bread. Then Satan took his abode in him, so that he was abashed and went out of the room."

From the copy-book of the boy R—— B——:

"Then Jesus Christ went with His disciples into the garden of Gethsemane to pray to God, and He said to His disciples: 'Wait for Me and do not sleep.'

"When Jesus came and saw that His disciples were asleep, He wakened them and said: 'You could not wait one hour for Me.'

"Then He went again to pray to God. He prayed to God and said: 'Lord, cannot this cup pass by?' and He prayed so long to God that He began to sweat blood. An angel flew down from heaven and began to fortify Jesus. Then Jesus returned to His disciples and said to them: 'Why are ye sleeping? The hour is coming when the Son of man will give Himself up into the hands of His enemies.'

"And Judas said to the high priest: 'Whom I shall kiss, that one take.'

"Then the disciples went after Jesus and they saw a crowd of people. Judas went up to Jesus and wanted to kiss Him. So Jesus says:

"'Art thou betraying Me by a kiss?' and to the people He says: 'Whom are ye seeking?'

"They said to Him: 'Jesus of Nazareth.'

"Jesus said: 'I am He.'

"With that word all fell."

## HISTORY AND GEOGRAPHY

Having finished the Old Testament, I naturally thought of teaching history and geography, both because these subjects are taught in all children's schools, just as I had learned them, and because the history of the Jews of the Old Testament seemed naturally to lead the children to the questions where, when, and under what conditions certain incidents had taken place, what Egypt was, and Pharaoh, and the Assyrian king, and so forth.

I began history, as is always done, with antiquity. But neither Mommsen, nor Duncker, nor all my efforts, were able to make it interesting. They felt no interest in Sesostris, in the Egyptian pyramids, and in the Phœnicians. I had hoped that questions, such as who the nations were that had anything to do with the Jews and where the Jews lived and wandered, would interest them; but the pupils were in no need of this information. The Pharaohs and Egypt and Palestine, which have existed sometime and somewhere, do not in the least satisfy them. The Jews are their heroes, all the others are unnecessary, superfluous persons. I did not succeed in making heroes out of the Egyptians and Phœnicians for lack of material. No matter how much in detail we may know how pyramids were built, in what condition and relation to each other the castes were, — *what good is all that to us?* — to us, that is, the children? In those histories there is no Abraham, Isaac, Jacob, Joseph, Samson. There were a few things which they remembered and liked in ancient history, such as Semiramis, and so forth, but that was retained only incidentally, not because it explained anything, but because it was artistic and fairy-like. But such passages were rare; the rest was dull, aimless, and I was compelled to abandon the study of universal history.

I was confronted with the same failure in geography as in history. I sometimes tell them anything that occurs to me from Greek, English, Swiss history, without any connection, and only as an instructive and artistic fable.

After universal history I had to experiment on our native Russian history, and I began that cheerless Russian history, which we know so well as neither artistic nor instructive, in the many remodellings from Ishímova to Vodovózov. I began it twice: the first time before having finished the whole Bible, and the second time after it. Before the Bible had been read, the pupils absolutely refused to remember the existence of the Igors and Olégs. The same thing is repeated now with the younger pupils. Those who have not yet learned to enter into the meaning of what is told them from the Bible, and to render it in their own words, will listen to it for five times and will remember nothing about Rúrik and Yarosláv.

The oldest pupils now remember Russian history and make notes of it, but nowhere near so well as they did with the stories from the Bible, and they ask for frequent repetitions. We tell them the stories from Vodovózov and from Pogódin's "Norman Period." One of the teachers was somehow carried away in his zeal, and, paying no attention to my advice, did not leave out the feudal period, and landed in the hopeless tangle and nonsense of the Mstislávs, Bryachislávs, and Boleslávs. I entered the class just as they were to recite. It is hard to describe what really happened. All were silent for a long time. Finally, those who were called out by the teacher began to speak, some of them more boldly and with a better display of memory. All their mental powers were directed toward recalling the "funny" names, but what each of them had done was a matter of secondary importance.

"So he, — what is it? — Barikav, is it?" began one, "went to, what do you call it?"

"Muslav, Lev Nikoláevich?" a girl helps him out.

"Mstisláv," I say.

"And put him to rout," proudly says one.

"Hold on, there was a river there."

"And his son collected an army and *smashed it to rout*, what do you call him?"

"I can't make it out," says a girl who has a memory like a blind person.

"It is such a funny thing," says Sémka.

"What is it, anyway, — Mislav, Chislav? The devil can't make out what it is good for!"

"Don't bother me if you do not know any better!"

"You know much! You are awfully clever."

"Don't push me!"

Those who have the best memories tried it once more and managed to say something if they were helped out. But all that was so monstrous, and it was such a pity to see these children (they were like hens to whom grain had been thrown out before and now sand is given, when they suddenly become perplexed, begin to cackle, are all in a flutter, and ready to pick each other's feathers), that the teacher and I decided never again to make such mistakes. We passed beyond the feudal period in continuing Russian history, and here is what comes of it in the copybooks of the older pupils.

From the copy-book of pupil V—— R——:

"Our ancestors were called Slavs. They had neither tsars, nor princes. They were divided into families, attacked each other, and went to war. Once the Normans fell upon the Slavs, and they conquered them, and levied a tribute. Then they say: 'Why are we living thus? Let us choose a prince, that he may rule over us.' They chose Rúrik, with his two brothers Sineús and Truvór. Rúrik settled in Ládoga, Sineús in Ízborsk with the Kríviches, Truvór at the Byelózero. When those brothers died, Rúrik took their places.

"Then two of them went to Greece,—Askóld and Dir, —and they stopped in Kíev and said: 'Who is ruling here?'

"The Kíevans said: 'There were three here: Ki, Shchek, and Khorív. Now they are dead.'

"Askóld and Dir said: 'All right, we shall rule over you.'

"The people agreed to it and began to pay tribute.

"Then Rúrik ordered cities and fortresses to be built, and he sent out the boyars to collect the tribute and bring it to him. Then Rúrik made up his mind to go to war against Constantinople with two hundred boats. When he rode up to that city, the emperor was not there. The Greeks sent for him. The people prayed to God all the time. Then the archpriest brought out the garment of the Holy Virgin and dipped it in the water, and there rose a terrible storm, and all the boats of Rúrik were scattered. Very few of them were saved. Then Rúrik went home and there died. There was left one son, Igor.

"When he was small Olég took his place. He wanted to conquer Kíev; he took Ígor with him and travelled straight down the Dnieper. On his way he conquered the cities of Lyúbich and Smolénsk. When they reached Kíev, Olég sent his messengers to Askóld and Dir to say that merchants had come to see them, and himself hid half of the men in boats, and half he left behind. When Askóld and Dir came out with a small retinue, Olég's army jumped out from underneath the boats and rushed against them. Then Olég lifted up Ígor and said:

"'You are no princes and not of a princely race, but here is the prince.'

"Then Olég ordered them to be killed and conquered Kíev. Olég remained there, made that city a capital, and called it the mother of all Russian cities. Then he ordered cities and fortresses to be built, and sent the boyars to collect tribute, and they brought it to him. Then he went to wage war with the neighbouring tribes, and he conquered very many of them. He did not want to wage war with peaceful men, but with brave men. Then he got ready to go against Greece, and we went down the Dnieper. When he had travelled down the Dnieper, he went over the Black Sea. When he reached Greece, his army leaped upon the shore and began to burn and pillage everything. Says Olég to the Greeks: Pay us a tribute,—a grívna for each boat.' They were glad and began to pay them the tribute. Here Olég collected three hundred puds and went home again."

From the copy-book of pupil V—— M——:

"When Olég died, Ígor, the son of Rúrik, took his place. Ígor wanted to get married. Once he went out to disport himself with his retinue,—he had to swim across the Dnieper. Suddenly he saw: a girl was swimming in a boat. When she reached the shore, Ígor said: Put me in.' She put him in. Then Ígor married her. Ígor wanted to distinguish himself. So he collected an army and went to war, straight down the Dnieper,— not to the right, but to the left, from the Dnieper into the Black Sea, from the Black Sea to the Caspian Sea. Ígor sent messengers to the kagan to let him pass through the field; when he should return from the war, he would give him half his booty. The kagan let him through

When they came near to the city, Igor ordered the people to come out on the shore, to burn and cut everything and to take prisoners. When they were through with their work, they began to rest. When they were through resting, they went home in great joy. They came up to the city of the kagan, — Igor sent to the kagan what he had promised. The people heard that Igor was coming from the war, so they began to ask the kagan to allow them to avenge themselves on Ígor, because Ígor had spilled the blood of their relatives. The kagan told them not to, but the people did not obey him and began to wage war, — there was a mighty battle. The Russians were worsted, and everything was taken away from them which they had conquered."

There is no vital interest in this, as the reader may see from the extracts quoted. Russian history goes better than universal history, only because they were accustomed to assimilate and write down what had been told them, and also because the question, "What is this for?" is less applicable here. The Russian people is their hero just as the Jewish nation has been. The Jewish, because it was God's favourite nation, and because its history is artistic. The Russian, although it has no artistic right to be their hero, because the national feeling speaks for it. But this instruction is dry, cold, and tedious. Unfortunately, the history itself very seldom gives occasion for the national sentiment to triumph.

Yesterday I went out from my class to the class of history in order to find out the cause of the animation which I could hear from the other room. It was the battle at Kulikóvo. All were agitated.

"Now that is history! It is great! — Listen, Lev Nikoláevich, how he scared away the Tartars! — Let me tell it to you!"

"No, I!" cried several children. "How the blood flowed in a stream!"

Nearly all were able to tell it, and all were enthusiastic. But if only the national feeling is to be satisfied, what will there be left of the whole history? The years 1612, 1812, and that is all. You cannot go through the whole of history by responding to the national feeling. I understand that it is possible to employ the historical tradition in order always to satisfy the artistic interest inherent in children, but that will not be history. For the instruction of history we need the preliminary development of the historical sentiment in children. How is that to be done?

I have frequently had occasion to hear that the teaching of history ought to be begun, not from the beginning, but from the end, that is, not with ancient, but with modern history. This idea is essentially true. How can a child be told and made interested in the beginning of the Russian realm, when he does not know what the Russian realm, or realm in general, is? He who has had anything to do with children ought to know that every Russian child is firmly convinced that the whole world is just like Russia, in which he is living; the same is true of a French or a German child. Why are children, and even grown-up, childishly naïve men, always surprised to hear that German children speak German?

The historical interest generally makes its appearance after the artistic interest. It is interesting for us to know the history of the foundation of Rome because we know what Rome was in her flourishing time, just as the childhood of a man whom we recognize as great is interesting. The antithesis of her might with an insignificant crowd of fugitives is for us the essence of history. We watch the evolution of Rome, having before our imagination the picture of that which she finally reached. We are interested in the foundation of the Moscow tsardom, because we know what the Russian Empire is. According to my observation and experience, the first germ of the historic interest makes its appearance as the result of the knowledge of contemporaneous history, and frequently as the result of a participation in it, through political interest, political opinions, debates, reading of newspapers, and therefore the idea of beginning history with the present must naturally present itself to every thinking teacher.

I made these experiments in the summer; I then wrote them down, and shall adduce one of them here.

The first lesson of history.

I had the intention of explaining at the first lesson in what way Russia differed from other countries, what its borders were, the characteristic of the governmental structure, of telling them who was reigning now, and how and when the emperor ascended the throne.

*Teacher.* Where do we live, in what country?

*A pupil.* In Yásnaya Polyána.

*Another pupil.* In the field.

*Teacher.* No, in what country is Yásnaya Polyána, and the Government of Túla?

*Pupil.* The Government of Túla is seventeen versts from us. Where is it? The Government is a Government and that is all there is to it.

*Teacher.* No. That is the capital of the Government, but a Government is something different. Well, what land is it?

*Pupil (who had heard geography before).* The earth is round like a ball.

By means of questions as to what country a German, whom they knew, had lived in before, and where they would get if they were to travel all the time in one direction, the pupils were led up to answer that they lived in Russia. Some, however, replied to the question where we should get if we travelled all the time in one direction, that we should get nowhere. Others said that we should get to the end of the world.

*Teacher (repeating the pupil's answer).* You said that

we should come to some other countries; where will Russia end and other countries begin?

*Pupil.* Where the Germans begin.

*Teacher.* So, if you meet Gústav Ivánovich and Karl Fédorovich in Túla, you will say that the Germans have begun and that there is a new country?

*Pupil.* No, when the Germans begin thick.

*Teacher.* No, there are places in Russia where the Germans are thick. Ivan Fórmich is from one of them, and yet that is still Russia. Why is it so?

Silence.

*Teacher.* Because they obey the same laws with the Russians.

*Pupil.* One law? How so? The Germans don't come to our church and they eat meat on fast-days.

*Teacher.* Not that law, but they obey one tsar.

*Pupil (skeptical Sémka).* That is funny! Why have they a different law, and yet obey the Tsar?

The teacher feels the need of explaining what a law is, and so he asks what is meant by "obeying a law, being under one law."

*Girl (independent manorial girl, hurriedly and timidly).* To accept the law means "to get married."

The pupils look interrogatively at the teacher. The teacher begins to explain that the law consists in putting a man in jail and in punishing him for stealing or killing.

*Skeptic Sémka.* And have not the Germans such a law?

*Teacher.* There are also laws with us about the gentry, the peasants, the merchants, the clergy (the word "clergy" perplexes them).

*Skeptic Sémka.* And the Germans have them not?

*Teacher.* In some countries there are such laws, and in others there are not. We have a Russian Tsar, and in the German countries there is a German Tsar.

This answer satisfies all the pupils and even skeptical Sémka.

Seeing the necessity of passing over to the explanation of the classes, the teacher asks them what classes of society they know. The pupils begin to count them out: the gentry, the peasants, the popes, the soldiers. "Any more?" asks the teacher. "The manorial servants, the burghers, the samovár-makers." The teacher asks them to distinguish these classes.

*Pupils.* The peasants plough, the manorial servants serve their masters, the merchants trade, the soldiers serve, the samovár-makers get the samovárs ready, the popes serve mass, the gentry do nothing.

The teacher explains the real distinction of the classes, but in vain tries to make clear the need of soldiers when there is no war on, — only as a protection of the state against attacks, — and the occupations of the gentry in government service. The teacher endeavours to explain to them in what way Russia differs geographically from the other countries by saying that the whole earth is divided into different states. The Russians, the French, the Germans, divided up the whole earth and said to themselves: "So far is mine, and so far is thine," so that Russia, like the other countries, has its borders.

*Teacher.* Do you understand what boundaries are? Let anybody explain them to me.

*Pupil (bright boy).* Beyond Túrkin Height there is a boundary (this boundary is a stone post standing on the road to Túla from Yásnaya Polyána and indicating the beginning of Túla County).

All the pupils are satisfied with this definition.

The teacher sees the need of pointing out the boundaries in a familiar locality. He draws the plan of two rooms and shows the boundary which separates them; he brings a plan of the village, and the pupils themselves recognize certain boundaries. The teacher explains, that is, he thinks that he explains, that as the land of Yásnaya Polyána has its boundaries, even so Russia has borders.

He flatters himself with the hope that all have understood him, but when he asks them how to find out how far it is from our locality to the boundaries of Russia, the pupils answer, without the least hesitation, that that is easy, that all that is necessary is to measure the distance with a yardstick.

*Teacher.* In what direction ?

*Pupil.* Just take it from here to the boundary and write down how much it is.

We again pass over to the drawings, plans, and maps. It is found that they need an idea of the scale, which is entirely absent from them. The teacher proposes to draw a plan of the village laid out along the street. We begin drawing on the board, but the village does not get on it because the scale is too large. We rub it out and begin anew on a small scale on a slate. The idea of scale, plan, boundary, is getting clearer. The teacher repeats all that has been said and asks what Russia is and where its ends are.

*Pupil.* The country in which we live and in which Germans and Tartars live.

*Another Pupil.* The country which is under the Russian Tsar.

*Teacher.* But where are its ends ?

*Girl.* There where the infidel Germans begin.

*Teacher.* The Germans are not infidels. The Germans, too, believe in Christ. (Explanation of religions and creeds.)

*Pupil* (*zealously, apparently happy to have recalled something*). In Russia there are laws that he who kills is put in jail, and there are all kinds of people, clergy-people, soldiers, gentry.

*Sémka.* Who feeds the soldiers ?

*Teacher.* The Tsar. That's why money is taken from everybody, for they serve for all.

The teacher explains what the Crown is, and manages

to make them repeat some way or other what boundaries are.

The lesson lasts about two hours. The teacher is convinced that the pupils have retained a great deal of what has been said, and continues his following lessons in the same strain, and convinces himself only much later that his method was wrong and that all that which he has been doing was the merest nonsense.

I involuntarily fell into the habitual error of the Socratic method, which in the German *Anschauungsunterricht* has reached the highest degree of monstrosity. I did not give the pupils any new ideas in these lessons, thinking all the time that I was giving them, and it was only due to my moral influence that I made the children answer as I pleased. *Russia, Russian*, remained the same unconscious tokens of something hazy and indefinite belonging to them, to us. *Law* remained the same unintelligible word. I made these experiments about six months ago and at first I was exceedingly well satisfied and proud of them. Those to whom I read them said that it was uncommonly good and interesting; but after three weeks, during which time I was not able to work in the school, I tried to continue what I had begun, and I convinced myself that what I had done before was nonsense and self-deception. Not one pupil was able to tell me what a boundary was, what Russia, what a law was, and what were the boundaries of Krapívensk County. Everything they had learned they had now forgotten, and yet they knew it all in their own fashion. I was convinced of my mistake; but what is not determined by me is whether the mistake consisted in the wrong method of instruction or in the very thought; maybe there is no possibility, up to a certain period of a general development and without the aid of newspapers and travel, of awakening in the child a historical and geographical interest; maybe that method will be found (I am still endeavouring to find it) by means of which it will be possible to do it. I know this much, that the method will in no way consist in what is called history and geography, that is, in studying out of books, which kills and does not rouse these interests.

I have also made other experiments in teaching modern history, and they have been very successful. I told them the history of the Crimean campaign, and the reign of Emperor Nicholas, and the year 1812. All this I told almost in a fairy-tale tone, as a rule, historically incorrect, and grouping the events about some one person. The greatest success was obtained, as was to have been expected, by the story of the war with Napoleon.

This class has remained a memorable event in our life. I shall never forget it. The children had long been promised that I should tell them history from its end, while another teacher would begin from the beginning, so that we should finally meet. My evening scholars had left me, and I came to the class of Russian history. They were talking about Svyatosláv. They felt dull. On a tall bench sat, in a row, as always, three peasant girls, their heads tied with kerchiefs. One was asleep. Míshka pushed me: "Look there, our cuckoos are sitting there,— one is asleep." And they were like cuckoos!

"You had better tell us from the end," said some one, and all arose.

I sat down and began to talk. As always, the hubbub, the groans, the tussling, lasted about two minutes. Some were climbing under the table, some on the table, some under the benches, and on their neighbours' shoulders and knees, and all was silent. I began with Alexander I., told them of the French Revolution, of Napoleon's successes, of his seizing the government, and of the war which ended in the peace of Tilsit. The moment we reached Russia there were heard sounds and words of lively interest on all sides.

"Well, is he going to conquer us too?"

"Never mind, Alexander will give it to him!" said some one who knew about Alexander, but I had to disappoint them, — the time had not yet come for that, — and they felt bad when they heard that the Tsar's sister was spoken of as a bride for Napoleon, and that Alexander spoke with him on the bridge, as with an equal.

"Just wait!" exclaimed Pétka, with a threatening gesture.

"Go on and tell us!"

When Alexander did not submit to him, that is, when Alexander declared war against him, all expressed their approbation. When Napoleon came against us with twelve nations, and stirred up the Germans and Poland, their hearts sank from agitation.

A German, a friend of mine, was standing in the room.

"Ah, you were against us, too," said Pétka (the best story-teller).

"Keep quiet!" cried the others.

The retreat of our army tormented the hearers, and on all sides were asked questions why? and curses were heaped on Kutúzov and Barclay.

"Your Kutúzov is no good!"

"Just wait," said another.

"Well, did he surrender?" asked a third.

When we reached the battle at Borodinó, and when in the end I was obliged to say that we did not gain a victory, I was sorry for them, — it was evident that I gave them all a terrible blow.

"Though our side did not win, theirs did not either!"

When Napoleon came to Moscow and was waiting for the keys and for obeisances, there was a clatter from a consciousness of being inconquerable. The conflagration of Moscow was, naturally, approved by all. Then came the victory, — the retreat.

"When he came out of Moscow Kutúzov rushed after him and went to fight him," I said.

"He made him rear up!" Fédka corrected me.

Fédka, red in his face, was sitting opposite me, and from excitement was bending his thin, tawny fingers. That is his habit. The moment he said that, the whole room groaned from a feeling of proud ecstasy. A little fellow in the back row was being crushed, but nobody paid any attention to it.

"That's better! There, take the keys now!" and so forth.

Then I continued about our pursuit of the French. It pained the children to hear that some one was too late at the Berézina and that we let them pass; Pétka even groaned with pain.

"I should have shot him to death for being late."

Then we even pitied a little the frozen Frenchmen. Then, when we crossed the border, and the Germans, who had been against us, joined us, some one recalled the German who was standing in the room.

"How is that? At first you are against us, and when the power is losing, you are with us!" and suddenly all arose and shouted against the German so that the noise could be heard in the street. When they quieted down, I continued telling them about our following up Napoleon as far as Paris, placing the real king on the throne, celebrating our victory, and feasting. But the recollection of the Crimean War spoiled our whole business.

"Just wait," said Pétka, shaking his fist, "let me grow up and I will show them!"

If we had now had a chance at the Shevardinó redoubt and at Mount Malakhóv, we should certainly have taken it back.

It was late when I finished. As a rule the children are asleep at that time. No one was sleeping, and the eyes of the little cuckoos were burning. Just as I got up

Taráska crawled out from underneath my chair, to my great astonishment, and looked lively and at the same time seriously at me.

"How did you get down there?"

"He has been there from the start," some one said.

There was no need asking him whether he had understood,—that could be seen from his face.

"Well, are you going to tell it?" I asked.

"I?" He thought awhile. "I will tell the whole thing."

"I will tell it at home."

"I too."

"And I."

"Is that all?"

"Yes."

All flew down under the staircase, some promising to give it to the Frenchmen, others rebuking the German, and others repeating how Kutúzov had made him rear up.

"*Sie haben ganz Russisch erzählt,*" the German who had been hooted said to me in the evening. "You ought to hear how they tell the story in our country! You have said nothing about the German struggles for freedom."

I fully agreed with him that my narrative was not history, but a fanciful tale rousing the national sentiment.

Consequently, as a study of history, this attempt was even less successful than the first.

In teaching geography I did the same. I first began with physical geography. I remember the first lesson. I began it, and immediately lost my way. It turned out, what I should never have suspected, that I did not know that which I wanted ten-year-old peasant boys to know. I could explain night and day to them, but was completely at a loss to explain summer and winter. Feeling ashamed of my ignorance, I studied up the matter; later I asked many of my acquaintances, educated people, and nobody, except such as had lately left school or as were teachers, was able to explain it to me well without a globe. I ask all my readers to verify this statement. I aver that out of one hundred people only one knows it, although all the children learn it. Having studied it up well, I again began to explain it and, as I imagined, had, with the help of a candle and a globe, given them an excellent idea of it. I was listened to with great attention and interest. (It gave them especial pleasure to know that which their fathers did not believe, and to be able to make a display of their wisdom.)

At the end of my explanation, skeptic Sémka, the most intelligent of all, stopped me with the question: "How is it the earth is moving and our house is all the time standing in the same spot? It ought to get off its old place."

I saw that I had in my explanations gone a thousand versts ahead of the most intelligent pupil; what kind of an idea must those have formed who were least intelligent?

I went back, — talked, drew, and adduced all the proofs of the sphericity of the earth: voyages around the earth, the appearance of the mast of a ship before the deck is seen, and so forth, and, consoling myself with the thought that now they must have understood, I made them write out the lesson. All wrote: "The earth is like a ball, — first proof — second proof;" the third proof they had forgotten and asked me to tell them. It was quite apparent that the main thing for them was to remember the "proofs." Not only once, or ten times, but a hundred times I returned to these explanations, and always without success. At an examination all pupils would answer the questions satisfactorily; but I felt that they did not understand, and, considering that I myself did not get a good idea of the matter before the age of thirty, I gladly excused them for their lack of comprehension. As I had taken it on faith in my childhood, so they now took my word that the earth was round, and so forth, though they did not comprehend a thing.

It is even now easier for me to understand — as my nurse had impressed it upon me in my first childhood — that earth and sky meet at the end of the world, and that there, at the end of the earth, the women are washing their linen, putting their beetles away upon the sky. Our pupils had long ago been confirmed, and they still persist in conceptions that are the very opposite to what I am trying to instil in them. It will be necessary for a long time to break down the explanations which they have, and all that world conception, which has not yet been impaired by anything, before they will be able to comprehend. The laws of physics and mechanics will be the first completely to shatter their old conceptions. But they, like me, like all the rest, began physical geography before they had had physics.

In the teaching of geography, as in all other subjects, the commonest, most serious and detrimental error is haste. We act as though we were so happy to have found out that the earth is round and moves around the sun that we hurry to inform the pupil of the fact. But what is really worth knowing is not that the earth is round, but the manner in which that information was obtained. Very frequently children are told that the sun is so many billions of versts distant from the earth, but that is not at all a matter of surprise or interest to the child. What he wants to know is how that was found out. If any one wants to talk about that let him tell about parallaxes. That is quite possible. The only reason why I dwelt so long on the roundness of the earth is because what is said about it refers to the whole of geography. Out of a thousand educated people, outside of teachers and pupils, one knows well why there is summer and winter, and where Guadeloupe is; out of a thousand children not one understands in his childhood the explanations of the sphericity of the earth and not one believes in the reality of Guadeloupe, and yet all are persistently taught both from early childhood.

After physical geography I began the parts of the world with their characterizations, and of that whole matter nothing was left but their vying in the ability to cry: "Asia, Africa, Australia;" and if I asked them: "In what part of the world is France?" (having told them but a minute before that England and France were in Europe) somebody called out that France was in Africa. I could see the question "Why?" in each dim vision, in every sound of their voices, whenever I began geography with them, — and there was no answer to that sad question "Why?"

Just as in history the simple thought was to begin with the end, so in geography the thought naturally occurred to begin with the schoolroom, with our native village. I had seen these experiments in Germany, and I myself, discouraged by the failure of the usual geography, took up the description of the room, the house, the village. As drawings of plans, such exercises are not devoid of usefulness, but it is not interesting for them to know what land lies beyond our village, because they all know that there is the village of Telyátinki. And it is not interesting to know what lies beyond Telyátinki, because there, no doubt, is just such a village as Telyátinki, and Telyátinki with its fields is absolutely uninteresting.

I tried to put up for them geographical guide-posts, such as Moscow, Kíev, but all that arranged itself so disconnectedly in their minds that they learned it by heart. I tried to draw maps, and that interested them and really aided their memories; but again the question arose why their memories should be aided. I also tried to tell them about the polar and equatorial regions, — they listened with pleasure and recited well, but they memorized only that which was not of a geographical nature in these stories. The main trouble was that the drawing of the plans of the village was drawing of plans, and not geography; the drawing of maps was drawing of maps, and not geography; the stories about animals, forests, icebergs, and cities were fairy-tales, and not geography. The geography was only a learning of something by heart. Of all the books, — Grúbe, Biernádski, — not one was interesting.

One little book, forgotten by all, which resembles a geography, was read with greater enjoyment than all the rest, and in my opinion is the best specimen of what ought to be done in order to prepare children for the study of geography and stir up the geographical interest in them. That book is "Parley," a Russian translation of the year 1837. That book is read, but mainly serves as a guiding string for the teacher, who in accordance with it tells what he knows of each country and city. The children recite, but rarely retain a name or a place on the map, which refers to the event described, — there are mainly the events alone that are left. However, this class belongs more properly to the category of conversations, of which we shall speak in their proper place. In spite of all the art with which the study of unnecessary names is masked in this book, in spite of all the care which we took with it, the children lately scented our purpose to inveigle them by pretty stories, and have acquired a positive distaste for this class.

I finally came to the conclusion that, in respect to history, there is not only no need of knowing the dull Russian history, but that Cyrus, Alexander the Great, Cæsar, and Luther are not necessary for the development of any child. All these persons and events are interesting for the student, not to the extent of their importance in history, but to the extent of the artistic composition of their activities to the extent of the artistic treatment of them by the historian, and even more so — not by the historian, but by the popular tradition.

The story of Romulus and Remus is interesting, not because these brothers were the founders of the mightiest empire in the world, but because it is entertaining, funny, and nice to hear about their having been nurtured by the she-wolf, and so forth. The story of the Gracchi is interesting because it is as artistic as the history of Gregory VII. and the humiliated emperor, and it is possible to get the pupils' attention by it; but the story of the migration of the nations will be dull and aimless, because its contents are not artistic, just as the story of the art of printing is not interesting, no matter how much we may try to impress the pupils with the idea that it forms an epoch in history, and that Gutenberg was a great man. Tell them well how matches were invented, and they will never agree with you that the inventor of matches was a lesser man than Gutenberg; in short, for the child, for the student in general, who has not yet begun to live, there does not exist the historical interest, let alone the interest of universal humanity. There is only the artistic interest. It is said that when all the material has been worked out, it will be possible to give an artistic exposition of all the periods of history, — I do not see it. Macaulay and Thiers may no more be given into their hands than Tacitus and Xenophon.

In order to make history popular, the artistic exterior is not sufficient; the historical phenomena have to be personified, just as tradition, sometimes life itself, sometimes great thinkers and historians, personify them. Children like history only when its contents are artistic. There is no historical interest for them, nor ever can be, consequently there can be no such a thing as history for children. History sometimes serves only as material for an artistic development, and so long as the historical interest is not developed, there can be no history. Bertet,

Kaydánov, after all, remain the only manuals. There is an old anecdote that the history of the Medes is dark and fabulous. Nothing else can be made out of history for children, who do not understand the historical interest. The contrary attempts to make history and geography artistic and interesting, Grúbe's biographical sketches, Biernádski, satisfy neither the artistic nor the historical demands, nor do they satisfy consistency and the historical interest, and at the same time with their details they expand to impossible dimensions.

The same is true of geography. When Mitrofánushka[1] was being persuaded to study geography, his mother said: "What is the use of teaching him all kinds of countries? His coachman will know how to get him there, when there is any need." There has never been brought forward a stronger argument against geography, and all the learned men of the world are unable to make any reply to this imperturbable argument. I am quite serious. What use was there in my studying about the river and city of Barcelona if, having lived thirty-three years, I have not once needed that information? But for the development of my mental powers, the most picturesque description of Barcelona and its inhabitants could do nothing, so far as I can see. What use is there in Sémka's and Fédka's knowing anything about the Maríinsk canal and the waterways if, as is to be supposed, they will never get there; but if Sémka should have an occasion to go there, it will make no difference whether he has studied it or not, for he will find out in practice, and he will find out well, all about this waterway. I am quite unable to see how, for the development of his mental powers, he will be helped by the knowledge that hemp goes down the Vólga, and tar comes up that river, that there is a harbour by the name of Dubóvka, and that a certain subterranean

[1] In Fon-Vízin's comedy, "The Minor."

layer goes to a certain place, and that the Samoyéds travel on reindeer, and so forth.

I have a whole world of mathematical and natural science information, of language and poetry, which time is too short to transmit; there is an endless number of questions from the phenomena of life surrounding me, to which the pupil demands an answer, and which I must answer before drawing for him pictures of the polar ice, of the tropical countries, of the mountains of Australia, and of the rivers of America.

In history and geography, experience tells us one and the same thing, and everywhere confirms our thoughts. Everywhere the teaching of history and of geography proceeds badly. In view of the examinations, the pupils memorize the names of mountains, cities and rivers, kings and emperors. The only possible text-books are, then, those by Arsénev and Obodóvski, Kaydánov, Smarágdov, and Bertet, and everywhere one hears complaints about the instruction in these subjects, and all are seeking for something new which they do not find.

It is curious to hear men recognize the incompatibility of the demands of geography with the spirit of the students throughout the world, and in consequence of this invent a thousand ingenious means (such as Sídov's method) in order to make the children remember words; but the simplest thought that the whole geography is unnecessary, that there is no need of knowing these words, never enters anybody's mind. All attempts at combining geography with geology, zoology, botany, ethnography, and I do not know with what else, and history with biography, remain empty dreams which result in such worthless books as that by Grúbe, which are of no use for the children, nor for youths, nor for teachers, nor for the public at large. Indeed, if the compilers of these seemingly new text-books of geography and history only thought what it is they want, and if they themselves were to apply their books to instruction, they would soon convince themselves of the impossibility of their undertaking.

In the first place, geography in connection with the natural sciences and ethnography would form such an extensive science that a whole life would not be sufficient for its study, and it would be even less a child study and much drier than geography. In the second, it is not likely that in another thousand years there will be enough material on hand for the writing of such a manual. Teaching the geography of Krapívensk County, I shall be compelled to give the pupils detailed information about the flora and the fauna and the geological structure of the earth at the north pole, and details about the inhabitants and the commerce of the kingdom of Baden, because I shall be in possession of this information ; and I shall hardly be able to say anything about the Byélev and Efrémov Counties, because I shall have no material in respect to them. But the children and common sense demand of me a certain harmoniousness and regularity of instruction. There is left, then, nothing else but to teach geography from Obodóvski's text-book, or not to teach it at all.

Just as the historical interest must first be roused for history, so the geographical interest must be evoked for the study of geography. But the geographical interest, from my observations and experiments, is roused either by the study of the natural sciences, or by travel, more particularly, in ninety-nine out of a hundred cases, by travel. As the reading of newspapers, and especially of biographies, and the sympathy with the political life of the nation generally serve as the first step in the study of history, just so travels serve as the first step in the study of geography. Both are now exceedingly accessible to every one and are easy in our day, — therefore we ought to be the less afraid of renouncing the old superstition about teaching history and geography. Our life is in our day so instructive in this respect that, if geographical and historical knowledge is really as necessary for our general development as it seems to be, life will always supply that defect.

Indeed, if we can renounce that old superstition, it will not appear so terrible to us that men may grow up without having learned in their childhood that there was such a man as Yaroslav, or Otho, and that there is such a place as Estremadura, and so forth. Have we not stopped teaching astrology, and dialectics, and poetics? And are they not giving up the study of Latin, without the human race growing any more stupid? New sciences are born, and in our time the natural sciences are being made popular; the old sciences have to drop off when they have outlived their utility, — not the sciences, but those sides of the sciences which with the birth of new sciences have become obsolete.

To rouse the interest and to know how the human race has lived and formed itself and developed in various countries; to rouse interest for the discovery of those laws by which humanity eternally moves; on the other hand, to rouse interest in the comprehension of the laws of the phenomena of Nature on the whole globe and of the distribution of the human race over it, — that is a different matter. Maybe the rousing of such interest is useful, but in order to attain this aim neither Ségur, nor Thiers, nor Obodóvski, nor Grúbe will add anything. I know two elements for that, — the artistic feeling of poetry and patriotism. But, in order to develop both, there have not yet been written text-books, and so long as there are none, we must seek, or waste our time and strength in vain, and torment the younger generation, making it learn history and geography simply because we have learned them. *Up to the university I not only see no need of the study of history and geography, but even a great injury in it.* What is beyond that I do not know.

## THE ARTS

In the report for the months of November and December of the Yásnaya Polyána school there now stand before me two subjects which have an entirely different character, and those are drawing and singing, — the arts.

If I did not start with the opinion that I do not know what is to be taught, and why this or that is to be taught, I should have to ask myself: Will it be useful for peasant children, who are placed under the necessity of passing all their lives in care about their daily bread, to study art, and what good is it to them? Ninety-nine out of every hundred will answer in the negative. Nor can one answer otherwise. The moment such a question is put, common sense demands the following answer: He is not to be an artist, — he will have to plough the ground. If he is to have any artistic needs, it will be above his strength to carry that persistent, untiring work which he must carry, and without carrying which the existence of the state would be unthinkable. When I say "he," I mean the child of the masses. Of course, it is insipid, but I rejoice at this insipidity, do not stop before it, but try to discover its causes. There is another great insipidity. This same child of the masses, every child of the masses, has just such a right, — what do I say? — a greater right to enjoy art than we have, the children of a happy class, who are not placed under the necessity of that untiring work, who are surrounded by all the comforts of life.

To deprive him of the right of enjoying art, to deprive me, the teacher, of the right of introducing him into that region of the better enjoyments, toward which his being strives with all the powers of his soul, is that greater insipidity. How are these two insipidities to be harmonized? This is not lyricism, of which I was reproached in the description of the walk which I gave in the first number, — this is logic. Every harmonization is impossible and is only a self-deception.

I shall be told, and I have been, if drawing is needed in a popular school, it can be admitted only as drawing from Nature, technical drawing, to be applied to life; the drawing of a plough, a machine, a building; free-hand drawing as a mere auxiliary for mechanical drawing. This common view of drawing is also held by the teacher of the Yásnaya Polyána school, whose report we offer. But it was the very experiment with teaching drawing in this manner which convinced us of the falseness and injustice of this technical programme. The majority of the pupils, after four months of careful, exclusively technical drawing, from which was excluded all drawing of men, animals, and landscapes, ended by cooling off considerably in respect to the drawing of technical objects and by developing to such an extent the feeling and need of drawing as an art that they provided themselves with their secret copy-books, in which they drew men, and horses with all four legs coming out of one spot. The same was true of music.

The customary programme of the popular schools does not admit singing beyond the singing of church choirs. The same thing takes place here: either it is a very dull and painful memorizing for the children, where certain sounds are produced by them, as though they were regarded merely as so many throats taking the place of the organ pipes, or there will be developed in them the feeling for the artistic, which finds its satisfaction in the balaláyka and the accordion and frequently in a homely song, which the pedagogue does not recognize, and in which he does not think it necessary to guide his pupils. Either one or the other: either art in general is injurious and unnecessary, which is not at all so, strange as it may appear at a first glance, or everybody, without distinction of classes and occupations, has a right to it and a right to devote himself to it, on the ground that art does not brook mediocrity.

The insipidity is not in that, but in the very putting of such a question as a question: Have the children of the masses a right to art? Asking this is like asking whether the children of the masses have a right to eat beef, that is, have they the right to satisfy their human needs? Now the question ought not to be in that, but whether the beef is good, which we offer the masses, or which we keep from them.

Even thus, when I offer the masses certain knowledge which is in our power, and when I notice the evil influence produced by it upon them, I do not conclude that the masses are bad, because they do not receive this knowledge, nor that the masses have not yet developed sufficiently to receive this knowledge and make use of it as we are making use of it, but that this knowledge is not good, not normal, and that we must with the aid of the masses work out a new knowledge, which will be more in accord with us, and with society, and with the masses. I conclude only that this knowledge and the arts live among us and do not seem injurious, but cannot live among the masses, and seem injurious to them only because this knowledge and the arts are not those which are needed in general, and that we live among them only because we are spoiled, because only those who harmlessly sit for five hours in the vitiated air of a factory or a tavern do not suffer from the air which would kill a newcomer.

I shall be told: "Who said that the knowledge and the arts of our cultivated society are false? How can you conclude from the fact that the masses do not receive them that they are false?" All such questions are solved very simply: Because there are thousands of us, and there are millions of them.

I continue the comparison with the well-known physiological fact. A man comes from the fresh air into a smoke-filled room, the air of which has been exhausted by breathing; his vital functions are still vigorous, for his organism has through breathing been fed by a large quantity of oxygen, which he has taken from the pure air. With the same habit of his organism he begins to breathe in the vitiated air of the room; the injurious gases are communicated to the blood in a large quantity, — his organism is weakened (frequently fainting and sometimes death ensue); at the same time hundreds of people continue to breathe and live in the foul air because their functions have become less vigorous, because, to express myself differently, they are weaker and live less.

If I am to be told that both classes of people live, and that it would be hard to decide whose life is more normal and better; that when a man comes out from a vitiated atmosphere into the fresh air he frequently faints, and vice versa, — the answer will be easy: not a physiologist, but a simple man with common sense, will ask himself where most people live, whether in the fresh air or in pestilential prisons, — and will follow the majority; and the physiologist will make observations on the sum total of the functions of both and he will say that the functions are more vigorous and the alimentation fuller with him who lives in the fresh air.

The same relation exists between the arts of the so-called cultured society and between the demands of the people's art: I am speaking of painting, and sculpture, and music, and poetry. Ivánov's painting will rouse in the people nothing but admiration for his technical mastery, but will not evoke any poetical, nor religious sensation, while this very poetical sentiment is evoked by a chap-book picture of John of Nóvgorod and the devil in the pitchers.[1] The

[1] We beg the reader to direct his attention to this monstrous picture, which is remarkable on account of the strength of the religio-poetic feeling expressed in it, and which bears the same relation to

Venus de Milo will rouse only a legitimate loathing for the nakedness and shamelessness of the woman. Beethoven's quartette of the latest epoch will appear only as a disagreeable sound, interesting perhaps because one plays on a big fiddle and the other on a small fiddle. The best production of our poetry, a lyrical composition by Púshkin, will seem only a collection of words, and its meaning the veriest nonsense.

Introduce a child from the people into this world; you can do that and are doing that all the time by means of the hierarchy of the educational institutions, academies, and art classes: he will feel, and will sincerely feel, the beauty of Ivánov's painting, and of the Venus de Milo, and of the quartette by Beethoven, and of Púshkin's lyrical poem. But, upon entering into this world, he will no longer be breathing with full lungs, — the fresh air, whenever he has to go into it, will affect him painfully and inimically.

As in the matter of breathing common sense and physiology will make the same reply, even thus in the matter of the arts the same common sense and pedagogy (not the pedagogy that writes programmes, but the one that endeavours to study the universal paths of education and its laws) will reply that he who is not living in the art-sphere of our educated classes lives better and fuller; that the demands made upon art, and the satisfaction which it gives, are fuller and more lawful with the masses than with us. Common sense will say that, because it sees a happy majority, mighty not merely in numbers, living outside that *milieu;* the pedagogian will observe the mental functions of the men who are living in our circles, and outside of them he will observe what happens when people are introduced into the vitiated air, that

modern Russian painting that the painting of Fra Beato Angelico has to the painting of the disciples of the school of Michelangelo. — *Author's Note.*

is, during the transmission of our arts to the younger generations, and on the basis of those syncopes and of that loathing which fresh natures manifest upon being introduced into an artificial atmosphere, and on the basis of the limitation of their mental functions, he will conclude that the demands that the people make upon art are more legitimate than the demands of a spoiled minority of the so-called cultured class.

I have made these observations in respect to the two branches of our arts, with which I am the more intimately acquainted and which I formerly loved very passionately, — music and poetry. Strange to say, I came to the conclusion that everything that we had been doing in those branches had been done along a false, exceptional path, which had no meaning and no future, and which was insignificant in comparison with those demands and even with those productions of the same arts, samples of which we find among the people. I convinced myself that a lyrical poem, for example, " I remember the charming moment," the musical productions, such as Beethoven's last symphony, were not as unconditionally and universally fine as the song of "Steward Vánka," and the tune of "Down the Mother Vólga;" that Púshkin and Beethoven please us, not because there is any absolute beauty in them, but because we are as much spoilt as Púshkin and Beethoven were, because Púshkin and Beethoven alike flatter our freaky irritability and our weakness. How common it is to hear the trite paradox that for the comprehension of what is beautiful there is needed a certain preparation! Who said that? How has that been proved? It is only an excuse, a way out from a hopeless situation, into which we have been brought by the falseness of the direction, by our art's belonging exclusively to one class. Why are the beauty of the sun, the beauty of the human face, the beauty of the sounds of a popular song, the beauty of an act of love and self-renunciation accessible to all, and why do they demand no preparation?

I know that for the majority everything I have said here will appear as the merest prattle, as the privilege of a boneless tongue, but pedagogy — free pedagogy — explains many questions by means of experiment, and by means of an endless repetition of one and the same phenomenon transfers the questions from the field of dreams and reflections into the territory of propositions based on facts. I have for years vainly endeavoured to transmit to the pupils the poetical beauties of Púshkin and of our whole literature; the same is being done by an endless number of teachers, — not in Russia alone, — and if these teachers watch the results of their efforts, and if they want to be frank, they will all confess that the chief effect of developing the poetical feeling has been to kill it, that the highly poetical natures have shown the greatest loathing for such explanations. I had struggled for years, I say, without being able to obtain any results, — and it was enough for me accidentally to open Rýbnikov's collection, and the poetical demand of the pupils found its full satisfaction, a satisfaction which, by calmly and without prejudice comparing any poem whatever with the best production of Púshkin, I could not help finding legitimate. The same happened to me in respect to music, of which I shall have to speak now.

I shall try and make a résumé of all said above. When the question is put whether the fine arts are necessary for the masses, the pedagogues generally become timid and confused (Plato was the only one who boldly decided the question in the negative). They say that they are necessary, but with certain limitations; that it is dangerous for the social structure to give all a chance to become artists. They say that certain arts and a certain degree of them may exist only in a certain class of society;

they say that the arts must have their own especial servants who are devoted to but one matter. They say that the highly gifted natures must have the chance to get away from the mass of the people and to devote themselves exclusively to the service of art. This is the greatest concession which pedagogy makes to the right of each individual to make of himself what he pleases. All the cares of the pedagogues in respect to the arts are directed toward attaining this one aim.

I regard all this as unjust. I assume that the necessity of enjoying art and serving art are inherent in each human personality, no matter to what race or *milieu* he may belong, and that this necessity has its rights and ought to be satisfied. Taking this assumption as an axiom, I say that if inconveniences and inconsistencies arise for each person in the enjoyment of art and its reproduction, the cause of these inconveniences lies not in the manner of the transmission, not in the dissemination or concentration of art among many or among a few, but in the character and direction of the art, upon which we must look with doubt, in order not to foist anything false upon the younger generation, and also in order to give that younger generation a chance to work out something new, both as to form and contents.

I now present the teacher's report in drawing for the months of November and December. This method of instruction, it seems to me, may be considered convenient for the manner in which the technical difficulties have been pleasantly and imperceptibly obviated for the pupils. The question of the art itself has not been touched upon, because the teacher, when beginning the instruction, had prejudged the question by deciding that it was useless for the children of peasants to become artists.

### DRAWING

When I nine months ago took up teaching drawing, I had no definite plan, neither as to how to distribute the matter of instruction, nor how to guide the pupils. I had neither drawings, nor models, except a few illustrated albums, which, however, I did not make use of during my course of instruction, limiting myself to simple aids, such as one may find in any village school. A painted wooden board, chalk, slates, and little square sticks of various lengths, which were used for object illustrations in teaching mathematics, — those were all the means we had during our instruction, which did not prevent us from copying everything that fell into our hands. Not one of the pupils had studied drawing before; they had brought to me only their ability to pass judgments, and they were granted full liberty to express themselves whenever and however they wished, hoping thus to discover what their needs were and then to form a definite plan of occupations. For the first lesson I formed a square out of four sticks and I tried to see whether the boys would be able without any previous instruction to draw that square. Only a few of the boys drew some very irregular squares, by expressing the solid sticks forming the square by means of straight lines. I was quite satisfied with that. For the weaker pupils I drew with chalk a square on the blackboard. Then we composed a cross in the same manner, and we drew it.

An unconscious, inborn feeling made the children generally discover a fairly correct correlation of the lines, although they drew the lines quite poorly. I did not deem it necessary to try to obtain a regularity in the straight lines in every figure, in order not to torment them in vain, and demanded only that the figure be copied. I intended, at first, to give the boys a conception of the relation of lines from their length and direction, rather than to trouble myself about their ability to make the lines themselves as regular as possible.

A child will learn to comprehend the relation between a long and a short line, the difference between a right angle and parallels, sooner than be able passably to draw a straight line.

By degrees we began, at the following lessons, to draw the corners of these square little sticks, and then we composed various figures out of them.

The pupils paid no attention whatever to the slight thickness of these sticks,— the third dimension,— and we drew all the time only the front view of the objects composed.

The difficulty of clearly presenting, with our insufficient material, the position and correlation of the figures compelled me, now and then, to draw figures on the board. I frequently united the drawing from Nature with the drawing of models, giving them some certain objects; if the boys were unable to draw a given object, I drew it myself on the board.

The drawing of figures from the board took place in the following manner: I first drew a horizontal or vertical line, divided it by points into different parts, and the pupils copied that line. Then I drew another or several other lines, perpendicular or slanting to the first, standing in a certain relation to the first, and divided into units of the same size. Then we connected the points of division of these lines by straight lines or arcs, and thus formed a certain symmetrical figure, which, step by step as it grew up, was copied by the boys. I thought that that would be advantageous, in the first place, because the boy learned objectively the whole process of the formation of the figure, and, in the second, because through this drawing on the board there was developed in him the conception of the correlation of lines much better than through the copying of drawings and originals. With such a process there was destroyed the possibility of copying directly, but the figure itself, as an object from Nature, had to be copied on a diminished scale.

It is nearly always useless to hang out before the pupils a large complete picture or figure, because the beginners will be positively confused before it, just as though they were before an object from Nature. But the very evolution of the figure before their eyes has a great significance. The pupils, in this case, see the skeleton of the drawing, upon which the whole body is later formed. The pupils were constantly called upon to criticize the lines and their relations, as I had drawn them. I frequently drew the lines wrong on purpose, in order to get an idea how much judgment they had formed about the correlation and regularity of the lines. Then again I asked the children, when I drew some figure, where some line ought to be added in their opinion, and I even made now one boy, now another, suggest some figure.

In this manner I not only roused a greater interest in the boys, but also a free participation in the formation and development of the figure; in this way the children's question, "Why?" which every child naturally asks himself in copying from an original, was obviated.

Their greater or lesser comprehension and their greater or lesser interest had the chief influence on the progress and the method of instruction, and I frequently abandoned that which I had purposely prepared for the lesson, only because it was foreign or dull to the boys.

So far, I had given them symmetrical figures to draw because their formation is easiest and most apparent. Then I, for experiment's sake, asked the best pupils themselves to compose and draw figures on the board. Although nearly all drew only after one given manner, it was, nevertheless, interesting to watch the growing rivalry, the judgment which they passed on the others, and the peculiar structure of their figures. Many of these drawings were peculiarly in harmony with the characters of the boys.

In each child there is a tendency to be independent, which it is injurious to destroy in any instruction, and which especially finds its expression in the dissatisfaction with the copying of models. By the above mentioned method, this independence was not only not killed, but even developed and strengthened.

If a pupil does not learn to create himself, he will always imitate and copy in life, because there are few who, having learned to copy, are able to make an independent application of such knowledge.

By always keeping to natural forms in drawing, and by frequently changing the objects, as, for example, leaves of a characteristic from, flowers, dishes and objects frequently used in life, and instruments, I tried to keep out routine and mannerism from our drawing.

With the greatest caution I approached the explanation of shades and shadows, because the beginner easily destroys the sharpness and regularity of figures by shading them too much, and thus gets used to a disorderly and infinite daubing.

In this manner I soon got more than thirty boys in a few months to learn quite thoroughly the correlation of lines in various figures and objects, and to render these figures in even, sharp lines. The mechanical art of line-drawing was soon evolved as if of its own accord. The greatest difficulty I had was to teach the children to keep their drawing-books and the drawings themselves clean. The convenience in rubbing out what has been drawn on a slate greatly enhances my difficulty in this respect. By giving the best, most talented boys copy-books, I obtained a greater cleanliness in the drawings themselves: for the greater difficulty in rubbing out compels them to be more careful and tidy with the material on which they are drawing. In a short time the best pupils reached such a clear and correct handling of the pencil that they could cleanly and regularly draw, not only straight-lined figures, but also the most fantastic compositions of curved lines.

I made some of the pupils control the figures of the others, when they were through with their own, — and this teacher's activity greatly encouraged the pupils, for they were at once able to apply that which they had just learned.

Of late I have been working with the oldest boys trying to get them to draw objects in different positions in their perspective, without clinging exclusively to the well-known method of Dupuis.

## SINGING

Last summer we returned from swimming. We were all in a happy mood. A peasant boy, the same that had been enticed by the manorial boy to steal books, a thickset boy with protruding cheek-bones, all covered with freckles, with bandy legs turned inward, having all the aspect of a grown-up sturdy peasant, but an intelligent, strong, and talented nature, ran ahead and seated himself in the cart that was driving in front of us. He took the lines, poised his cap jauntily, spit out sidewise, and started a drawn-out peasant song, and he sang with such feeling, such sobbing sounds, such lamentings! The boys laughed.

"Sémka, Sémka! What a fine singer he is!"

Sémka was quite serious.

"Don't interrupt my song," he said, in a peculiar, feignedly hoarse voice, during an interval, and just as seriously and evenly proceeded to sing. Two of the more musical boys sat down in the cart with him, and fell in with him and carried the refrain. One of them seconded now at an octave or sixth, another at a third, and it was all charming. Then other boys joined them, and they began to sing "As under such an apple-tree," and they made a noise, but there was not much music.

With that evening the singing began. Now, after eight months, we sing "The angel lamented" and two cherubical songs, numbers four and seven, the whole common mass, and small chorus songs. The best pupils (only two) take down in writing the tunes of the songs which they know, and almost read music. But up to the present what they sing is not anywhere near so good as the song which they sang when returning from the swimming. I say this with no ulterior purpose, not in order to prove anything,— I simply state a fact. Now I am going to tell how the instruction proceeded, with which I am comparatively satisfied.

At the first lesson I divided all up into three voices and we sang the following chords:

We succeeded in this very soon. Each sang what he pleased. One would try soprano, and then would pass over to tenor, and from tenor to alto, so that the best pupils learned the whole chord do-mi-sol, some of them even all three chords. They pronounced the notes as in French. One sang mi-fa-fa-mi, another do-do-re-do, and so forth.

"I declare that is fine, Lev Nikoláevich!" they said, "it even makes something shake in the ear. Let us have some more!"

We sang these chords at school, and in the yard, and in the garden, and on the way home, until late into the night, and could not tear ourselves away from this occupation or have enough of our success.

On the following day we tried the gamut, and the more talented went through it all, while the poorer ones could hardly get as far as the third. I wrote the notes on a staff in the alto-clef, the most symmetrical of clefs, and gave them the French names. The next five or six lessons proceeded just as merrily; we also succeeded in getting new minor keys and the passes to the majors, — "Kyrie eleison," "Glory be to the Father and Son," and a song for three voices with piano accompaniment. One-half of the lesson was occupied with that, the other half with the singing of the gamut and the exercises, which the pupils themselves invented, "do-mi-re-fa-mi-sol," or "do-re-re-mi-mi-fa," or "do-mi-re-do-re-fa-mi-re," and so forth.

I soon noticed that the notes on the staff were not clear to them, and I found it necessary to use figures instead. Besides, for the explanation of intervals and the variation of the tonic scale, the figures present greater conveniences. After six lessons some of them took the intervals by order, such as I asked them for, getting up to them by some imaginary gamut. They were particularly fond of exercises in fourths, — do-fa-re-sol, and so forth, up and down. Fa (the lower dominant) struck them more especially by its force.

"What a whopper of a fa!" said Sémka. "It just cuts clean."

The unmusical boys soon fell away, while with the musical boys the class lasted as much as three or four hours. I tried to give them an idea of time by the accepted method, but the matter proved so difficult that I was compelled to separate time from tune and, writing down the sounds without the measure, to analyze them, and then, having written down the time, that is, the measure without the sounds, to analyze one beat by tapping the finger, and only then to combine the two processes together.

After a few lessons, when I tried to render myself an account of what I had been doing, I came to the conclusion that my method of instruction is almost the same as Chevet's method, which I had seen in practice at Paris, — a method which I had not adopted at once simply because it was a method. All those who are teaching singing cannot be urged too much to read that work, on the outer cover of which it says in large letters "*Repoussé à l'unanimité*" and which now is sold in tens of thousands of copies throughout Europe. I saw in Paris striking examples of success with that method when taught by Chevet himself: an audience of from five to six hundred men and women, sometimes of between forty and fifty years of age, were singing in absolute harmony and *à livre ouvert*, whatever the teacher gave them to sing.

In Chevet's method there are many rules, exercises, prescribed courses, which have no significance whatever, and the like of which every intelligent teacher will invent by the hundred on the battle-field, that is, during the class; there is there a very comical, though it may be a very convenient, method of keeping time without the sounds, for example, at four fourths the pupil says ta-fa-te-fe, at three fourths the pupil says ta-te-ti, at eight eighths ta-fa-te-fe-te-re-li-ri. All that is interesting, as one of the means by which music may be taught, interesting as the history of a certain musical school, but these rules are not absolute and cannot form a method. But in Chevet there are thoughts remarkable on account of their simplicity, three of which form the essence of his method:

(1) An old idea of expressing the musical signs by means of figures, first introduced by Jean Jacques Rousseau in his "*Dictionnaire de musique.*" Whatever the

opponents of this method of writing may say, any teacher of singing may make this experiment, and he will always convince himself of the immense advantage of figures over the staff, both for reading and writing. I taught with the staff about ten lessons, and only once pointed out the figures, telling them that it was the same, and the pupils always ask me to write the figures for them, and always themselves write the figures. (2) A remarkable idea, exclusively belonging to Chevet, which consists in teaching the sounds independently of time, and vice versa. Having but once applied this method to instruction, everybody will see that that which had appeared as an insuperable difficulty will now appear so easy that he will only marvel how it is such a simple thought had not occurred to any one before. How many torments the unfortunate children would be saved, who sing in the archiepiscopal and other choirs, if the conductors only tried this simple thing, — to make the student, without singing, strike with a little stick or with his finger that phrase which he is to sing: four times a whole note, once a quarter note or two eighths, and so forth, then sing, without counting time, the same phrase, then again sing a measure, and then all together.

For example, it is written:

The pupil will first sing, without counting time, do-re-mi-fa-sol-mi-re-do; then he, without singing, but only striking the note of the first measure, says, one, two, three, four; then, on the first note of the third measure he strikes twice and says, one, two, and the second note of the third measure, saying, three, four, and so forth; then he sings beating time, while the other pupils read aloud.

That is my method which, like Chevet's, cannot be prescribed; it is convenient, but there may be discovered more convenient methods still. The main thing is to separate the study of time from sound, though there may be an endless number of ways to accomplish this.

Finally, Chevet's third great idea consists in making music and its study popular. His method of instruction fully realizes this aim. And that is not only Chevet's wish and my assumption, but an actual fact. I saw in Paris hundreds of labourers with horny hands, sitting on benches, underneath which lay the tools with which they were returning from their shops, singing from music, comprehending and enjoying the laws of music. As I looked at these labourers, I could easily imagine Russian peasants in their place, if Chevet but spoke Russian: they would sing in just the same fashion, would just as easily understand everything he was saying about the common rules and laws of music. We hope to have an occasion to say something more about Chevet, and more especially about the importance of popularized music, especially singing, as a means for uplifting the decaying art.

I now pass over to the description of the progress of instruction in our school. After six lessons the goslings were separated from the sheep; there were left only the musical natures, the amateurs, and we passed over to the minor scales, and to the explanation of intervals. The only difficulty was to find and distinguish the small second from the large. Fa was called a "whopper" by the pupils, do was just such a "crier," and so I did not have to teach them, — they themselves felt the note into which the small second resolved itself, and so they felt the second itself. We easily found that the major scale consisted of a sequence of two large, one small, three large, and one small seconds. Then we sang "Glory be to God" in the minor scale, and by ear got up to the scale which turned out to be minor; then we found in that scale one large, one small, two large, one small, one very large, and one small second. Then I showed them that it was possible to sing and write a scale beginning with any sound, that when it does not come to large or small second, when necessary, we may place a sharp or flat. For convenience' sake I wrote out for them a chromatic scale of the following kind:

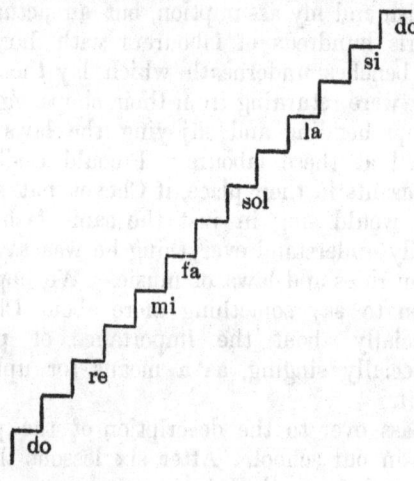

Along this staircase I made them write all kinds of major and minor scales, beginning with any note whatever. These exercises amused them very much, and the progress was so striking that two of them frequently passed their time between classes in writing out the tunes of the songs which they knew. These pupils are continually humming the motives of some songs which they cannot name, and they hum them sweetly and tenderly, and, above all, they now second much better and cannot bear to hear all the children sing inharmoniously together.

We had hardly more than twelve lessons during the

winter. Our instruction was spoiled by ambition. The parents, we, the teachers, and the pupils themselves, wanted to surprise the whole village,— to sing in the church; we began to prepare the mass and the cherubical songs of Bortnyánski. It seemed to be more amusing for the children, but it turned out quite differently. Although the desire to be in the choir sustained them, and they loved music, and we, the teachers, put forth our special effort in this subject and made it more compulsory than the rest, I often felt sorry, looking at some tiny Kiryúshka in torn leg-rags, as he rolled off his part, "Secretly fo-o-o-o-orming," and was requested to repeat it ten times, which finally vexed him so much that he beat the music with his fingers, insisting that he was singing right.

We once travelled down to the church and had a success; the enthusiasm was enormous, but the singing suffered from it: the lessons were growing tedious to them, and they fell out by degrees, and it was only at Easter that it was possible after great effort to get together a choir. Our singers began to resemble archiepiscopal singers, who frequently sing well, but with whom, on account of that skill, all desire for singing is killed, and who absolutely know nothing of notes, though they think they do know. I have frequently seen those who come out of such a school undertake to study themselves without knowing anything about notes, but they are quite helpless the moment they try to sing that which has not been shouted into their ears.

From the small experience which I have had in the instruction of music, I have convinced myself:

(1) That the method of writing the sounds down in figures is the most convenient.

(2) That teaching time independently of sound is the most convenient method.

(3) That, in order that the musical instruction should leave traces and should be cheerfully received, it is

necessary from the very start to teach the art, and not the skill of singing and playing. Young ladies may be made to play Burgmüner's exercises, but the children of the people it is better not to teach at all than to teach mechanically.

(4) That the aim of the musical instruction for the pupils must consist in transmitting to them that knowledge of the common laws of music which we possess, but by no means in the transmission of that false taste which is developed in us.

(5) That the aim of teaching the masses music must consist in transmitting to them such knowledge of the common laws of music as we possess, but by no means in transmitting to them that false taste which is developed in us.

# LINEN - MEASURER

History of a Horse

1861

# LINEN-MEASURER

Dedicated to the Memory of M. A. Stakhóvich [1]

## I.

THE sky rose higher and higher; the dawn spread farther and farther; the dull silver of the dew grew whiter; the sickle of the moon looked ever more lifeless; the forest resounded more sonorously — People began to get up, and in the manorial horse-yard could be heard ever more frequently snorting, rummaging in the straw, and even the whining neigh of horses crowded together and fussing about something.

"Hold on! You will have time! Are you hungry?" said the old herdman, quickly opening the creaking gates. "Back!" he shouted, swinging his arm toward the mare that was pushing her way through the gate.

Herdman Néster was dressed in a Cossack short coat, girded with an ornamented leather belt; his whip was swung over his shoulder, and his bread was wrapped in a scarf stuck into his belt. He carried a saddle and a bridle in his hands.

The horses were not in the least frightened and offended

[1] This subject was under consideration by M. A. Stakhóvich, and communicated to the author by A. A. Stakhóvich. — *Author's Note.*

by the frivolous tone of the herdman; they looked as
though it did not make much difference to them, and
leisurely walked away from the gate; only one bay,
shaggy-maned mare dropped an ear and rapidly turned
her back to him. Upon this occasion a young mare, who
was standing behind her, and who was not at all concerned
in the matter, whined and kicked her hind legs at the
first horse she ran across.

"Hoa there!" the herdman cried out even louder and
more threateningly, marching toward the corner of the
yard.

Of all the horses that were in the enclosure (there were
more than one hundred of them), the least impatience
was displayed by a piebald gelding, who was standing
alone in the corner under a penthouse, and, blinking with
his eyes, was licking the oak bark of the carriage shed.

It is impossible to tell what pleasure the piebald gelding
found in this, but his expression was serious and thoughtful while he was doing it.

"Lazybones!" the herdman turned to him, again in
the same tone, as he walked up toward him and placed
the saddle and the glossy saddle-cloth on the manure pile
near by.

The piebald gelding stopped licking and, without stirring, for a long time looked at Néster. He did not laugh,
nor get angry, nor frown, but only moved his own belly,
drawing a very deep breath, and turned away. The
herdman put his arm around his neck and put the bridle
on him.

"Why are you sighing so?" said Néster.

The gelding switched his tail, as though to say: "Oh,
nothing, Néster."

Néster put the saddle-cloth on him, whereat the horse,
evidently to express his dissatisfaction, dropped his ears,
for which he was only scolded as a "good-for-nothing"
and had his belly-band tightened.

At this the gelding puffed himself up with anger, but Néster put his finger into the horse's mouth, and gave him such a kick in his belly with the foot that he had to let out his breath. And yet, when the girth was tightened on him, he once more dropped his ears and even looked around. Although he knew that it would do him no good, he considered it his duty to show that it was not agreeable to him, and that he would always express his dissatisfaction with it. When he was saddled, he put forth his swollen right leg and began to chew the bit, again for some special reason, for he ought to have known that there could be no taste to a bit.

Néster climbed on the gelding over a short stirrup, unwound his whip, straightened out his coat from under his knee, seated himself in the saddle in a peculiar attitude, such as coachmen, gentlemen riders, and herdmen assume, and pulled the reins. The gelding raised his head, expressing his willingness to proceed when ordered, but he did not stir from the spot. He knew that before starting Néster would make no end of fuss, giving orders to Váska and calling out to the horses. Indeed, Néster began to shout:

"Váska! Oh, Váska! Have you let out the mares, eh? Where are you going, devil? Hoa there! Are you asleep? Open the gate! Let the mares get out first!" and so forth.

The gate creaked. Váska, angry and sleepy, holding a horse by the bridle, was standing near the gate-post and letting out the horses. The horses began to pass out one after another, cautiously stepping over the straw and sniffing at it: there were fillies, yearling stallions, suckling colts, and mares great with young, cautiously, one by one, carrying their bellies through the gate. The young mares crowded together, sometimes two and three at a time, placing their heads over each other's backs and tripping through the gate, for which they each time were rebuked by the herdmen. The suckling colts now and then darted under the legs of strange mares, neighing sonorously in response to the short whinny of the mares.

A young playful mare bent her head downward and sidewise the moment she got out of the gate, kicked up with her hind legs and whinnied; but she did not dare to run ahead of old, dappled gray Zhuldýba, who, as always, was walking cautiously, in a slow and heavy step, at the head of all the horses.

In a few minutes the animated enclosure was sadly deserted; the pillars towered gloomily under the empty penthouse, and there could be seen nothing but crumpled and dung-covered straw. No matter how familiar this picture of desolation was to the piebald gelding, it must have affected him with melancholy. He slowly lowered and raised his head, as though greeting some one, drew a sigh, as much as the girth permitted him to do so, and, dragging his crooked and stiff legs, shambled after the herd, carrying old Néster on his bony back.

"I know: as soon as we get out on the road, he will strike fire and will light his wooden pipe with the brass trimming and with the little chain," thought the gelding "I am glad of it, because early in the morning, while the dew is on the ground, this odour is pleasant to me and reminds me of many pleasant things; the only annoying thing is that the old man with his pipe becomes quite dashing, imagining that he is somebody, and sits down sidewise, by all means sidewise, — and it is there where it pains me. However, God be with him! It is not the first time I have had to suffer, to afford somebody pleasure; I have even come to derive a certain equine pleasure from it. Let the poor fellow put on style! He feels courageous only when nobody sees him. Let him sit sidewise!" reflected the gelding, as he, stepping cautiously with his crooked legs, walked in the middle of the road.

## II.

HAVING driven the herd to the river, near which the horses were to graze, Néster climbed down from the gelding and unsaddled him. The herd had in the meantime begun to scatter over the untrampled meadow, which was covered with dew and with a mist rising alike from the meadow and the encircling river.

Having taken off the bridle from the piebald gelding, Néster scratched him under his neck, in response to which the gelding, to express his gratefulness and pleasure, closed his eyes.

"He likes it, old dog!" said Néster.

But the gelding did not like that scratching in the least, and only out of delicacy of feeling pretended that it pleased him; he shook his head in sign of consent.

But suddenly, Néster, entirely unexpectedly and without any cause, perhaps supposing that too great a familiarity might give the piebald gelding a wrong idea about his importance,— Néster, without any warning, pushed away from him the head of the gelding, and, swinging the bridle, struck the gelding a very painful blow on his lean leg with the buckle of the bridle and, without saying anything, went up a mound to the stump near which he generally sat.

Though this deed grieved the piebald gelding, he did not show it, and, slowly swaying his scanty tail and sniffing at something and browsing just for pastime, walked over to the river.

He paid no attention to what the young mares, yearling stallions, and suckling colts, enjoying the early morning, were doing all around him. Knowing that it was healthiest, especially at his age, first to take a good drink on an empty stomach, and then only to go to eating, he selected a spot near the shore, where it was steepest and clearest, and, wetting his hoofs and fetlocks, dipped his muzzle in the water and began to suck in the water through his torn lips, to expand his full sides, and from pleasure to swing his scanty piebald tail on the bald stump.

A quarrelsome bay mare, who always teased the old fellow and caused him all kinds of annoyances, even now came up to him in the water, as though attending to some affair of hers, but, in reality, only in order to roil the water before his very nose. But the piebald gelding had had his fill and, as though not noticing the intention of the bay mare, one after another drew out his feet which were sunk in the mud, tossed his head, and, walking away from the youthful crowd, began to eat. Sprawling his feet in all kinds of fashion, and trampling down no more grass than was necessary, he, without unbending himself, ate exactly three hours. When he had eaten so much that his belly hung down like a bag from his lean, steep ribs, he balanced himself on his four sore legs so as to experience the least amount of pain, especially in his right fore leg, which was weaker than the rest, and fell asleep.

There is an old age which is majestic, and another which is homely, and another still which is pitiful. And there is also an old age which is both homely and majestic. The old age of the piebald gelding was precisely of that order.

The gelding was tall, not less than two arshíns three vershóks[1] in height. His hair was dappled black, that is, it had been, but now the black spots had become of a dirty bay hue. His piebaldness consisted of three spots: one, on the head, extending as a crooked white spot from one side of the nose down to the middle of the neck. His

[1] An arshín is about 2 feet, 4 inches; a vershók is 1-16 arshín.

long bur-matted mane was white and brownish in spots. Another spot extended down the right side as far as the middle of his belly; the third, on the crupper, took in the upper part of the tail and went down to the middle of the flanks. The rest of his tail was whitish and checkered.

His large bony head, with deep hollows over the eyes and a pendent, torn, black lower lip, hung low and heavily on his emaciated and bent neck, which looked as though made of wood. Back of the pendent lower lip could be seen a blackish tongue turned to one side and the yellow stumps of the ground-down lower teeth. The ears, of which one was slit, hung low on both sides and lazily moved from time to time, in order to scare away the pestering flies. One tuft of his forelock, which was still long, hung behind his ears; his open brow was sunken and curly; on the spacious jowls the skin hung down in bags. On the neck and head the veins were connected in knots, which twitched and trembled at every touch of a fly. The expression of his face was that of austere patience, deep thought, and suffering.

His fore legs were bent archlike at the knee; both hoofs were swollen, and on one leg, on which the piebald spot reached down to the middle, there was at the knee a swelling of the size of a fist. His hind legs were in a better condition, but the hair was worn off the haunches and refused to grow out again. All the legs looked disproportionately long on account of the thinness of the body.

The ribs, though flat and declivitous, stood out from the body, and were so covered by skin that the skin seemed to have stuck fast to the intervals between the ribs. The withers and the back had a variegated appearance from old blows, and on the back there was a still freshly swollen and festering sore; the black tail stump, with its clearly defined vertebræ, was long and almost bare. On the bay crupper, near the tail, there was a scar of the size of the palm of the hand, as though from a bite, which was overgrown with white hair. Another scarred sore could be seen on the shoulder.

His hocks and tail were soiled from the chronic disorder of his stomach. The hair, though short, stood in tufts all over his body. And yet, in spite of the hideous old age of this horse, one involuntarily stopped and reflected, looking at him, and a connoisseur would have said at once that he had been a fine horse in his day. A connoisseur would also have said that there was only one stock in Russia which could produce such broad bones, such immense kneepans, such hoofs, such slender leg bones, such a well-built neck, and, above all, such a head bone, such large, black, bright eyes, and such thoroughbred ganglia of veins about the head and neck, and such a thin skin and such hair.

Indeed, there was something majestic in the figure of that horse, and in the terrible combination of the repulsive signs of his decrepitude, which was the more apparent through the variegated colour of his skin, and of his manner and expression of self-confidence and calm, which are peculiar to conscious beauty and strength.

Like a living ruin, he stood alone in the midst of the dew-drenched meadow, while not far from him could be heard the tramping, snorting youthful neighing and whinnying of the scattered herd.

## III.

The sun had risen above the forest and now shone brightly on the grass and on the bends of the river. The dew was drying up, collecting in drops; the last of the morning mist passed away as light smoke. The cloudlets were becoming curly, but there was as yet no wind. Beyond the river stood green rye, curling into pipes, and there was an odour of fresh verdure and of blossoms.

A cuckoo was calling hoarsely in the forest, and Néster, lying on his back, was counting the number of years he was to live yet. The larks rose over the rye and the meadow. A belated hare lost his way among the herd, jumped out into the open, sat down near a bush, and began to listen. Váska had fallen asleep, with his head in the grass; the mares made a still larger circle about him and scattered over the meadow. The old mares, snorting, made a bright path over the dew and looked for places where they might remain unmolested; they no longer ate, but only tasted some choice pieces of grass. The whole herd was imperceptibly moving in one direction.

And again old Zhuldýba, walking with measured step in front of the rest, showed the possibility of going farther. Young black Fly, who had just had her first colt, kept whinnying all the time and, raising her tail, snorted at her lilac colt. Young Atlas, with smooth and glossy hair, lowered her head in such a way that the black, silky forelock covered her brow and eyes; she was playing with the grass — now biting it off, now throwing it away — and striking the ground with her dew-drenched foot with shaggy fetlock.

One of the older colts, no doubt imagining he was playing some game, was now running around his mother for the twenty-sixth time, raising his short, curly tail in the shape of a panache, while she calmly continued to browse, having become accustomed to her son's character, and only occasionally looking at him awry with her large black eye.

One of the smallest colts, a black, big-headed little fellow, with forelock towering surprised between his ears and a little tail turned to one side, as it had been in his mother's womb, stood with pricked ears and dull glance, without stirring from the spot, looking fixedly at the colt who was frisking and prancing about, — it is hard to tell whether he was envying him or condemning him for what he was doing.

Some of the colts were suckling, hitting their mothers' teats with their noses; some, without any apparent reason, did not respond to their mothers' calls, but ran in an awkward, mincing trot in this opposite direction, as though looking for something, and then, no one knew why, stopped and neighed in a despairingly penetrating voice; some lay stretched out in a row; some were learning to eat grass; and some again were scratching themselves behind their ears with a hind leg.

Two mares with young were walking apart from the rest and, slowly dragging their legs along, were still eating. It was evident that their condition was respected by the rest, and none of the younger horses dared to approach and disturb them. If some frisky colts happened, nevertheless, to come near to them, one motion of the ear and tail was sufficient to show them all the indecency of their behaviour.

The yearling stallions and fillies pretended to be grown up and sedate, and but rarely leaped about or joined the jolly company. They ate the grass with all due propriety, stretching out their clipped swanlike necks, and switching their little tufts as though they were tails. Just like the grown-up ones, some of them lay down, rolled, or scratched each other.

The jolliest company was composed of the two and three-year-old fillies and of the maiden mares. They were going all together as a merry maiden crowd. Among them could be heard tramping, whinnying, neighing, and snorting. They came together, placed their heads over each other's shoulders, sniffed at each other, jumped about, and, now and then raising their tails with a 'trumpet-like flourish, proudly and coquettishly raced in front of their companions in a half-trot, half-amble.

The first beauty and the first instigator of fun among all this youth was the mischievous bay mare. Whatever she undertook to do, the others did; wherever she went, a whole crowd of beauties followed her. The mischievous mare was in an unusually playful mood on that morning. The happy mood had come over her, just as it comes over people. Even at the watering-place, when she had played her prank on the old gelding, she ran down in the water, pretending to have been frightened by something, and with a loud snort raced down the field so that Váska was compelled to gallop after her and after the others that had started off with her. Then, having eaten a bit, she began to roll, and then to tease the old mares by running up in front of them; then she separated a suckling colt from his mother, as though wishing to bite him. The mother was frightened and stopped eating, while the little colt whinnied in a pitiful voice; but the mischievous mare did not touch him at all: she only scared him some, thus affording a spectacle to her companions who were looking sympathetically at her tricks. Then she undertook to turn the head of a gray horse which a peasant was driving in a plough over the rye-field, far away on the other side of the river. She took up a proud attitude, somewhat to one side, raised her head, shook herself, and neighed in a sweet, tender, and drawn-out voice. In this neighing there was expressed mischief, and feeling, and a certain sadness. There was in it both the desire and the promise of love, and the pining for it.

There a corn-crake, leaping from place to place in the thick reeds, was passionately calling for his mate; there the cuckoo and the quail were singing love, and the flowers were sending their fragrant dust over the wind to each other.

"I am young, and beautiful, and strong," said the neighing of the mischievous one, "but I have not been allowed so far to experience the sweetness of that feeling; not only have I not been allowed to experience it, but not one lover, not one, has ever seen me."

And the significant neighing resounded sad and full of youth and was borne over the meadow and over the field, and reached the gray horse in the distance. He raised his ears and stopped. The peasant struck him with his bast shoe, but the gray horse was spelled by the silvery sound of the distant neighing, and himself neighed. The peasant grew angry, jerked the lines, and gave him with the bast shoe such a kick in his belly that he stopped in the middle of the neighing and moved on. But the gray horse felt both happy and sad, and from the distant rye-field the sounds of an incipient passionate neighing and of the angry voice of the peasant were for a long time borne to the herd.

If the mere voice could have turned the head of the gray horse so as to make him forget his duty, what would have happened to him if he could have seen the whole beautiful form of the mischievous mare as she, pricking her ears, expanding her nostrils, drawing in the air, ready to run, and trembling with her whole youthful and beautiful body, was calling him.

But the mischievous one did not dwell long on her impressions. When the voice of the gray horse died away, she gave another scornful neigh and, lowering her head, began to paw the earth, and then went away to waken and tease the piebald gelding. The piebald gelding was the constant martyr and butt of this happy youth. He suffered more from this youth than from people. He had done no wrong to either. People needed him, but why did the young horses torment him?

## IV.

He was old, they were young; he was lean, they were plump; he was sad, they were merry. Consequently he was an entire stranger to them, an entirely different being, and there was no reason for pitying him. Horses pity only themselves and only exceptionally those in whose hide they can imagine themselves. But was it the piebald gelding's fault that he was old and haggard and homely?

One would think not, but according to equine sense he was blameworthy, and those only were right who were strong, young, and happy, those with whom everything was still ahead, those whose every muscle quivered and whose tails rose up straight from every unnecessary tension. It may be that the piebald gelding himself understood that, and in his quiet moments agreed with them that he was blameworthy for having lived his life and that he had to pay for that life; but still he was a horse, and so he frequently could not repress a consciousness of insult, sadness, and provocation, whenever he looked at the youth tormenting him for that to which they themselves would be subject at the end of their lives. Another cause of the pitilessness of the horses was an aristocratic feeling. All of them, on their father's or mother's side, derived their genealogy from the famous stud Cream, while the piebald gelding was of an unknown origin, having come from the outside, where three years before he had been bought in the market-place for eighty roubles in assignats.

The bay mare, pretending to be taking a walk, went up

to the very nose of the piebald gelding and pushed him.
He knew what it was, and, without opening his eyes,
dropped his ears and showed his teeth. The mare turned
her back to him and looked as though she was going to
kick him. He opened his eyes and went away. He was
no longer asleep, and so began to eat. Again the mischief-maker, accompanied by her companions, walked
over to the gelding. A two-year-old, white-spotted mare,
a very stupid beast, who in everything and always imitated the bay mare, went with her and, as is always the
case with imitators, put on too thick that which the mischief-maker had been doing. The bay mare generally
walked over to him as though attending to her own business, and passed in front of his nose, without looking at
him, so that he was positively unable to tell whether he
ought to get angry or not, and so it was really funny.

This she did even now, but the white-spotted mare,
who was following her and who was in an unusually
frisky mood, struck the gelding with her breast. He
again showed his teeth, screeched, and with an agility
which one could not have expected of him made for her
and bit her in the flank. The white-spotted mare kicked
up her hind legs with all her might and gave the old
gelding a painful blow on his lean, bare ribs. The gelding groaned and wanted to rush at her once more, but
changed his mind and, drawing a deep sigh, went away.

No doubt all the youth of the herd regarded as a
personal insult the impudence which the piebald gelding
had allowed himself to offer to the white-spotted mare,
for they positively gave him no chance to eat the rest of
the day, nor did they give him a moment of rest, so that
the herdman had to bring them several times to their
senses, and he was unable to make out what the matter
with them was.

The gelding was so much insulted that he himself went
up to Néster when the old man was getting ready to

drive the herd home, and felt himself happier and calmer when he was saddled and mounted.

God knows what the old gelding was thinking of as he was carrying old Néster on his back. Whether he was resentfully thinking of the impudent and cruel youth, or whether, with a contemptuous and taciturn pride, characteristic of old persons, he forgave his offenders, — he in no way manifested his reflections on his whole way home.

That very evening friends had come to see Néster, and, as he was driving the herd past the huts of the manorial servants, he noticed a cart with a horse, tied to his porch. Having driven in the herd, he was in such a hurry that he did not take off the saddle, but let the gelding out into the yard, called out to Váska to unsaddle the herding-horse, closed the gate, and went to his friends.

Whether on account of the insult offered to the white-spotted mare, Cream's great-grandchild, by the "mangy trash," bought at a horse-market and knowing neither his father nor his mother, and the consequent offended aristocratic feeling of the whole enclosure, or whether the gelding in his high saddle, without the rider, presented an odd and fantastic spectacle to the horses, — certainly something unusual took place that evening in the enclosure. All the horses, young and old, ran after the gelding, with grinning teeth, driving him about the yard; there were heard the scunds of hoofs striking against his lean sides and heavy groans. The gelding could stand it no longer, — he could no longer escape the blows. He stopped in the middle of the yard; in his face there was expressed the disgusting, feeble fury of impotent old age, then despair; he dropped his ears, and suddenly something happened which made all the horses grow silent. The eldest of the mares, Vyazopúrikha, went up to the gelding, sniffed at him, and drew a sigh. The gelding, too, drew a sigh.

. . . . . . . . . .

## V.

In the middle of the yard lighted up by the moon stood the tall, lean figure of the gelding with the high saddle, with the big knob of its bow. The horses stood motionless and in profound silence all about him, as though they had found out something new and unusual from him. Indeed, they did find out from him something new and unusual.

This is what they learned from him.

. . . . . . . . .

### FIRST NIGHT

"Yes, I am the son of Darling I. and of Bába. My name according to the pedigree is Muzhík I. I am Muzhík I. according to the pedigree, but nicknamed Linen-measurer, called so by the crowd for my long and flowing gait, the like of which there was not in all Russia. There is no more thoroughly bred horse in the whole world than I am. I should never have told you so. What good would it do? You would never have recognized me, just as Vyazopúrikha, who was with me at Khryénov, has not recognized me before this. You would not have believed me even now if Vyazopúrikha were not my witness. I should never have told it to you. I do not need your equine compassion. But you asked for it. Yes I am that Linen-measurer whom the connoisseurs of horse-flesh are looking for and cannot find, that Linen-measurer whom the count himself knew and whom he got rid of from his stud for having outran his favourite, Swan.

. . . . . . . . .

"When I was born, I did not know what 'piebald' meant,—I thought I was a horse. The first remark about my hair, I remember, startled me and my mother.

"I must have been born at night; in the morning I was all licked clean by my mother and could stand on my feet. I remember, I was all the time wanting something, and everything seemed exceedingly wonderful and, at the same time, exceedingly simple. Our stalls were in a long, warm corridor, with grated doors, through which everything could be seen.

"My mother offered me her teats, but I was still so innocent that I nudged her with my nose, now between her forelegs, and now at her udders. Suddenly my mother looked back at the grated door, and, putting her leg over me, stepped aside. The groom of the day was looking at us·through the grate.

"'I declare, Bába has had a colt,' he said, and began to draw back the door-bolt.

"He walked over the fresh bedding and embraced me.

"'Look here, Tarás,' he called out, 'and see how piebald he is,—just like a magpie.'

"I darted away from him and fell on my knees.

"'What a little devil!' he said.

"My mother was anxious, but did not defend me; she only drew a deep, deep breath and walked a little aside. The grooms came to look at me. One ran away to announce the fact to the keeper of the stable.

"All laughed, looking at my piebald spots, and gave me all kinds of names. Neither I nor even my mother understood the meaning of these words. Up till then there had not been among us or among all my relatives a single piebald horse. We did not think there was anything wrong about it. All then praised my build and my strength.

"'See how quick he is!' said a groom. 'You can't hold him.'

"After awhile the keeper came, and he marvelled at my colour; he even seemed to be aggrieved.

"'I wonder after whom this monster takes,' he said. 'The general will not leave him in the stud. O Bába, you have played me a nice trick.' He turned to my mother. 'If you had had a white-spotted one, I should not have minded it so, but no, this one is all piebaid!'

"My mother made no reply and, as always in such cases, again drew a sigh.

"'What devil does he take after? Just like a muzhík!' he continued. 'He can't be left in the stud! It is a shame! And yet he is a fine colt, he is fine!' said he, and so said all, looking at me.

"A few days later the general himself came; he looked at me, and again all seemed to be horrified and rebuked me and my mother for the colour of my hair.

"'And yet he is a fine colt, he is!' said all who saw me.

"Until spring we all lived separated in the mare stable, each with his mother; occasionally, when the snow began to melt in the sun on the roofs of the stables, mother and I were let out in a broad yard bedded with fresh straw. Here I for the first time became acquainted with all my near and distant relatives. Here I saw all the famous mares of that time come out with their young from different doors. Here was old Dutchy, Fly, Cream's daughter, Reddy, riding-horse Complaint,— all the famous mares of that time, all were gathered there with their young, walking about in the sun, rolling on the fresh straw, and sniffing at each other, like any common horses.

"The sight of that enclosure, filled with the beauties of that time, I have never been able to forget. There was also that very Vyazopúrikha, who then was a yearling filly,— a sweet, lively, merry little horse; but, no insult being meant to her, although now she is regarded by you as a remarkable thoroughbred, she then was only one of the worst horses of that breed. She will herself tell you so.

"My variegated colour, which had so displeased the men, found great favour with the horses; they all surrounded me, admired me, and played with me. I began to forget the words of the men and felt happy. Soon I learned the first sorrow of my life, and the cause of it was my mother. When it began to melt, and the sparrows twittered under the roofs, and spring could be felt more strongly in the air, my mother began to change her treatment of me.

"All her manner was changed. Now she suddenly without any cause began to play, running about in the yard, which did not at all comport with her respectable age; now she fell to musing and started to neigh; now she bit and kicked her sister mares; now she began to sniff at me and snort out in dissatisfaction; and now, as she went out into the sun, she put her head over the shoulder of her cousin Tradeswoman, and for a long time scratched her back while lost in thought, and kept driving me away from her teats.

"Once there came the keeper of the stable, who ordered that a halter be put on her and that she be taken out of the stall. She neighed, and I answered her and made a dart for her, but she did not even look back at me. Groom Tarás put his arms around me just as they were closing the door after my mother had been led out.

"I bolted and threw the groom down on the straw, but the door was closed, and I only heard the receding neighing of my mother. But in that neigh I no longer heard a call for me, but something different. To her voice there came in response a mighty voice, that of Good I., as I later learned, who, with two grooms by his sides, was going to meet my mother.

"I do not remember how Tarás got out of my stall: I was too sad, for I felt that I had for ever lost the love of my mother. And it was all because I was piebald, I thought, recalling the words of the people about the colour of my hair, and I became so infuriated that I began to beat my head and my knees against the wall of the stall, and continued doing so until I began to perspire and had to stop from exhaustion.

"After awhile my mother returned to me. I heard her run up the corridor to our stall in a trot, and with an unusual gait. The door was opened for her, and I did not recognize her, — she looked so much younger and prettier. She sniffed at me, snorted, and began to whinny. I could see by her whole expression that she did not love me.

"She told me about Good's beauty and about her love of him. These meetings were continued, and the relations between me and my mother grew colder and colder.

"Soon we were let out to grass. Then I learned new joys, which took the place of my mother's lost love. I had companions and friends. We learned together to eat grass, to neigh like grown horses, and, raising our tails, to gallop in circles about our mothers. That was a happy time. I was forgiven everything; all loved me, admired me, and looked condescendingly at everything I did. That did not last long.

"Soon after something terrible happened to me."

The gelding heaved a terrible sigh, and walked away from the horses.

The dawn had long crimsoned the sky. The gate creaked, and Néster came in. The horses scattered. The herdman fixed the saddle on the gelding and drove out the herd.

## VI.

#### SECOND NIGHT

The moment the horses were all driven home, they again gathered about the piebald gelding.

"In the month of August mother and I were separated," began the gelding, "and I did not experience any special grief. I saw that my mother was heavy with a younger brother, famous Usán, and I was no longer to her what I had been. I was not jealous, but I felt that I was getting colder toward her. Besides, I knew that, leaving my mother, I was going to enter into the common division of colts, where we were stationed two and three at a time, and whence a whole lot of us young colts were let out into the open. I stood in the same division with Dear. Dear was a riding-horse, and later on the emperor rode him, and he was represented in paintings and in statues. But at that time he was still a simple colt, with soft, glossy hair, a swanlike neck, and legs as straight and thin as strings. He was always jolly, good-natured, and kind; he was always ready to play, to lick, and to joke either horse or man.

"We involuntarily became friends, living together, and that friendship lasted during the whole time of our youth.

"He was cheerful and frivolous. He even then began to fall in love and play with the mares, and he laughed at my innocence. To my misfortune, I from egotism began to imitate him, and soon was carried away by love. That early weakness of mine was the cause of the greatest change in my fate. It happened so that I was carried away —— Vyazopúrikha was one year older than I; we were specially friendly with each other, but toward the end of autumn I noticed that she began to be shy of me.

"But I will not tell all that unfortunate story of my first love; she herself remembers my senseless transport which ended for me in the most important change in my life.

"The herdmen began to drive her away and to strike me. In the evening I was driven into a special stall, where I neighed all night long as though having a presentiment of what was to happen on the following day.

"In the morning the general, the keeper, the grooms, and the herdmen came to the corridor where my stall was, and there was raised a terrible hubbub. The general shouted to the keeper; the keeper vindicated himself by saying that he had given no order to let me out, but that the grooms had done so on their own account. The general said that he should have them all flogged, but that the young stallions should not be kept. The keeper promised that everything would be done. They grew quiet and went away. I did not comprehend a thing, but I saw that something was to be done with me.

. . . . . . . . . . .

"On the following day I for ever stopped neighing,— I became what I now am. The whole world was changed in my eyes. Nothing gave me any pleasure: I pondered over myself and began to brood. At first everything annoyed me. I even ceased to eat, to drink, and to walk, and, of course, play was out of the question. Now and then it would occur to me to give a kick, take a run, start a neigh; but immediately the terrible question arose before me: What for? Why? and my last strength was gone.

"Once I was being led around in the evening, as the herd was driven from the field. At a distance I saw a cloud of dust with the indistinct familiar contours of all our mares. I heard a merry whinnying and tramping. I stopped, although the rope of the halter, by which the groom was pulling me, was cutting the nape of my neck, and began to look at the approaching herd, as one looks at the happiness which is for ever lost and will not return.

"They were coming nearer, and I could tell one after another all the beautiful, majestic, healthy, well-fed horses whom I knew so well. Some of them also looked at me. I did not feel any pain from the jerking of the groom's halter. I forgot myself and involuntarily neighed from old habit and ran in a trot; but my neighing sounded sad, ridiculous, and insipid.

"They did not laugh in the herd, but I noticed that many of them turned away from me out of politeness. They were obviously disgusted, and sorry, and ashamed, and, above all, I appeared so ridiculous to them. What they found so ridiculous was my thin, inexpressive neck, big head (I had grown lean in the meantime), my long, clumsy legs, and the stupid trotting gait, with which I, from old habit, started to make evolutions about the groom. Nobody replied to my neighing, — all turned away from me. I suddenly understood all; I understood how I had once and for all become a stranger to them, — I do not remember how I reached home with the groom.

"I had even before begun to show an inclination toward seriousness and reflection, and now a complete transformation took place in me. My piebald spots, which had produced such a strange contempt in people for me, and my peculiar position in the stud, which I began to feel but was quite unable to explain to myself, caused me to brood over myself.

"I pondered on the injustice of men, who condemned me because I was piebald; I pondered on the inconstancy of maternal and, in general, of woman's love, and its dependence on physical conditions; and, above all, I pondered on the qualities of that strange race of animals, with whom we are so intimately connected and whom we call men, — those qualities from which sprang that peculiar position of mine in the stud, which I felt but could not understand.

"The meaning of that peculiarity and of the human qualities on which it was based was revealed to me on the following occasion:

"It was in winter, during the holidays. I had not been given anything to eat or drink during the whole day. As I later learned, this was due to the fact that our groom was drunk. On that day the keeper of the stable came in to my stall and, upon seeing that I had no feed, began to call the absent groom all kinds of bad names.

"On the next day the groom came with a companion of his to our stall to give us hay. I saw that he was unusually pale and sad; especially in the expression of his long back was there something significant and provoking compassion.

"He angrily threw the hay over the railing. I stuck my head over his shoulder, being eager to eat; but he struck me with his fist such a blow on the point of my nose that I jumped away. Then he kicked me in the belly with his boot.

"'If it had not been for that mangy one,' he said, 'nothing would have happened.'

"'What is the matter?' asked the other.

"'The devil knows whether they have sold him or have given him away. If I had starved the count's horses, it would not have mattered, but how did I dare to give no feed to *his* colt. "Lie down," says he, and then they started walloping me! What has become of Christianity? They pity an animal more than a man. He must be an infidel: he himself did the counting, the barbarian! The general has never flogged me like that!

He has made swales on my whole back,—he evidently has no Christian soul!'

"What they were saying about flogging and Christianity, I understood well, but at that time I could not make out what was meant by the words 'his colt,' from which I saw that people assumed a certain connection between me and the keeper. Wherein this connection consisted I could not understand then. Only much later, when I was separated from the rest of the horses, did I comprehend what it meant. At that time I was absolutely unable to understand what was meant by calling *me* the property of a man. The words 'my horse' had reference to me, a living horse, and seemed as strange to me as the words 'my land,' 'my air,' 'my water.'

"But these words had an enormous influence upon me. I never stopped thinking of them, and only much later, after the most varied relations with men, did I finally come to understand the meaning ascribed by people to these strange words.

"People are guided in life, not by deeds, but by words. They love not so much the ability to do or not do something, as the ability to apply certain conventional words to all kinds of objects. Such words, which are regarded as very important by them, are 'my, mine,' which they say about different objects, beings, and things, even about the earth, about people, and about horses. About any one thing they have agreed to let just one man call it 'mine.' And he who, according to this game, agreed among them, is able to say 'mine' about the greatest number of things is regarded as the happiest. Why it is so, I do not know, only it is so. Formerly I used to attempt to explain it by some advantage which they derive from it, but that has proved to be unjust.

"Many of those people who, for example, called me their horse, did not ride on me, but entirely different persons rode on me. Nor did they, but others, feed me.

And again, it was not those who called me their horse who did kindnesses to me, but coachmen, veterinarians, and, in general, strangers.

"Having later expanded the circle of my observations, I convinced myself that even in respect to things other than horses the idea of 'mine' had no other foundation than a low, animal, human instinct, called by them the feeling or right of property. A man says 'my house,' and never lives in it, but only cares about the building and the maintenance of the house. A merchant says 'my shop, my draper's shop,' for example, and has not any clothes of the best cloth that there is in his shop.

"There are people who call the land their own, though they have never seen that land, and have never walked over it. There are people who call other people their own, and who have never seen those men; and the only relation which they bear to these people is to do them harm.

"There are people who call women their own women, or wives; but these women live with other men. And people strive in life not after doing good, but after calling as many things as possible 'theirs.'

"I am now convinced that in this lies the essential difference between men and us. Therefore, not to mention other advantages which we have over men, we by this alone may say that we stand higher than men in the scale of living beings; the activity of men, at least of those with whom I have had any relations, is guided by words, while ours is guided by deeds.

"It was this right to speak of me as 'my' horse which the keeper had acquired, and for which he had the groom flogged. That discovery affected me powerfully and, combined with those thoughts and reflections, which my piebald appearance called forth in men, and with the melancholy, called forth in me by the treason of my mother, caused me to become the serious and thoughtful gelding that I am.

"I was thrice unhappy: I was piebald, I was a gelding, and people imagined about me that I did not belong to God and to myself, as is proper for all living beings, but that I belonged to the keeper.

"There were many consequences of this belief of theirs. The first of these was that they kept me separate, fed me better, oftener took me out by the line, and hitched me up much earlier.

"I was hitched up the first time in my third year. I remember how the keeper himself, who imagined that I belonged to him, the first time began to hitch me up with a crowd of grooms, expecting violence or resistance from me. They tied me up with ropes as they took me down between the shafts; they put on my back a broad cross of leather straps and tied it to the shafts, so as to keep me from kicking, whereas I was only waiting for a chance to show them my willingness and love of work.

"They were surprised to see me go like an old horse. They began to drive me, and I began to exercise trotting. I made ever greater progress with every new day, so that in three months the general himself, and others, praised my gait. But, strange to say, even because they imagined that I was not theirs, but the keeper's, my gait had for them an entirely different meaning.

"My brother colts were driven in races, their records were kept, and people came out to see them, and they were driven in gilt sulkies, and expensive horse blankets were thrown over them. I travelled in the common carts of the keeper to help him attend to his business at Chesménka and other hamlets. All that was caused by the fact that I was piebald, and, chiefly, because I was, in their opinion, not the count's, but the keeper's own.

"To-morrow, if we are alive, I will tell you the chief

consequence that this right of property, which the keeper imagined he had, had for me."

All that day the horses treated Linen-measurer with respect. But Néster's treatment was as rude as before. The gray horse of the peasant, coming up to the herd, again neighed, and the bay mare again flirted with him.

## VII.

### THIRD NIGHT

The moon arose, and its narrow sickle illuminated the figure of Linen-measurer, who was standing in the middle of the yard; the horses were crowding around him.

"The chief wonderful consequence of my being not the count's or God's, but the keeper's," continued the piebald gelding, "was that that which forms our main desert, — namely our rapid gait, — became the cause of my expulsion. Swan was being driven on the track, as the Chesménka keeper drove up to the track with me. Swan went past us. He was a fine trotter, but he was showing off a great deal, and did not have that agility which I had worked out in myself, which was that at the touch of one foot the other should immediately be lifted, so that not the slightest effort should be lost in vain, but that every exertion should send me ahead.

"'Well, shall I try my piebald?' he called out; and when Swan came abreast with me he let me go. He had already the impetus ahead of me, and so I fell behind at the first turn; but in the second I began to gain on him, came nearer to his vehicle, came abreast of him, ran ahead, — and outstripped him.

"They tried a second time, — and the same took place. I was even in better trim, and this terrified all. The general asked to have me sold as far from him as possible, so that he might never hear of me.

"'For if the count finds out, there will be trouble,' he said.

"And so I was sold to a horse dealer as a centre horse. I did not stay long with the horse dealer. A hussar, who came to buy remounts, took me with him. All that was so unfair, so cruel, that I was glad when I was taken away from Khryénov, and when I for ever parted from that which was familiar and dear to me. I felt too painfully my situation among them. For them there was love, honour, freedom; for me labour, humiliation, work to the end of my life! Why? Because I was piebald, and because for that reason I had to become somebody's horse — "

Linen-measurer was unable to proceed with his story upon that evening. In the enclosure there happened something that stirred up all the horses. Tradeswoman, a mare late with young, who had been listening to the beginning of the story, suddenly turned around and slowly walked over to the shed; there she began to groan so loud that all the horses directed their attention to her; then she lay down, then rose again, and again lay down. The old mares understood what the matter was, but the young horses were agitated, and, leaving the gelding, surrounded the sick mare.

On the morrow there was a new colt who was quivering on his legs. Néster called the keeper, and the mare with her colt was taken to a stall, while the horses were driven out without them.

## III.

#### FOURTH NIGHT

In the evening, when the gate was closed and all quieted down, the piebald continued as follows:

"I have had opportunity to make many observations, both on men and on horses, during the time that I passed from hand to hand. Longest of all I stayed with two masters, with a prince, an officer of hussars, and later with an old woman who lived near the Church of St. Nicholas, the miracle-worker.

"With the officer of hussars I passed the best time of my life.

"Although he was the cause of my ruin, although he never loved any one or anything, I have always loved him for that very reason.

"What I liked in him was that he was handsome, happy, rich, and therefore loved nobody.

"You must understand that exalted equine feeling of ours! His coldness, my dependence on him, added special strength to my love for him. 'Kill me, drive me to death,' I used to think in our good days, 'I will only be the happier for it.'

"He had bought me of the horse dealer, to whom the keeper had sold me for eight hundred roubles. He bought me for the reason that nobody had any piebald horses.

"That was my best time.

"He had a mistress. I knew it because I took him to her every day, and sometimes drove them out together.

"His mistress was a beauty, and he was handsome, and his coachman was handsome. And I loved them all for it. And I had an easy life with them.

"My life passed like this: In the morning the groom came to groom me — not the coachman, but the groom. The groom was a young boy taken from the village. He opened the door, let the horse evaporations go out, threw out the dung, took off the blankets, and began to curry my body, and to deposit white rows of the dandruff on the deals of the floor, which was all knocked up by my sponges.

"I jestingly bit his sleeve and pawed the ground.

"Then we were led, one after another, to a vat filled with cold water, and the lad took delight in his work, in the smooth piebald spots, the leg, as straight as an arrow, with its broad hoof, and the glossy crupper and back, which looked smooth enough to lie down upon.

"Hay was put in behind the high railing, and oats were poured into the oak crib. Then Feofán and the chief coachman came.

"The master and the coachman were very much alike. Neither the one nor the other was afraid of anything nor loved anybody, but himself, and for this both were loved by all. Feofán wore a red shirt and plush trousers and a sleeveless coat. I used to be glad to see him come into the stable on a holiday, all pomaded and wearing his sleeveless coat, and call out:

"'Well, beast, have you forgotten me?' and he would strike me with the fork-handle on my flank, not painfully, but just as a joke.

"I immediately saw that it was a joke and, dropping my ears, gritted my teeth.

"We had a black stallion who went in a span. At night I was hitched with him. This beast did not know what a joke was and was as mean as a devil. I stood by his side, one stall from him, and he frequently bit me, not in jest. Feofán was not afraid of him. He simply walked up straight to him and shouted so loud that I thought he would kill him, but no, he would go on and would put the halter on him.

"Once he and I, driving in a span, drove down Blacksmith Bridge. Neither the master nor the coachman was frightened: they laughed, shouted to the people, and checked us in, and turned — and he did not crush any one.

"In their service I lost my best qualities and half of my life. Here they ruined me by watering me too much, and they foundered me. Still, in spite of it all, that was the best part of my life! They would come at midnight, harness me up, grease my hoofs, wet my mane and forelock, and put me between the shafts.

"The sleigh was of woven reed with velvet cushions; the harness had small silver buckles, the lines were of silk, and so was the netting. The harness was such that when all the traces and straps were in place and hitched, it was impossible to make out where the harness ended and the horse began.

"I was generally harnessed up in the shed. Then Feofán, broader at his hips than at his shoulders, came out, carrying a red belt under his armpit; he examined the harness, sat down, fixed his caftan, put his foot in the stirrup, made some joke, hung his whip over his wrist, just for appearances, for he never gave me the whip, and said: 'Come now!'

"Playing at every step, I moved out of the gate; and the cook, who came out to throw out the swill, stopped on the threshold, and a peasant, who brought wood into the yard, opened wide his eyes. He drove me out and some distance away, and stopped. Then lackeys came out, and other coachmen came up. And they began to chat. There they all waited: we frequently had to stand for three hours at the entrance; sometimes we would be driven about and brought back to the same place to wait.

"Then there was a stir in the vestibule, and gray Tíkhon, wearing a dress coat over his paunch, came out and called out: 'The carriage!' Then there was not that stupid manner of saying 'Forward!' as though I did not know that we drove forward and not backward; Feofán smacked his tongue and drove up.

"And the prince stepped out leisurely, carelessly, as though there was nothing remarkable in that sleigh, nor in the horse, nor in Feofán, who bent his back and stretched out his arm in an attitude in which he could not, it seemed, persevere long. The prince came out in his helmet and military overcoat with a gray beaver collar, which concealed the ruddy, black-browed, beautiful face that ought never to have been concealed. He came out clattering with his sabre, his spurs, and the brass heels of his galoshes, stepping over the carpet, as though in a hurry and paying no attention to me or to Feofán, though all but him looked at us and admired us.

"Feofán smacked his tongue, I pulled at the traces, and we moved up, as was proper, at an amble, and stopped; I looked sidewise at the prince, and shook my thoroughbred head and fine forelock.

"The prince was in a good mood; now and then he jested with Feofán. Feofán replied to him, barely turning toward him his handsome head, and, without dropping his hands, made a barely perceptible movement with the lines, which I understood well, and one, two, three — I ran ahead, quivering with every muscle and throwing up the snow and the mud against the front part of the sleigh.

"They did not have then the stupid manner of calling 'Oh!' as though the coachmen were in pain, but they called out the intelligible 'Come now! Look out!'

"'Come now! Look out!' Feofán called, and the

people stepped aside and stopped, and craned their necks, looking at the beauty of the horse, and at the handsome coachman, and at the handsome master.

"I was particularly fond of running ahead of a trotter. When Feofán and I saw some harness ahead of us, which seemed to be worthy of our effort, we, flying like a whirlwind, began slowly to gain on the vehicle. Already I, throwing the mud on the back of the sleigh, am even with the passenger and snort right over his head, and now I am even with the horse's saddle-cloth, with the arch, and I do not see him and only hear behind me his receding voice.

"And the prince and Feofán and I, we were all silent, and pretended to be simply driving, attending to our business, and not noticing those whom we met on the way driving quiet horses.

"I loved to outstrip a good trotter, but I also liked to meet such a horse. One moment, a sound, a glance, and we were driving in different directions, and again we were off all alone, each attending to his business —"

The gate creaked and the voices of Néster and Váska were heard.

### FIFTH NIGHT

The weather began to change. It looked gloomy; there had been no dew in the morning, and it was hot, and the gnats were very pestering. The moment the herd was driven in, the horses gathered about the piebald gelding, and he finished his story as following:

"My happy life soon came to an end. I lived thus only two years. Toward the end of the second winter there happened the most joyful incident for me, and soon after my greatest misfortune.

"It was during Butter-week. I took the prince to the races. Atlas and Steer were racing. I do not know what they were doing in the booth, only he came out and ordered Feofán to drive into the track.

"I remember I was placed on the track by Atlas's side. Atlas was driving with a sulky, while I was pulling a city sleigh. I outstripped him in turning. Laughter and a roar of applause greeted me.

"When I was led out, a crowd followed me up. Some five men offered the prince thousands for me. He only laughed, displaying his white teeth.

"'No,' he said, 'that is not a horse, but a friend of mine; I sha'n't take mountains of gold for him. Good-bye, gentlemen!'

"He opened the boot, and seated himself in the sleigh.

"'To the Ostózhenka!'

"There was the house of his mistress. And we flew —

"That was our last happy day. We arrived there. He called her 'his own.' But she loved another, and had gone away with him. He learned that at her house. It was five o'clock, and he, without unhitching me, went after her. They did to me what they had never done before: they gave me the whip, and made me gallop.

"For the first time I took a wrong step, and I felt ashamed and wanted to redeem myself; but suddenly I heard the prince calling out in a strange voice, 'Go!' and the whip swished and struck me, and I darted forward striking my foot against the iron of the sleigh front.

"We caught up with her twenty-five versts away. I brought him there, but I trembled all night long and could not eat anything. In the morning I was given water to drink. I drank it and I ceased for ever to be the horse I had been.

"I was ailing, and they tormented and maimed me,— people call it curing. My hoofs came off, I had swellings, and my legs bent, my chest sank in, and there appeared a weakness and indolence in all my limbs.

"I was sold to a horse dealer. He fed me on carrots and something else, and made something of me which was not like myself, but which could deceive one who was not experienced. I had no longer any strength, and all my trotting qualities were gone.

"Besides, the horse dealer tormented me every time when purchasers came, by coming into my stall and beating me unmercifully with a whip and frightening me, so that he nearly drove me mad. Then he rubbed down the whip-marks and led me out.

"An old woman bought me from the horse dealer. She drove all the time to the Church of St. Nicholas the Miracle-worker, and flogged the coachman. The coachman wept in my stall. And I learned that tears have an agreeable salt taste. Then the old woman died.

"Her clerk took me to the country and sold me to a shopkeeper; then I ate too much wheat and grew more ailing still.

"Then I was sold to a peasant. There I ploughed, getting hardly anything to eat, and I got my leg hurt by the ploughshare. I was again ill.

"I was swapped off to a gipsy. He tormented me fearfully, and finally he sold me to the clerk here, and here I am —"

All were silent. It began to sprinkle.

## IX.

Upon returning home the next evening, the herd came upon the master with a guest. When near the house Zhuldýba looked askance at two male figures: the one was the young master in a straw hat, — the other, a tall, fat, bloated military. The old mare looked awry at the men and, bearing off to one side, passed by them; the others — the young horses — were confused and at a loss what to do, especially when the master purposely went with his guest among the horses, and they talked and pointed something out to each other.

"This one here I bought of Voéykov, — the dappled gray horse," said the master.

"And this young black mare with the white legs, whose is she? She is nice," said the guest.

They looked over a number of horses, running ahead of them and stopping them. They also noticed the little bay mare.

"This breed is left with me from the Khryénov riding-horses," said the master.

They were not able to examine all the horses as they walked by. The master called out to Néster, and the old man, hurriedly urging up the piebald gelding by striking his sides with the heels of his boots, galloped forward. The piebald gelding limped on one leg, but he ran in such a way that it was evident that he would under no consideration murmur, even though he should be asked to run to the end of the world with the expenditure of all his strength. He was even ready to gallop at full speed, and made the attempt at it with his right leg.

"Now this mare here, I dare say, is such that you will hardly find a better one in all of Russia," said the master, pointing to one of the mares.

The guest praised her. The master ran in agitation, now ahead of the horses, now to one side of them, pointing all the time to them and telling their story and the pedigree of each horse.

The guest was apparently tired of listening to the host, and he invented questions just to show that he was interested in all such things.

"Yes, yes," he said, absent-mindedly.

"You look at her," said the host, without replying. "Look at her legs!— She cost me a lot, but I have a three-year-old one from her that is already trotting."

"Does he trot well?" asked the guest.

In this manner they took up nearly all the horses, and there was nothing more to show.

"Well, shall we go now?"

"Yes."

They went through the gate. The guest was glad that the show was over and that he was going to the house where there would be something to eat, drink, and smoke, and he looked visibly happier. Passing by Néster, who, sitting on the piebald horse, was still waiting for orders, the guest struck the piebald's crupper with his big fat hand.

"He is a beauty," he said. "I had just such a piebald horse,— do you remember my telling you about him?"

The host heard that it was not his horse he was talking about, so he paid no attention, and continued to look at his herd.

Suddenly he heard a stupid, weak, old neighing right above his ears. It was the piebald that was neighing;

as though confused, he stopped without finishing his neigh.

Neither the host nor the guest paid any attention to this neighing and they went to the house.

Linen-measurer had in the bloated old man recognized his favourite master, Serpul hovskóy, the one that had been so immensely rich and handsome.

## X.

* * * * * * * * * *

IT continued to sprinkle. The enclosure looked gloomy, but in the master's house it was quite different. There the table was set for a luxurious evening tea in a luxurious drawing-room. The host, the hostess, and the guest were sitting at the table.

The hostess was pregnant, which was quite apparent from the size of her abdomen, from her straight and strained attitude, from her fulness, and, especially, from her large eyes, which were meekly and solemnly turned inward. She was sitting at the samovár.

The host held in his hands a box of ten-year-old, extra fine cigars, such as, according to his words, no one else had, and was getting ready to boast of them to his guest.

The host was a handsome man of about twenty-five years, — fresh-looking, well-fed, well-groomed. He was dressed at home in a new, loose, strong suit made in London. Large, expensive trinkets hung down from his watch-chain. The shirt-studs were of massive gold, with turquoises. He wore a beard à la Napoleon III., and the mouse-tails were pomaded and stuck out as well as though they had been fixed in Paris.

The hostess wore a dress of silk gauze, with large bouquets of various colours; she had large golden hairpins of a peculiar pattern in her thick, blond, beautiful, though not all her own, hair. On her hands there were many bracelets and rings, all of them expensive ones.

The samovár was of silver, and the tea service was fine. A lackey, magnificent in his dress coat and white waistcoat and neckerchief, stood like a statue at the door, waiting for orders. The furniture was of bent wood and bright in colouring; the wall-paper was dark, with a large flower design.

Near the table, a remarkably fine greyhound tinkled with his silver collar; they called him by an uncommonly difficult English name, which was badly pronounced by both, as neither of them knew any English.

In the corner an inlaid piano stood among flowers. Everything gave an impression of novelty, luxury, and rarity. Everything was good, but on everything there was an imprint of superabundance, wealth, and absence of spiritual interests.

The host was a high-flier, of an extremely sanguine temperament, one of those who never give out, who travel about in sable fur coats, who throw expensive bouquets to actresses, drink the most expensive wines with the newest labels in the most expensive hotels, offer prizes in their name, and keep the most expensive —

The guest, Nikíta Serpukhovskóy, was a man of more than forty years, tall, fat, bald-headed, with large moustache and side-whiskers. He must have been very handsome. Now he seemed to have fallen physically, morally, and monetarily.

He had so many debts that he was compelled to serve, in order not to be put in a hole. He was now on his way to the capital of a Government as a chief of a stud. Distinguished relatives had obtained this place for him.

He was dressed in a military blouse and blue trousers. The blouse and trousers were such as only a rich man would have made for himself; the same was true of his linen; his watch was of an English make. His boots had strange soles a finger's width in thickness.

Nikíta Serpukhovskóy had in his lifetime squandered a fortune of two millions, and was still 120,000 in debt.

From such a performance there is always left that swing of life which gives one a chance to get things on credit and to pass almost in luxury another ten years.

The ten years were coming to an end, and the buoyancy was giving out, and Nikíta was beginning to find it hard to live. He was beginning to take to drinking, that is, to get drunk on wine, which had never happened to him before. As a matter of fact, he never began or ended drinking. Most perceptible was his fall in the restlessness of his glance (his eyes were beginning to flit unsteadily) and in the lack of firmness in his intonations and movements. This restlessness was the more striking in that it had evidently come to him within a short time, for it was obvious that he had long been accustomed not to be afraid of anybody or anything, and that now he had, within but a very short time, through heavy suffering, reached that dread which was so much out of keeping with his nature.

The host and the hostess noticed it; they exchanged glances which showed that they understood each other and only delayed until bedtime a detailed discussion of the subject, and that they endured poor Nikíta. They treated him with great attention.

The sight of the happiness of the young host humbled Nikíta and made him morbidly envy the host, as he recalled his irretrievable past.

"Mary, does not the cigar incommode you?" he said, turning to the lady, in that peculiar tone which is acquired only through experience, that polite, friendly, but not quite respectful tone, which people, who know the world, use toward mistresses in distinction from their wives. He did not exactly want to offend her; on the contrary, he just now wished rather to curry the favour of the host and the hostess, though he would not have acknowledged the fact to himself. It was simply because he had become accustomed to speak to women in that tone. He knew that she herself would have been surprised, even offended, if he had treated her as a lady. Besides, he had to preserve a certain shade of a respectful tone for the real wife of his equal.

He always treated such women with respect, not because he shared any of those so-called convictions that were preached in periodicals (he never read such trash) about the respect due to the personality of each man, about the meaninglessness of marriage, and so forth, but because all decent people did so, and he was a decent, though a fallen, man.

He took a cigar. But the host awkwardly took a whole handful of cigars and offered them to him.

"No, you take this! You will see how they are."

Nikíta brushed aside the cigars with his hand, and in his eyes there was something like a gleam of offence and shame.

"Thank you." He took out his cigar-holder. "Try mine!"

The hostess was quick-witted. She noticed it and hastened to talk to him.

"I am very fond of cigars. I should smoke myself, if all about me did not smoke."

And she smiled her beautiful, kindly smile. In response he gave her a weak smile. Two of his teeth were lacking.

"No, you take this one," continued the dull-witted host. "I have others that are weaker. Fritz, bringen Sie noch *eine* Kasten," he said, "dort zwei."

The German lackey brought him another box.

"What kind do you like? Big ones? Strong cigars? These are very good. Take them all." He kept pushing them into his hand.

He was evidently glad that he had some one to whom he could make a boast of the rare things which he possessed, and he did not notice anything. Serpukhovskóy lighted his cigar and hastened to continue the conversation which they had begun.

"So, how much was it you paid for Atlas?" he asked.

"He cost me a great deal,—not less than five thousand. At least I am secure on him. What colts he gets, I tell you!"

"Do they trot?" asked Serpukhovskóy.

"They trot well. His colt took three prizes this year: in Túla, in Moscow, and in St. Petersburg; he raced with Voéykov's Raven. The rascal of a jockey made four missteps, or else he would have left him behind the flag."

"He is a little raw. There is too much Dutch blood in him, that's what I will tell you," said Serpukhovskóy.

"Well, and what about the mares? I will show them to you to-morrow. I gave three thousand for Dobrýnya. For Amiability I gave two thousand."

The host began once more to figure up his wealth. The hostess saw that it was painful to Serpukhovskóy and that he only feigned to be listening.

"Won't you have another glass of tea?" asked the hostess.

"No," said the host, continuing to talk. She arose; the host stopped her, and embraced and kissed her.

Serpukhovskóy began to smile as he looked at them with what to them appeared as an unnatural smile, but when the host arose and, embracing her, went with her up to the portière, Nikíta's face suddenly changed; he heaved a deep sigh, and on his puffed-up face there was suddenly expressed despair. Even malice could be seen on it.

The host returned and, smiling, sat down opposite Nikíta. They were silent for awhile.

## XI.

"YES, you said you bought it of Voéykov," said Serpukhovskóy, as though carelessly.

"Yes, Atlas, I told you so. I wanted to buy some mares from Dubovítski, but there was nothing but trash left."

"He has gone up the flue," said Serpukhovskóy. He suddenly stopped and looked about him. He recalled that he himself owed twenty thousand to that man who had gone up the flue. And when it came to talking about people who had gone up, he was certainly one of whom they would say that. He laughed.

Both were again silent. The host was rummaging through his brain for something to brag of before his guest; Serpukhovskóy was trying to say something which would show that he had not yet gone up the flue. But the minds of both were dulled, although they tried to brace themselves with cigars.

"How would it be if I had a drink of something?" thought Serpukhovskóy. "I must by all means have something to drink, or else the tedium he is causing me will kill me," thought the host.

"Are you going to stay here for a long time yet?" asked Serpukhovskóy.

"About another month. Well, are we going to have supper, eh? Fritz, is it ready?"

They went into the dining-room. Here a table was placed under a hanging lamp. On it stood candles and all kinds of unusual things: siphons, unusual wine in decanters, unusual appetizers, and brandy. They drank and ate, and drank again, and ate again, and then they struck up a conversation. Serpukhovskóy grew red in his face, and began to talk without timidity.

They were talking about women, mentioning the gipsies, ballet-dancers, and French women that this or that one had.

"Well, have you given up Matier?" asked the host.

"I have not given her up, but she has given me up. Ah, my friend, it makes me feel bad to think what I have spent in my lifetime. Nowadays I am really happy when I have one thousand roubles at a time, and I am really glad to get away from everybody. I can't stand it in Moscow. What is the use of mentioning it?"

It annoyed the host to hear Serpukhovskóy talk. He wanted to talk about himself and to brag, while Serpukhovskóy wanted to talk about himself, about his brilliant past. The host filled a glass of wine for him and was waiting for him to finish it, so as to tell him all about himself, about how much better his stud was arranged than anybody else's, and how his Mary loved him not for his money merely, but with her whole heart.

"I wanted to tell you that in my stud —" he began. But Serpukhovskóy interrupted him.

"There was a time, I must say," he began, "when I loved to live well, and when I knew how to do it. You are talking about trotting, — tell me which is your liveliest horse?"

The host was glad to have an opportunity to tell him something about his stud, and so he began to speak; but Serpukhovskóy again interrupted him.

"Yes, yes," he said. "You keepers of the stud are doing it all for vanity's sake, and not for pleasure, for life's sake. It was not so with me. I told you to-day that I had a carriage-horse, one that had the same kind of spots that your herdman's piebald horse has. Oh, what a horse he was! You can't possibly know: that was in the year forty-two, — I had just arrived in Moscow; I went to a horse dealer where I saw the piebald gelding. He had good qualities. I liked him. The price? One thousand roubles. I liked him, so I took him and began to drive him out. I have never had such a horse, nor will you ever have such a one. I have never known a better horse in size, in strength, and in beauty. You were a boy then, so you cannot have seen him, but you may have heard of him, I suppose. All Moscow knew him."

"Yes, I have heard of him," the host said, unwillingly, "but I wanted to tell you about my — "

"So you have heard. I bought him just as he was, without his pedigree, without his record; only later I learned what he was. Voéykov and I made it out. He was a colt by Darling I., Linen-measurer, he just measured linen. On account of his piebald spots he was taken out of the Khryénov stud and given to the keeper of the stable, who castrated him and sold him to a horse dealer. There are no such horses nowadays, my friend! Ah, what a time that was! Oh, my youth!" He sang a line of a gipsy song. He was getting under the influence of the liquor. "Ah, it was a fine time! I was twenty-five years old, had eighty thousand roubles yearly income, not a gray hair on my head, and my teeth like pearls — Whatever I undertook came out well for me, and now all is ended — "

"There was not that mettle then," said the host, making use of the interruption. "Let me tell you that my first horses have begun to trot without — "

"Your horses! There was more mettle in them in those days — "

"How so?"

"There simply was. I remember how I once drove out to the races with him. I had put up no horses. I did not like trotters, — I had thoroughbreds: Count Cholet, Mohammed. I drove the piebald gelding. I had a fine lad of a coachman, — I loved him. Well, he has ruined himself by drinking. So I arrived. 'Serpukhovskóy,' they said, 'when will you provide yourself with trotters?' — 'The devil take your lubbers! I have a carriage piebald that will outrun all your trotters.' — 'No, he won't.' — 'I will wager one thousand roubles.' They took the wager, and we let them run. He beat them by five seconds. I won the one thousand rouble wager. That is nothing! I once made one hundred versts in three hours with a tróyka of thoroughbreds. All Moscow knows about it."

And Serpukhovskóy began to lie so glibly and so uninterruptedly that the host was not able to put in a single word, and remained sitting opposite him with a melancholy countenance; to divert himself he now and then filled his guest's glass and his own with wine.

Day was beginning to break. They were still sitting. The host felt unspeakably dull. He arose.

"It is time to go to bed," said Serpukhovskóy, rising and tottering. He went, puffing, into the room set aside for him.

. . . . . . . . .

The host was lying with his mistress.

"No, he is impossible. He is drunk and keeps lying without interruption."

"And he is making court to me."

"I am afraid he will ask me for some money."

Serpukhovskóy was lying undressed on his bed and puffing away.

"It seems to me I have been telling him a lot of lies," he thought. "Well, it does not make much difference! The wine is good, but he is a big swine. There is something of the merchant in him. I, too, am a big swine," he said to himself, bursting out into a laugh. "First I kept her, now she keeps me. Yes, the Winkler woman keeps me, — I take money from her. Serves him right. Still, I must undress myself. I can't get my boots off."

"Hoa there!" he called out; but the man who was given him as an attendant had gone to bed long before.

He sat down, pulled off his blouse, his waistcoat, and somehow managed to get his trousers off; but he was for a long time unable to get his boots off, because his soft belly was in his way. Finally he somehow managed to pull one off; on the other he worked and worked, and puffed, and became exhausted. He kept that one boot on and rolled down on his bed and began to snore, filling the room with the odour of tobacco, wine, and nasty old age.

## XII.

If Linen-measurer recalled anything that night, Váska distracted him. He threw a blanket over him, and galloped away. He kept him until morning at the door of a tavern, near a peasant horse. They licked each other. In the morning he went to the herd and kept scratching himself all the while.

"It itches dreadfully," he thought.

Five days passed. The veterinary surgeon was called. He joyfully said:

"The itch, — be pleased to sell him to the gipsies."

"What is the use? Cut his throat and make an end of him this very day."

It was a calm, clear morning. The herd went into the field. Linen-measurer was left behind. There came a strange, lean, black, dirty man in a black caftan with some kind of stains upon it. It was the flayer. He took hold of the strap of the halter which was on Linen-measurer, and, without looking at him, led him away. Linen-measurer went calmly, without looking around, dragging his legs along as always, and catching his hind feet in the straw.

Upon emerging from the gate, he wanted to make for the well, but the flayer jerked him by the halter and said: "What is the use?"

The flayer and Váska, who was walking behind, came to a ravine back of the brick-kiln and stopped, as though there was anything peculiar in that very common place; the flayer gave the lines to Váska, took off his caftan, rolled up his sleeves, and fetched a knife and a whetstone out of his boot-leg.

The gelding turned his head to the halter line, wishing to chew it from tedium, but he could not reach it. He drew a sigh and closed his eyes. His lower lip hung down; his ground-down yellow teeth could be seen, as he fell asleep under the sound produced by the grinding of the knife. Only his swollen leg, spread sidewise, kept quivering. Suddenly he felt that he was seized by his jowls and that his head was raised up. He opened his eyes. There were two dogs before him. One was sniffing in the direction of the flayer; the other was sitting and watching the gelding, as though expecting something from him. The gelding looked at them and began to rub his cheek-bone against the hand which was holding him.

"No doubt they want to cure me," he thought. "Let them!"

And, indeed, he felt that they were doing something to his throat. It pained him; he shuddered and gave a kick with his foot, but repressed himself and waited to see what was coming —

The next he felt was a liquid mass coming down in a stream over his neck and breast. He heaved a deep sigh and felt better, much better.

The whole weight of his life was taken from him!

He closed his eyes and began to lower his head, — nobody was holding him. Then his feet quivered, his whole body tottered. He was not so much frightened as surprised —

Everything was so new to him. He was surprised, darted forward, upward — But, instead, his legs, moving from the spot, got entangled, — and he began to fall sidewise. He tried to straighten himself, but only rushed forward and fell on his left side.

The flayer waited until the convulsions all stopped; he drove away the dogs, which had moved up, took hold

of the gelding's legs, turned him on his back, and, telling
Váska to hold one leg, began to flay him.

"And it was a horse, too," said Váska.

"If it had been fed better, the hide would have been
all right," said the flayer.

The herd came up hill in the evening, and those who
were walking on the left side could see something red
down below, and near it the dogs busy about something,
and crows and vultures flying about. One dog, pressing
its paws against the carrion and shaking its head, was
with a crackling noise tearing away that which it had
taken hold of.

The bay mare stopped, stretched her head and neck,
and for a long time kept sniffing the air. It was with
difficulty that she was driven away.

At dawn, big-headed wolf cubs howled joyfully in a
ravine of the old forest, in an overgrown wold. There
were five of them: four of them were of nearly the same
size, and one little one had his head larger than his body.
A lean, moulting she-wolf, dragging her full belly with
the flabby teats on the ground, came out of the bushes
and sat down opposite the wolf cubs. The cubs stood in
a semicircle around her. She went up to the smallest
one and, lowering and bending down her snout, made
several convulsive motions and, opening her sharp-toothed
jaws, strained herself and vomited up a large piece of horse-
flesh. The larger cubs rushed up to her, but she moved
threateningly toward them and offered everything to the
little one. The little one, as though in anger, grabbed
the horse-flesh with a growl and, holding it under him,
began to devour it. The she-wolf in the same manner
vomited up to the second, the third, until all five had
some, and then lay down opposite them to rest herself.

A week later only a large skull and two femurs were
lying about near the brick-kiln; everything else had been
devoured. In the summer, a peasant, who collected

bones, carried away the bones and the skull and put them to use.

Serpukhovskóy's dead body, which had been walking about and eating and drinking in the world, was put away much later. Neither his skin, nor his flesh, nor his bones were of any use to anybody.

Just as for twenty years his walking dead body had been a great burden to everybody, even so the putting away of his body in the earth was only an unnecessary trouble to the people. He had long ceased to be of any use to anybody, and was only a nuisance to everybody; and yet the dead that bury the dead found it necessary to clothe the puffed-up decaying body in a good uniform and good boots, to place him in a new, good coffin, with new tassels on its four corners, then to put this new coffin in another coffin of lead, and to take him down to Moscow, and there to dig up old human bones, and in that very spot to put away his rotting and worm-eaten body, in the new uniform and clean boots, and to cover all up with earth.


THE END.

www.ingramcontent.com/pod-product-compliance
Lightning Source LLC
Chambersburg PA
CBHW011745220426
43667CB00019B/2912